IN

THE

NEW

WORLD

# IN THE NEW WORLD

## The Making of a Korean American

## Peter Hyun

A Kolowalu Book

UNIVERSITY OF HAWAI'I PRESS

HONOLULU

First published by University of Hawai'i Press 1995

Printed in the United States of America

00 99 98 97 96 95   5 4 3 2 1


**Library of Congress Cataloging-in-Publication Data**

Hyun, Peter, 1906–1993.
  In the new world : the making of a Korean
American / Peter Hyun.
      p.   cm.
    ISBN 0–8248–1648–X
    1. Hyun, Peter, 1906–1993.
    2. Korean Americans—Hawaii—Biography.
   I. Title.
   DU624.7.K67H983   1995
996.9'004957'0092—dc20            94–30661
                                  CIP


University of Hawai'i Press books are printed
on acid-free paper and meet the guidelines for
permanence and durability of the Council on
Library Resources


*Designed by Paula Newcomb*

# Contents

# Foreword

Peter Hyun's *Man Sei! The Making of a Korean American* was published by the University of Hawai'i Press in 1986. *Man Sei!* was the story of Peter's life in Hawaii, Korea, and Shanghai and ended when he was seventeen and returning to Hawaii and the New World. In 1987 he began to write the story of his adult life in America.

Peter Hyun's illness in 1993 interrupted the final editing of the manuscript of *In the New World: The Making of a Korean American.* Using the comments of the readers and University of Hawai'i Press editor Pamela Kelley, we assumed the task of working with Peter to improve the flow of the narrative. Together, with Peter, we completed a new draft of the manuscript.

Following the submission of the final version, Peter entered the hospital with a terminal illness. His wife, Luisa Stuart Hyun, his children, and University of Hawai'i Press helped select the illustrations from Peter's archives. Occasionally, names were changed to protect an individual's privacy.

Special thanks go to Luisa Stuart Hyun. Her love and support for Peter during the twenty-eight years of their marriage made this book possible.

Edward D. Beechert
Alice M. Beechert

# Preface

I am Peter's youngest brother. My background is somewhat the reverse of Peter's. Peter, born in 1906 in America, was raised in Korea, and I, born in Korea in 1917, was raised in America. This juxtaposition of birth and upbringing has given me an inside American view of my brother's transformation from Korean to American, a story he tells with humor and perception in this, his second book.

In his first book, *Man Sei!*, Peter tells the story of his life in Korea. There he witnessed the funeral of the last Korean king and the massacre on March 1, 1919, of men, women, and children who demonstrated for the declaration of Korean independence from Japanese colonial rule.

A few months later, our mother, a tiny woman less than five feet in height, bribed Japanese officials, gathered her eight children ranging in ages from infancy to sixteen, and fled across the border, across Manchuria, across half of China into Shanghai by train and by foot, with the older children carrying the younger. Alice was born in 1903; Elizabeth, in 1905; Peter, the oldest boy, in 1906; Soon Ok, in 1907 (she died in Shanghai in 1922); Paul, in 1913; Joshua, in 1915; I was born in 1917; Mary, born in 1919, was a babe in arms.

In Shanghai the family met our father, who was engaged in uniting immigrant Korean leaders from China, Manchuria, Siberia, Korea, and Hawaii and who eventually engaged in electing the officers of the provisional government of Korea. Peter witnessed the dedication of Korea's independence fighters who were under constant threat of kidnapping and assasination from Japanese agents, and he saw for the first time Europeans and Americans who lived in a grand style in the various international zones in Shanghai.

Peter knew of the physical torture of our mother by the Japanese police who sought the whereabouts of her husband. Peter saw her steadfastness during the long, dangerous journey through Manchuria and China. Peter watched the members of the Shanghai Committee carrying on the work of an absentee provisional government despite their growing poverty and lack of personal glory, and in spite of the danger to their own lives. Thus Peter learned that sincerely good-hearted persons put the welfare of the people above personal gain. Peter used this principle later in his unusually high achievements in America.

In *Man Sei!* Peter told of his childhood and youth. *In the New World* begins in 1924, when Peter, at age seventeen, and Elizabeth returned to Hawaii with Mary, age five, and me, age seven. In Hawaii he experienced fully the spirit and customs of his new world in the style of Hawaiian aloha.

Peter grew up with a definite identity. He was Korean. His early life was that of a Korean among Koreans. He did not grow up wondering, What am I? Am I Korean? Am I American? Peter grew up proudly in the embrace of Korean culture, which was one of his inner resources.

Peter also grew up learning to seek the courage to change his inner life. He saw our parents, both raised in the very strict Confucian traditions of the Korean official class in the late nineteenth century, change to become devout Christians and advocates of American democracy.

When our father and mother sat together for a public dinner at the same table, the church courtyard was filled to overflowing by people who wished to witness the breaking of a Korean tradition in favor of a Christian and democratic practice. Thus the courage of our father to change his daily habits to conform with his beliefs set a standard of truth for Peter. This was another of Peter's resources.

For Korean immigrants of the present day, I hope *In the New World* will provide insight and hope. The Korean American, inheritor of two grand cultures, can help give the world troubled by ethnic hostilities the truth that integration of cultures can be a joyous and powerful blessing.

David Hyun

# PROLOGUE

My father was among the first Koreans to acquire a Western education, studying not only its language but its religion—Christianity. Because of his knowledge of English and his theological background, my father was hired by the East-West Development Company in 1903 to lead a group of Korean immigrants to Hawaii. His young wife accompanied him. In a strange land, the Koreans settled in various sugar plantation camps and began working in the cane fields for their living. Traveling from camp to camp, my father looked after their welfare, and by conducting religious services, cared for their spiritual needs as well. Impressed with his leadership, the Methodist Mission in Hawaii ordained him as a traveling preacher. His young wife, a daughter of a royal physician in the palace, besides giving birth to three children—two girls, Alice and Elizabeth, and a boy, Peter—helped their family budget by washing and mending the working men's clothes.

In 1907, when Japan's aggression in Korea became ominous, my father and mother returned to Korea with their three Hawaii-born children; at nine months old, I was the youngest. Accepting the pastorship of the Jung Dong First Methodist Church, he devoted his life to preaching, teaching, and always encouraging the people to fight for their freedom and national independence.

Throughout its four thousand-year history, time and again, Korea was overrun and occupied by would-be conquerors: Genghis Khan and his Mongol hordes, Chinese emperors of various dynasties, and the Russians under the czar. But the Korean people always rose up shouting, *"Man Sei!"* "Long Live Korea!" and repelled the invaders.

1

Once again in 1919, the cry of *"Man Sei!"* thundered across the "Land of the Morning Calm." The Koreans cast off the yoke of the ruthless Japanese colonial rule and declared their freedom and independence. My father was one of the organizers of that uprising. With a price on his head, he fled to Shanghai, and there, together with a group of other Korean patriots in exile, helped to establish the free Korean Provisional Government. In 1920, the rest of our family left Korea to join him in Shanghai. As the vice-minister of foreign affairs, Father traveled the world, to Moscow, Washington, D.C., and China, seeking recognition and aid for the new government. In urging the establishment of a League of Nations, President Woodrow Wilson said: "A general association of nations must be formed under specific convenants for the purpose of affording mutual guarantees of political independence and territorial integrity to great and small states alike" (XIV of Wilson's fourteen points). However, the world turned its back on Korea. After five years of hand-to-mouth existence, the Korean Provisional Government was forced to close its doors. From the cabinet ministers down, all the brave revolutionaries scattered for self-preservation.

Fortunately for my father, he was appointed as the minister of the Korean Methodist Church in Honolulu, Hawaii. He didn't have to go alone to start work in his new church. Sister Alice, who returned from Korea after her brief marriage had failed, was anxious to go with him. She had married Chung, a fellow student she had met in Japan, in Shanghai in 1921. Her belief that she and Chung could accomplish a great deal in helping Korea and its people turned out to be a mistake. Living on Chung's large family estate with an inherited family fortune was his undoing; he not only became a hopeless drunk, but reverted to the old feudal ways of treating his wife. Finally convinced she could not save him, Sister Alice had to fight to save herself. As soon as she regained her strength after the birth of a baby girl, she let Chung know that she was leaving him. He didn't seem much concerned, but he would not allow my sister to take her baby with her. It was not easy, but rather than holding on to her baby, she extricated herself and returned alone to Shanghai, hoping she could rebuild her damaged life. What better way than to travel to Hawaii with Father toward a new life?

Six months after their departure from China, Father sent money saved from his meager salary to his family still in Shanghai. Sister

Soon-Ok had died in 1922 but there were still seven children. It was not enough money for all of us to go to Hawaii, so my mother arranged to send Elizabeth and me with the younger children, David, age seven, and Mary, age three. In 1924 we sailed for Honolulu on an American Dollar Line steamer called the *President Wilson*.

I left behind all of my seventeen years of life in Korea and China; all the mountains and rivers in Korea, all the hunger and pain in China, and all my relatives and friends. Fifteen days and nights crossing the Pacific gave me ample time to dream. I dreamed of my life in the New World. I dreamed of new hopes and new aspirations.

This sequel to *Man Sei!* is the story of what happened in the New World; of what happened to those dreams.

# 1

## NEW

## WORLD

At last, I was nearing the New World. So near, I could almost reach out and touch it. It was May 1924; I was seventeen years old. I'd never forgotten the dreams I had dreamed and the stories I had heard of this New World of America: a land where all the people were free and happy, a land of riches in abundance for everyone, a land where the streets were paved with gold, and where a newspaperboy could rise to become the president of the country!

But even as I was approaching this New World, the fear would not leave me: This strange land looming before me—was it real or a vanishing dream?

When we left behind the ancient land of Korea in 1920, we left all our family treasures; the priceless scrolls, screens, silverware. Even more precious were my beloved grandfather and grandmother, our dear aunts and uncles, and my childhood playmates, all of whom we left behind. Still, I gladly left behind the cruel world of Japanese rulers. No longer would I have to bow to the emperor of Japan each morning in school. And no longer would I be jeered at and called vulgar names by the Japanese children of Seoul.

My tiny mother had escaped this world with her eight young children and journeyed to China to find a new home. But China was no heaven either. My family, along with several hundred other Korean exiles, huddled in the tenements of Shanghai for mutual protection and survival. Like my father, all the Koreans gathered there were revolutionaries with prices on their heads, fighting for the overthrow of Japanese rule in Korea. The price they paid for their struggle was heavy—privation, often verging on starvation.

For me, the cutting pain, more than hunger, was the insults heaped on us by the Chinese people: *"Wang Guo Loo! Wang Guo Loo!"* "Lost Country Slaves! Lost Country Slaves!" This painful epitaph was hurled at us in the most unexpected places and moments. On street corners, in the market places, all types of Chinese, young and old, shouted it at us. Now I had to reassure myself that this painful world of China, too, was left behind when I sailed across the Pacific Ocean.

No fear! The New World we were approaching nearer and nearer was real; the good ship SS *President Wilson* was gliding into the Honolulu harbor. A strange and happy sight! A group of young Hawaiian boys were following our ship in the water, swimming and diving for the coins tossed by the passengers. On the pier, I could see a throng of colorfully dressed people, and a band in white uniforms playing strangely haunting music. When we neared the pier, all the passengers rushed out on deck and leaned against the rail, causing the big ship to visibly list dockside. They began to wave and scream as roars came from the pier.

Sister Elizabeth and I, holding onto little Brother David and baby Sister Mary, squeezed ourselves into a tight space at the rail. We scanned the crowd below, desperately searching for our father and Sister Alice. It was hopeless; there were too many people packed together in a mass. What impressed me were the bright colors the people were wearing. And for another, I couldn't detect a single beggar among the crowd.

Suddenly I screamed, "Papa! Papa! Sister! Sister!"

"Where? Where?" Sister Elizabeth and the little ones clustered around me.

"There! There!"

Following my pointing finger, they finally discovered them and began yelling, "Papa! Papa! Sister! Sister!" Frantically, we waved our arms and jumped up and down, up and down. Sadly, they couldn't see us; they just stood there with worried frowns on their faces. How sad! When would we meet them face to face? The moment we got off the ship, I assured myself.

"All third-class (steerage) passengers! Prepare to get off the ship!" The order was bellowed in three languages (Japanese, Chinese, English) over a loud speaker. Leaving the little ones on the deck with strict instructions not to move, Sister Elizabeth and I rushed down to the hold, picked up our bundles, and ran back up on the deck. Brother David and baby Sister Mary were holding on to each other, trembling and crying softly. Loaded down with bundles and holding on to the little ones, we managed to stagger down the gangplank and finally step down on land. That's when the beautiful image of the New World showed its first small crack.

Instead of Father and Sister Alice, we were met by a very gruff man in uniform who ordered us to follow the line of people—all steerage passengers—and get on board a waiting truck. Indeed, a strange way to welcome new arrivals; but who were we to question the New World custom? When the truck was fully loaded, it rumbled off the dock. Where were we being taken? Will Papa and Sister Alice be able to find us? The truck was now traveling along the road, but we were so tightly packed, I couldn't see any scenes on the street except occasional flashes of some drab, windowless buildings.

Finally, the truck stopped in front of a large two-story building. A uniformed man opened the iron gate, and after we passed through, he closed it again. With the rest of the people, we jumped off the truck, being careful to lift our little ones down. We were led into a large hall furnished only with rows of wooden benches. I hoped this was where we would meet our father and sister. But what a strange place, and what a strange custom!

But even more puzzling was the heavy steel door that only the man in uniform could open with a key. And why the iron bars in every window? Was this a prison? Have we traveled for fifteen days across the Pacific only to be imprisoned? Even if Hawaii was only an outpost, it was a part of America. How could they explain the rude and inhospitable treatment of the new arrivals to their land? There had to be some explanation. I should be more patient.

As time passed the situation did not improve; instead, it became more puzzling and humiliating. Women and girls were separated and taken to another part of the building while the men and boys were moved to a huge dormitory upstairs where lines of double-decked wooden beds filled the entire room. It was like the steerage hold aboard the ship we had just left. Moreover, it surely meant we would be kept here overnight. But how much longer?

In the morning, little Brother David and I were taken to a hospital-like room where my whole body was checked and examined; the same for little Brother David. The next day, we were taken to another hospital room. There they stuck a needle in my arm and drew some of my blood. When it was little Brother David's turn, I held him on my lap and shielded his eyes with my hand to save him from the sight of the ugly needle. We were then given vaccinations; another frightening ordeal for my little brother. But why these repetitions? We had gotten all the examinations and injections in Shanghai only a fortnight ago. Then, still another day was spent with interrogations regarding my passport and other documents that I had never seen before.

The only redeeming feature throughout the ordeal was the three meals we received daily. We ate, not sitting on the floor as in the steerage, but on a bench at a long wooden table. I was also thankful for the use of the toilet that cleaned itself after each use! On the morning of the fourth day I heard the metal door rattle, and a man in uniform stuck his head in, shouting, "All right, you can all go now!"

We were stunned. Go? Go where? In a stupor, I held little Brother David's hand and walked out to the hallway. Standing in the middle of the adjoining room, we found Sister Elizabeth and baby Sister Mary, who appeared as dumbfounded as we were. We had not seen or known the fate of each other for four days. Speechless, we just touched each other as though disbelieving we were together again. We walked down the hallway to face another door. But this was only a wooden door, and no uniformed man was guarding it. We walked into a large sunlit room that had windows without bars. Out of the crowd gathered there, Papa and Sister Alice rushed toward us, followed by other Korean men and women. Clinging to Papa's legs, little Brother David and baby Sister Mary began to cry, and then, embracing each other, we all cried.

Thankfully, we were led out of the building onto the street. For the first time since we got off the ship, I saw the clear blue sky and the little shop windows and people walking by whose faces showed not a care in the world. We approached a line of automobiles parked on the street, and everyone got in the cars and settled down. We drove off slowly as though in a parade—a fitting celebration of our arrival in the New World. Only nineteen days ago in Shanghai, riding in a car through city streets was unimaginable.

I was all eyes following the rapidly moving scenes. The most unusual sight was the row of palm trees lining both sides of the street.

I had never seen them except in the pictures of Bible stories. Our caravan came to a halt in front of Father's church. I recognized it instantly from the picture Father had sent to us. It was even more beautiful than in the picture. A large, arched window with two smaller ones at either side graced the white front wall. Wide, inviting steps at both ends of the building led up to the entrances. I was anxious to enter and see the inside, but the people who had come to welcome us were leaving, and I joined the family to thank them. They took turns shaking hands: first with Father, Sister Alice, then with Sister Elizabeth, little Brother David, baby Sister Mary, and finally me. That was my first lesson in American custom; shaking each other's hands before departing. Strange—in China we shook not the others' hands but our own when meeting or taking our leave.

Now we could go and enter our new home, "the minister's house." It was only steps away from the church. Of all the many houses we had lived in, in Korea and China, this was a palace. A half dozen wide steps led us up to the porch, which ran the whole length of the house. In China, ten people could easily sleep in such a large space. The porch was empty except for two strange-looking chairs. I sat down in one and was startled by the chair tilting backward. I moved forward and the chair moved with me. Amused, I kept moving back and forth, back and forth. Some kind of plaything for children, I guessed.

The large front door was divided in the center and opened on either side. Inside, I stood in the center of the room and just stared at everything: the enormous size of the room, the pictures on the walls, beautiful lamps and rugs on the floor. The only time I had ever seen such a room was when I visited an American missionary's home in Nanking, China. This room was even bigger and more inviting. At one end, the walls were lined with shelves filled with books. Space in front of the shelves was occupied by an unusual large desk and a semicircular chair. The desk had a wooden cover that rolled up to open and rolled down to close. I sat in the chair to discover that it could not only tilt back and forth but also spin in either direction! But the biggest surprise was the sight of a telephone resting on a little table by the side of the desk. The only private telephones I saw in China were in big hotel lobbies, on a bank official's desk, or in the police station. It delighted me to picture Papa sitting on his tilting chair, lifting the receiver of the telephone and talking to anyone, anywhere, anytime.

Sister Alice took us on a tour of the house, being very gentle in instructing us what to do and not do. Every room was filled with wonders: beds with bouncing mattresses, brightly-colored blankets over each bed, and a pretty lamp at every bedside. In each room there was a separate little room set in the wall where all the clothing could be kept on things called "hangers."

The parts of the house that intrigued me the most were the kitchen and the bathroom. For cooking, there was no need to build a fire; one only had to turn a little knob for an instant fire to cook all the food without suffocating smoke and streaming tears. Beside this magical stove, all the food preparations were done on a spacious counter—peeling, cutting, and chopping. And conveniently attached to the counter was a sink with faucets of hot and cold water. All the bowls and plates, pots and pans could be washed here.

Sister Alice was preparing lunch for us. I watched at her side, fascinated by the many different items of food that she took out of a large white box standing on the kitchen floor. Smiling at my curiosity, she said, "This big box is called 'refrigerator.'"

"Oh," I said, delighted to learn. "Rib . . . rib . . . no, reef . . . reef . . ." I gave up. "The name of the box is too long," I said.

"That's all right," Sister Alice laughed, "you will learn soon enough." She then patiently explained, "The inside of the re-fri-ge-ra-tor is very cold, and the food we keep in it won't get spoiled. We can even get ice out of the re-fri-ge-ra-tor whenever we want to." I had heard of such magical things in America, but never dreamed of having them in my own house.

The bathroom was no less fascinating. The Americans seemed to have used their talent and resources not only for constructing tall buildings and giant warships, but also for taking care of little, everyday human needs. After living in China, where wooden barrels were used to collect human waste, the idea of using a shiny white porcelain bowl and pressing a little lever after each use to have it emptied, washed, and refilled with fresh water again was beyond my wildest imagination!

And the wonders didn't cease. There was also a large, oblong porcelain tub, which could be filled with water at whatever temperature one liked. You could then lie in the warm water and soak for as long as you wished. And as though that were not enough luxury, another device was added for bathing. The water pipes—both cold and hot—were raised overhead and attached to a funnel with tiny holes. When the water was turned on, it poured out of the tiny holes in a spray. At first, it felt very strange to have water sprayed on my naked body, but I soon found it pleasurable and became addicted.

Sister Alice called us to lunch; this was my first meal in the New World, with my family. We were led to a large, round table in a spacious room. In China, we had our meals in the same little room where some of us studied and slept. Out of a handsome cupboard with a wide mirror Sister Alice brought out pretty, painted plates and all the eating utensils—not chopsticks, but metal forks, knives, and little spoons. She also handed each one of us a white, folded paper; its name was "napkin."

Then, out of the kitchen, Sister Alice brought a large platter filled with steaming food and a wonderful aroma trailing her. Papa offered a brief prayer—a short but touching grace. Taking turns, we passed our plates, and Sister Alice served the food.

"What's this?" I asked, pointing at a large round piece of meat.

"That's called 'ham-bur-ger,'" she said slowly for my benefit.

"Oh, ham-bur-ger," I repeated, I thought perfectly. Strange to eat a large piece of meat all by itself, even though its taste was surprisingly good.

"And what's this, Sister?"

"That's fried potatoes." And pointing at a red bottle she said, "Pour some catsup over it."

I understood "cat" but not "catsup." I had never eaten potatoes in my life with or without catsup. But I followed Sister's instructions and found the potatoes not bad, especially with some catsup. The dish that shocked me was called "salad." I took a mouthful and almost spat it out. It was raw vegetables! So, the Americans ate raw vegetables like cows and goats.

I might have expected Sister Alice to serve a real Korean dish. The *bee-bim-bap*—rice mixed with cucumber, broiled meat, chili sauce, and sesame oil—was a welcome sight. However, what made our first meal in the New World perfect was the dish of *kim-chee,* the indispensable Korean pickled cabbage. This heart-warming lunch ended with ice cream and cookies.

"Dessert," Sister Alice called it, giving glasses of milk to everyone.

"Milk!" I was mystified.

"Yes, milk," Sister Alice explained. "In America, not only babies but grown-ups, too, drink milk every day."

The first Sunday in Father's church in Honolulu was an eventful day. Children began arriving early in the morning for their Sunday school. They were all American-born Koreans. They looked Korean, but they could neither speak nor understand Korean. They circled around me and stared as if I were a new member of the zoo. They bombarded me with questions, in English, of course, of which I could understand very little, and I kept talking to them in Korean, which only provoked their laughter. So, other than intently staring at each other, our communication was minimal.

I felt more comfortable at the morning service. Not only did Father preach in Korean, but the congregation was mostly first-generation Korean immigrants. I had no trouble communicating with them. It had been many years since I last heard one of Father's sermons. As I listened, I remembered those thrilling sermons I had heard at the Jung Dong First Methodist Church in Seoul. The theme for Father's sermon today was "Human Family." Of course, he alluded to the recent reunion of his own family. The powerful ring in his voice was still there as he expressed his joy in our reunion. Then he continued, "But under God, there is only one human family: Let us always be together; we must never stray or be lost." Father's sermons never failed to arouse a mysterious, thrilling sensation in me. Listening to him once again, I felt proud to be my father's son.

After the service, in the afternoon, I was "baptized" in the restless waves of the Pacific Ocean. A group of boys and girls—all close to my age—invited me, then begged and cajoled me to join them; they were beach bound. They brushed aside all my excuses: never been to a beach before, don't know how to swim, don't have a bathing suit. Yes, they had an extra bathing suit, and they would take good care of me. Their sheer exuberance swept me away, and I found myself in their automobile, not knowing quite how to respond to all their boisterous jubilance.

"Peter," the boy driving the car announced, "this is the famous Waikiki Beach!" The girls peeled off their dresses, revealing scanty and colorful bathing suits, and dashed off to the beach. Slowly, I took my clothes off and put on the black bathing suit they gave me. I felt like the so-called "fish out of water," but I pretended to be quite comfortable and followed the boys.

I was startled to see a mass of people on the beach; I had never seen such a sight. Men and women, boys and girls, all scantily clad in tight-fitting outfits, were screaming, laughing, splashing, and having a wonderful, frolicking time. I watched with keen interest to see what nationalities they might be. With only their bathing suits on, it was impossible to distinguish the Koreans from the Chinese; the Japanese from the Hawaiians. Even those with light yellow hair and sun-browned skin couldn't be set apart from the Orientals.

The girls from our church saw me standing alone and rushed out of the water and took my hands. "Come on, Peter," they screamed, "let's get in the water!" I didn't understand. So they repeated over and over very slowly, which didn't help. But their motions and gestures were unmistakable; they were dragging me into the ocean! I was terrified by the rushing waves, but said, "Okay! Okay!"—the American expression I had just learned from the Sunday school children. The girls pulled me farther and farther into the water, and to my dismay, it became deeper and deeper. A mountainous wave was rushing toward me. Helplessly, at the last moment, emulating the boys I saw, I dove headlong into the wave; it was so powerful that it threw me over backward. Terrified, I staggered out of the water.

"That's good, Peter! That's very good!" The girls gathered around me jumping and clapping. With their encouragement and my newfound bravery, I went back in the water and met the oncoming wave. Bang! Again, I was thrown backward. I tried it again and again and again and again, each time meeting the same fate. After that Sunday's baptismal, I learned the secret of diving into the crest of the wave to avoid being tossed over backward.

"Let's go have a hot dog!" someone yelled.

"Come on, Peter, let's go!" The girls took charge of me and dragged me across the lawn.

"Hot dog?" I understood the words but had no idea what they meant. I was more than a little curious. Do the Americans eat dogs? I asked myself. We found a shady spot under tall pine trees, and the girls and I settled down on the soft grass while the boys ran off to fetch the hot dogs. What they brought back was neither hot nor dogs. Everyone began eating with gusto. Gingerly, I took a bite of mine. It tasted strange, but after several more bites, I decided I liked the taste of the hot dog.

This first Sunday in Honolulu was an unforgettable day filled with adventures. Returning home with the boys and girls in the car, I felt tired but elated. I saw and learned so much; learned so many new English words, watched the American families at play on the beach, and tasted new American food. If the days ahead were as rich and rewarding, in a short time I would find myself quite comfortable and at home in this New World.

After a quick "shower," I joined the family and sat at the dinner table. Sister Alice served us yet another foreign dish.

"What's this?" I asked.

"It's Irish stew," she told us.

The Irish stew taken with Korean rice and *kim-chee* produced a wonderfully harmonious taste. Papa announced at the table that there would be a party following the evening service—a party to celebrate our arrival from China. It would be held in the "recreation hall," which was a part of the two-story dormitory Father had built behind the minister's house. He had built it to provide housing for young Koreans who came to Honolulu from the outer islands to attend college. Father was a well-known builder. He had built many churches in his early missionary days in Hawaii, and now he was building once again.

The evening service was quite brief. The congregation adjourned to the recreation hall, a spacious room with chairs set against the walls. I was disappointed that there were no young people; only the elderly were gathered there. To start the party, a tall lady with great dignity delivered a moving speech welcoming us. She was deeply thankful and happy that we had "escaped from China" and joined our father and sister. I learned that her name was Mrs. Dora Moon, a devout Christian leader from Korea and staunch supporter of Father's work. She concluded her speech by reminding all that Mrs. Hyun—our mother—and two other children, Joshua and Paul, were still in China. She prayed they, too, would join us soon. As was customary in all social gatherings of Koreans, many other speeches followed—speeches expounding the proud history of the Korean people, decrying their sufferings under the Japanese ruler, extolling their undying commitment to achieve freedom and national independence.

I had heard the same speeches many times over in Shanghai. The monotony was finally broken by a speaker who really impressed me, chiefly because she was so beautiful. She was Mrs. Wella Chung, the daughter of Mrs. Moon and married to a man who owned a furniture store, and reputedly quite rich. It was her daughter, Ai-Young, who had dragged me into the wild waves of Waikiki Beach that afternoon. In a lilting, musical voice the beautiful lady told us how proud and happy she was to "embrace us" in their fold. She hoped both Elizabeth and I would conduct the sorely needed classes and teach their children Korean language and history.

Not too soon, Mrs. Moon rose and put an end to the speech making. "Now, let's have a real party," she said. She knew the men and women with talents, and she called on each one in turn to render their specialties—singing sad Korean folk songs or telling funny old folk tales. I was pleased to discover that the Koreans in Hawaii sang the same songs and told the same old folk tales as the Koreans in Shanghai.

Now it was Father's turn to respond. He stood up and thanked the members of his church for their help in bringing his four children from China. When his wife and two children left in China finally joined them, he said, he would once more have his whole family together and be able to live and work with complete peace of mind. Then at the urging of his followers, he agreed to sing his favorite Korean folk song—the "Harvest Song"—also known as the "Rice-pounding Song." I was thrilled to hear him sing again; it had been many years since I last heard him. When he finished with a long, punctuating note, everyone joined in resounding applause.

Someone's suggestion that the newly arrived son of the minister also sing a song was met with enthusiastic response. Modestly, I stood up and bowed to everyone politely. "I am not very good at singing," I said, "so instead, I'll do a scene and give you a glimpse of life in Shanghai." As an introduction, I explained that the city of Shanghai was carved into various foreign "concessions," and each was ruled under foreign laws and foreign police. This is an advantage to the lawbreaker, sometimes. When the street peddler sees a policeman approaching, he only has to pick up his stand and run across the street to a different national concession. The policeman would shake his fist as a warning but could not cross the boundary and pursue the lawbreaker. But at times, the police of the two national concessions would approach at the same time and be able to arrest the poor peddler.

That's when the big scene would take place; whose prisoner is the lawbreaker? The argument would heat up among the policemen of four nationalities: French, English, Annamese, and Sikh. It was done entirely in gibberish and pantomime. But the distinct accents and gestures of each nationality were unmistakable: the English policeman with a haughty and disdainful air, and his swallowed words rolling out of his tight-lipped mouth; the excitable French policeman, whose rapid-fire words sounded as though they were passing through his nose; the lyrical and melodic sounds of the Sikh policeman of India, who is determined to claim the prisoner; and the high, falsetto voice of the Annamese policeman from Indochina, whose monotonous staccato speech baffles everyone. This irreconcilable encounter reaches its climax when the policemen lose their patience, shouting at each other and gesticulating all at the same time.

At the height of the shouts and snorts, the whines and singsong obbligatos, I brought the scene to an abrupt end. The audience was silent for a long moment. Then they broke into loud applause. My first appearance in America as an actor was a roaring success!

Once again, time passed quickly and I was faced with a new dilemma: How could I cope with all the strange things of the New World surrounding me? Where and how could I direct my future? I began to realize that I would have to abandon many of my cherished ideas and beliefs. No enemies to face daily, no guerrillas, and no "Young Revolutionary Society" here. Great changes took place overnight; we no longer worried about our next meal, and, without being rich, we could still attend school. I would have to reshape my thoughts and feelings and try to become a part of this new land and its way of life.

My gravest concern was my education. Just in elementary school, I had to completely change my language twice—from Korean to Japanese, then to Chinese. Now, I was faced with the need to change my language once more—to English. It seemed an insurmountable task. From now on, all my learning both in and out of school would have to be done in this strange new language. But where and how would I begin? In the year 1924 there were no special considerations for students from foreign countries. The term "bilingual education" in the American school system would not be heard for nearly fifty more years.

So it was entirely up to me; I had to somehow find the answers to the countless puzzles of the English language. I found myself wrestling with English words through all my waking hours—their sounds, meaning, and spelling, not to mention the many variations and changes of each word. The only relief from this preoccupation was at the end of the day when I went to bed and fell asleep. For then I would have my dreams, and in my dreams I could speak my own language, Korean.

The most discouraging thing about learning English was that the more I studied, the more complicated it became. I could never be sure of the words I learned because sometimes new heads or tails would be attached to the words, or they changed into different words altogether. A simple word like "eat" had such complex variations that it didn't seem possible I could ever master its use. In English "eat" changed to "ate," "eaten," or "will eat." In Chinese, the word "eat" was constant regardless of time. Chinese did add, "eat today," "eat yesterday," or "eat tomorrow," making it perfectly clear when the eating was done.

When I finally learned the three tenses of the verb, I was confronted with more complicated variations. I had to learn to add still other adjuncts: "have eaten," "had eaten," "will have eaten," and on and on ad infinitum. Sometimes the word had to be preceded by "to" or end with "ing." It wreaked endless havoc, and that was only one word!

The conjugation of verbs haunted me for over a year before I began to grasp the subtleties of the tenses. But the verb was only one part of the English speech; there were seven other parts, each with its own peculiar and mysterious rules. Moreover, studying and memorizing the rules were of no great help, for each rule, more often than not, became nullified by exceptions to the rule.

All these struggles and anguish had to do with book learning. There was another, even more painful side of learning: spoken English. No matter how hard I tried, all that I spoke sounded wrong. Both in and out of the classroom, whenever I said something, everyone laughed. Evidently, the English I spoke came out of my mouth sounding foreign and comical. But nobody would tell me how I could improve. I was conscious of my inability to produce the sound of "the"; it always sounded like "dih" or "duh." Finally, when I was able to approximate the "the" sound, I encountered the baffling complexities of "accents." There wasn't any rule about the aggravating problem of accents. There were no logical explanations why "pro-nounce" should change to "pro-nun-ci-a-tion" nor why "nation" should become "na-tion-al-i-ty." All I could do was to try to imitate and remember.

Enduring all the aggravations and pain, I worked hard, determined to master the art of placing the accent over the right syllable. One day in the classroom, I was anxious to test my mastery. It happened to be the day after the lunar eclipse. The whole English class was discussing it. I raised my hand, was called upon, and stood up.

"It was a strange fino-menon," I said rather proudly.

Dead silence.

"What did you say, Peter?" the teacher asked.

"It was a strange fino-menon," I repeated.

"How do you spell it?" The teacher appeared puzzled.

"P-h-e-n-o-m-e-n-o-n." I remembered the spelling, fortunately.

"Oh," the teacher smiled, "you mean 'phe-nom-e-non'." The class burst into roaring laughter.

One day, I asked my English teacher, Mrs. Anderson, who was very kind and understanding, to show me how I could speak my new language without being laughed at.

With a look of pity she said, "Come and see me after school." In our private session, she said, "I think you are really serious about learning to speak English. So, I am going to give you some advice. To speak English, you must pronounce and articulate the sound of every syllable of every word. And in order to do that, you must use all your physical mechanisms—your mouth, your lips, your jaws, your teeth, and your tongue." She gave a vivid demonstration of what she meant.

I was amazed. Such a manner of speaking completely violated all the proper speaking manners I had learned in Korea: keep your face expressionless, don't reveal your emotions when you speak, and so on, until one could cultivate the perfectly immobile face of a cultured person. Now I had to forsake all the discipline and training and learn to speak in a different form; with a wide-open mouth, bare teeth, and flipping tongue—in general, with a contorted face. It was embarrassing even to try.

There was no alternative and no easy answer. I had to suffer through every obstacle and master this impossible language as quickly as possible. I was blessed with one salvation: I was not afraid. As a true "Oriental," I was supposed to be polite and shy. Instead, I was bold and daring. I didn't remain in the background; I was in the center of all happenings. I didn't hesitate and stutter; I spoke up, not minding people laughing at what I said. The more mistakes I made, the more I learned. Such an attitude and approach resulted in two significant benefits. First, it helped to silence those who laughed at my English, and second, I gained a considerable measure of confidence.

The New World taught me another lesson as puzzling as its language. Those with a smooth and fluent tongue did not necessarily march on the road to success. The more important possession, it seemed, was the size of the wallet in one's pocket. I discovered that the boys with lots of money were the ones who wore stylish clothes and kept company with the best-looking girls. Money also seemed to carry other hidden powers: respect of others and all kinds of advantages. Such high regard for money was contrary to my childhood upbringing. In Korea, I was taught to be disdainful not only of money, but of all material possessions. By tradition, the most honored one in the Korean society was not the richest, but the teacher, and the lowliest was the tradesman who handled money. But inexorably, I was drawn into the American way of life. I felt the need to find money, and quickly!

I soon found my first opportunity. Thanks to a Korean foreman, I found a job in the Dole pineapple cannery. I had to get up before dawn, eat a quick breakfast—usually a bowl of cornflakes—catch a bus to the cannery, and punch a time card before 7:00 A.M. My job was to stand at a tub of running water into which the conveyor dumped pineapples already peeled and cored. Wearing long rubber gloves, I had to wash the fruit in the tub and place it on the next conveyor, which carried it to the slicing machine. The rubber gloves were for protection, but at the end of the day, I would have painful burns on my hands caused by the pineapple acid, which ate away tiny holes in the gloves.

Making money, even in this rich land, demanded hard work.

Standing in front of a wet tub and washing pineapples for eight hours with a half-hour break for lunch and two ten-minute breaks during the day not only sapped all my energy but drained my spirit as well. I had to devise some means of overcoming the monotony. While working, I tried to imagine that I was in Seoul on New Year's day, flying my kite on the hillside. Then I tried imagining I was playing soccer in Shanghai with my "little revolutionaries". It was hopeless; no amount of imagination could compete with the rattling of the machinery and the endless tumbling of pineapples. In desperation, I began to sing. The noise of the machines drowned the sound so that I could sing at the top of my voice. It worked. So as I worked, I sang all day— all the songs I knew in Korean, Japanese, and Chinese. The women sitting at the conveyor packing sliced pineapples would stare at me and laugh, wondering, no doubt, what made me so happy washing pineapples all day.

I worked all through the summer—the peak of the pineapple season. This was perfectly suitable for the Dole Company, since all the work could be done by students on vacation, and at the lowest possible wages. As a newcomer, I was paid 22.5 cents an hour. After paying for the bus fare and lunch at the cafeteria, I earned almost $1.50 a day. My weekly earnings were entrusted to Sister Alice for safekeeping.

Already in my mind I had decided how I would spend my hard-earned American dollars. From my earliest childhood I had always dreamed of playing a violin. One day, I saw the most beautiful violin in a shop window and went in and asked for its price. I was told: "Sixty-five dollars!"

On the last day of work, I took all the money Sister Alice had kept for me, and when the workday was over, I hurried straight to the music store. I floated out of the store with the violin under my arm. Would any of my friends in Shanghai believe that I owned my own violin?

But now how do I learn to play it? Going to a violin teacher was beyond my reach; it would be too expensive, and I had no more money. I bought a self-teaching book, and with it I learned to tune the instrument, draw the bow across the strings, and use my fingers to produce the notes. I was thrilled! But I had to be careful and be sure there was no one in the dormitory when I practiced, for I was sure if they heard the interminable scratchings of the violin they would tear me limb from limb. After some time, when I could make decent sounds and learned to play the first song—"Home Sweet Home"—I dared to play when I knew the boys were in their rooms. When I finished, they appeared at my door and paid me the highest compliment: "Say, Peter, that's not bad!"

Washing pineapples for eight hours a day every day for three months had helped to fulfill my dearest childhood dream!

The summer quickly passed; it was time to prepare for school. What school could I attend? I had two options: to go to an elementary school, where I could improve my English, or attend the public high school, where, with my meager English, I would be hopelessly lost. I was saved from either fate by my discovery of a private high school especially for boys like me from foreign countries. I registered as a freshman at Iolani High School. I learned later that Sun Yat-sen, the founder of the Republic of China, was an alumnus of this school.

The subjects included biology, algebra, civics, and English. In the classrooms I understood very little of what the teachers were saying. Only in algebra class could I follow the daily lesson because I had already studied algebra in China. Solving the problems of $x$, $y$ and $z$ could be done in Chinese as well as in English. It was a different story in my biology and civics classes. Learning the names of animal parts, some in Latin, was like tackling yet another language. The class in civics was a jungle; to learn the strange names of the "bureaus," "branches," and "departments" of American government was nightmarish enough, but to remember the names and duties of all the officials was an unfathomable puzzle.

And the class in English was a pitch-dark tunnel; I groped, stumbled, and floundered to find my way out. Each week, I had to read a book and turn in a book report. I would never forget my first book report; it was on *Ivanhoe*. I didn't have the remotest idea who or what *Ivanhoe* was. I used three dictionaries: Korean-English, Japanese-English, and Chinese-English, and it took an hour to finish reading one page. At that rate, it would have taken me at least six months to finish reading, never mind the written report. I had to find a shortcut. I befriended a senior student, bribed him, and begged him to write the report for me. Mercifully, the school year came to an end, and to my great surprise, my report card showed passing grades in all subjects. I was pleased to know that when the new school term started in the fall, I would be a sophomore.

Once more, the summer vacation meant a chance to make money. I was now a veteran at the Dole Company and received a pay raise—two cents an hour, making it 24.5 cents an hour. Well, I thought, I wasn't a "dumb foreigner" any more. I was learning to "hustle" for bigger money. There was a can-stacking department in the cannery that was managed by a Korean. He hired only Koreans and taught them how to stack pineapple cans to a height of twelve feet. I was hired as a learner.

Two men worked as a team. We began from the floor by stacking four cans on top of each other, covering an area six feet wide and four feet deep. When the first layer of four cans was finished, inch-wide wooden slats were placed between the rows of cans. Then four more cans were stacked on top of the slats. More slats and more cans were stacked until they reached a height of six feet. Then a second row of cans was stacked in front of the first until it reached a matching height. Now, a wooden platform was hoisted and placed on top of the front rows. One of us climbed up to the platform and got ready to pile the cans for another six feet on top of the back rows. This was accomplished by coordinated flowing movements of the team; the one below picked up four cans and placed them on the platform while the one above picked them up and stacked them. The continuous bending and lifting, bending and lifting of the two men did not stop until the cans reached the height of twelve feet. Then, we paused only to drink some water out of the gallon can we kept at the side. With a deep breath, we would start all over again from the bottom.

A lot of tricks and technique were involved in stacking pineapple cans. In fact, we considered it an art. First, I had to learn to pick up four cans at a time—quite a bit of artistry involved there. Then I had to learn how to flip them so that instead of falling, they landed on top of each other. After mastering all the basics, I had to develop the art of bending and lifting continuously, without any wasted motion. By perfecting and accelerating the rhythmic motion, my partner and I were able to stack, depending on the size of the cans, between thirty to fifty thousand cans a day. We worked at such a furious pace because we were on contract labor; the more cans we stacked, the more money we made. We were paid twenty-five cents for every thousand cans. For a daily average of forty thousand cans stacked, we earned ten dollars; five dollars for each of us. That was very big money! It sure beat the $1.50 I had earned standing at a wet tub and washing pineapples for eight hours.

Flushed with the prospect of amassing a fortune, I paid little attention to the terrible physical strain, especially on my back. Little did I suspect that I would suffer with a damaged spine for the rest of my life. But at the time I was elated. When the summer ended, even after all the money spent for movies and *saimin* (noodles), I had saved one hundred dollars!

In March 1925, the third and the last shipment of our family arrived from Shanghai—Umma [variation of Western "mama"] with my two younger brothers, Paul and Joshua. Of course, they, too, were locked up in the U.S. Immigration cells for three days and nights. We were overjoyed to see them freed and walking out of the familiar brick building. Also, naturally, a delegation from Father's church was there to welcome the last of the Hyun refugees. I was appalled by the appearance of my mother and my two brothers; they looked so shabby and stark. Umma's Chinese blouse and skirt, and my brothers' imitation boy scout outfits made them look so strange. Could it be that in such a short time I had become accustomed to seeing all the people in neat and colorful clothes? Though hard to imagine, on my arrival in Honolulu I, too, must have looked that foreign.

Entering our new home, we were eager to show them how much we knew about America. Little Brother David showed off by talking to them in English, and baby Sister Mary changed into different dresses and paraded before Umma, who nearly broke down and cried. Father took us all into his church and proudly showed the newcomers the pipe organ, patted and caressed the shiny wooden benches, and pointed at the stained glass windows. Then he said, "Let us pray." We stood with our heads bowed, and father in a low, soft voice murmured a prayer: He thanked the Lord for his united family and asked for His divine guidance for our future.

Of course, there had to be another party to celebrate the latest arrivals. After a short Sunday evening service, the congregation once more filled the recreation hall. I could see Umma unperturbed and calmly acknowledging all the greetings. Brother Paul was as alert as ever, his eyes darting here and there to see who might be watching him. But Brother Joshua was a picture of befuddlement; he looked doubtful that this was really the last stop in the family exodus.

Following the usual patriotic speeches extolling the proud history of Korea and its people, Mrs. Dora Moon offered a formal greeting to the latest Hyuns. She concluded by saying, "To Mrs. Hyun, Hawaii is not new. She had been here as a pioneer over twenty years ago, and had given birth to three of her children. Since then, she has been fighting for her husband's church, fighting for her children, and fighting for Korea's freedom."

Acknowledging the prolonged applause, my adorable, diminutive mother stood up. With a faint, wry smile, she said, "Yes, in Korea, I had to fight the Japanese police. And in China, to save our pennies, I had to fight the tradesmen. But now, I don't know whom I will have to fight here in Honolulu."

"Oh, no! No more fight! No more fight!" the people cried out in protest, and everyone, including Umma, joined in laughter. Mrs. Moon then turned to my two younger brothers and asked for some words. To my surprise, Brother Paul, the shy one, stood up and announced that he wished to sing for them an old Chinese folk song. Even before the enthusiastic applause could die down, he began to sing in perfect Chinese. His rendition of an ancient Chinese love song was vibrant and passionate. Everyone loved it.

Now it was my silent but wise Brother Joshua's turn. The persistent clamor finally forced him to stand up. After a long pause, he said (in Korean, of course), "To tell the truth, I don't know where I am."

Another burst of laughter.

Joshua then asked the audience, "What am I doing here?" So silencing everyone, he sat down. I felt so proud of my brothers, I gladly gave them my bedroom and moved into one of the rooms in the dormitory.

One question lingered and gnawed at me: What should I do with the hundred dollars I had saved? Of course, I should keep it and keep saving more for college. But that seemed so far away, and I really wanted to own an automobile. But be realistic, I said to myself; how could I buy an automobile with one hundred dollars? Then, as though providence had ordered it, at the dinner table Father mentioned that a Korean man wished to sell his car for one hundred dollars. I was at the man's house the next day. The deal was closed quickly.

"Do you know how to drive?" he asked.

"No," I said, "but you could show me."

The man led me to the garage and pointed at his car, a Model-T Ford. I gave him the money, and he handed me the papers and the key. We climbed in and the man explained how to use the three foot pedals: one to go forward, two together to go backward, and the third to slow down or stop the car.

"What are these?" I asked, pointing at the two long levers under the steering wheel.

"The one on your left is the choke which you use for starting the car in the morning when the engine is cold."

"Do I pull it down or push it up?" I asked.

"You pull it down to start the engine, and when it has run for a while, you push it up." Then he took hold of the lever on the right, saying, "You push this down like this to go faster and push it up like this to slow down."

Cranking to start the engine was the biggest challenge; it required strength as well as some know-how. After several misses, the engine started with a roar. I rushed in and stepped on the two pedals. The car backed out of the garage while I steered to turn it around. The man stood with his mouth open while I stepped on the forward pedal and drove off, waving at him.

I had to drive through some city streets to reach home in time for dinner. I took my seat at the table and struggled to calm myself. I tried but couldn't eat. Papa and Umma glanced at each other suspiciously. I pretended not to notice them and went through the motions of eating.

Sister Alice finally put down her fork with a bang and asked; "All right, Pedro-ya, what's the matter?"

"Sister," I answered slowly, "I bought a car." I thought I was being very calm, but my voice betrayed me.

Then everyone screamed in unison, "YOU BOUGHT WHAT?!"

Much more calmly now, I said, "I bought a car—a pretty Ford."

Everyone was either too stunned or reluctant to believe me.

"Well, come follow me and I'll show you." I led them out to the porch, and pointing, I said, "There! That's my car. Isn't it pretty?"

Now believing but overwhelmed, they shouted,

"Where did you get it?"

"How much did it cost?"

"Who drove it here?" and so on and so on.

When the family calmed down somewhat, I offered to take them all for a ride. They were hesitant, but I set them at ease with my confident air. Five people piled in beside me, and three little ones were put on their laps. Starting the car without a hitch and slowly driving away with my whole family in the car was a most exhilerating feeling. Of course, I chose the most popular drive—to Waikiki Beach. I reached the beach safely, circled Kapiolani Park, and, as the sun began to set, headed home.

"Oh, the night blooming cereus are in full bloom," someone cried. "Could we drive by to see them?"

"Why not?" I said, and changed my direction toward Punahou School. The stone wall surrounding the school there, now at the height of season, would be covered with the brilliant, exotic flowers that bloom only at night. It was a great annual attraction. As I approached, we were suddenly engulfed by a forest of cars moving in both directions: The whole Honolulu population must have been there. I managed to keep the engine running, and after painfully slow progress, began to get out of the traffic jam.

That's when the engine coughed and coughed and finally died. I jumped out of the car and furiously began to crank; it wouldn't start. I began to feel nervous and was losing my grip. I kept cranking; the engine showed no signs of life. Horrible thoughts flashed through my mind: Out of gasoline? Suppose I got arrested for blocking traffic? Even worse, suppose I got arrested for driving without a license?

Spurred on by the thought of imminent disaster, I found new strength and cranked on. A miracle! The engine coughed and coughed and finally started. I jumped in, held my breath, and drove off. I don't believe I breathed again until we arrived home and I parked the car in back of the church. Everyone was jubilant. The children jumped up and down and clapped their hands. Papa and Umma stood silently watching me with proud smiles on their faces. The highest reward was uttered by Sister Alice: "Pedro-ya! Oh, Pedro-ya! We have never had such a wonderful time!"

And that was my first lesson in the pains and pleasures of owning an automobile in America.

# 2

# AMERICANIZATION

At unguarded moments in 1926, memories of Shanghai would leap into my mind. The picture of my departure aboard the SS *President Wilson* was still vivid. And the faces of those who had come to bid me farewell, my "little revolutionary" comrades, young boys and girls, still haunted me. I could hear their voices: "Peter, you will forget us. You will forget Korea—you will become an American!" And just as clearly, I could hear my own shouted answer: "No, never! I'll never forget you! I'll never forget Korea!" I began to ask myself why I hadn't also assured them, "No, I'll never become an American."

Since arriving in Hawaii, in a very short time I had gone through astounding changes. I ate different kinds of food—no more rice gruel for breakfast. No; instead I drank fresh orange juice and ate ham and eggs and toast with butter and jam. I also ate enormous chunks of meat called steak, and raw vegetables. It wasn't only what I ate, but how much I ate—as much as I could eat, and I didn't go to sleep hungry. Is this being Americanized?

To be sure, there were other changes: I wore newer and better clothes; I also wore a different kind of haircut. Perhaps the most startling change was my luxurious personal possessions: a beautiful violin, which I was learning to play, and an automobile, which I drove to and from school. Indeed, I had to be undergoing the process of Americanization.

The all-embracing experience, however, was learning and speaking the new language. It was imperative for me to learn English as speedily as possible. I was jeered and laughed at for my "funny"

English, but undaunted, I kept stammering and making up m
kind of English.

Soon, I began to hold my own at parties—Oh, how the people
in Hawaii loved parties!—began to understand more of what was
happening at the movies, and even began to make people laugh with
jokes I made up in English. Out of all the ingredients in the process
of Americanization, learning to speak the language of the land had
to be the most vital one. Still, it was not the complete answer. All the
changes I had experienced so far had to do with things outside of
me—with the objective world.

They did not reach my inside world: my thoughts, feelings,
and beliefs—my identity. Such disturbing introspection, however,
became more and more infrequent. The scenes of Shanghai, Nanking, and Seoul were receding and becoming fainter and fainter. I
became preoccupied more and more with the daily new discoveries,
all very enthralling and exciting: eating new foods in new places,
meeting new friends and visiting their American-style homes, learning new English words and new slang—these occupied my mind
through all my waking hours.

I was also beginning to come in close contact with girls. In
Korea, any relationship with girls was governed by the teachings of
Confucius that boys and girls should be separated when they reach
the age of six.

The first time I ever saw men and women holding each other
and dancing in public was in Shanghai. One evening I happened to
pass by the French Club and heard loud orchestral music. Not seeing
the watchman at the gate, I walked in. In a great pavilion, under
dimly lit lights, men and women were clinging to each other and
whirling around and around with the music. It was so embarrassing, I
couldn't look at them directly, but I could see that the faces of some
men and women almost touched each other. I saw enough and
walked away. At home, I told my mother what I had seen.

"Barbarians!" she snorted.

And here I was in Hawaii, dating and dancing with no feeling
of shame or embarrassment. Was I becoming so free like the rest of
the Americans? Or was I joining the "barbarians"?

I began to discover a sensation that I had never felt before—a
tingling whenever I found myself alone with a girl. What's more, I
didn't feel ashamed, and I didn't have to fight anyone as I did in

Shanghai when I was accused of kissing a girl. Then I learned to dance, to embrace a girl close to me and glide, sway, and whirl in rhythm with the music.

I discovered English also meant learning new attitudes and relations, and learning, above all, a different sense of values. English was not only a language; it was a way of life. My attitude toward the elders and the authority, including the teachers, was no longer born of fear and submission. There were no separate polite forms of speaking to parents and elders or authorities as with the Korean language. In Korean, every expression and communication varied, depending on the comparative age and status. One spoke one way to a younger or an inferior person; quite another way to a person of equal age and status. And the expression changed totally when addressing an older person. Here in America, I used the same words with my elders as with my friends. In such insidious and subtle ways, my relations with everyone were placed on equal terms.

My attitude toward girls and women was also changing. There was no moral dictum. Boys and girls grew up together, went to school together, played together. And when they reached high-school age, fifteen or sixteen, they began playing the "dating" game. It followed a pattern: A boy would single out a certain girl in school, church, or even on the street and begin paying singular attention to her. Such attention was mutually recognized and acknowledged without the exchange of a single word. The silent communication could also be initiated by a girl. None too soon, there could be the first verbal exchange, such as, "What's your name?" "Where do you live?" Or a bolder one might even express his admiration: "You are so pretty!"

The next stage of the dating game was to make a date; that is, an engagement to meet together alone. This was the crucial stage. The boy should not appear too bold and brazen nor the girl too eager or too reticent. The boy shouldn't be discouraged by the girl's first rejection or even subsequent ones. That was part of the game. My God! If he were seriously interested in dating the girl, he had to prove it with perseverance and persistence. And the girl, attuned to all the wiles of the boy's approaches, would respond with apparent reserve—neither too quickly nor too slowly.

Both the boy and the girl would know when the time was ripe to meet and to choose a place and time to consummate the date. The date would usually wind up in a movie or at the beach. But should their relationship continue and grow sufficiently, they would even spend their date inside a car parked in a dark lane or under the shadows in the park.

Innocently, I asked my friend one day, "What could they do sitting in the car in the dark all night?"

My friend shot back, "You dumb *yabo* (old-fashioned Korean) —what would you do with a pretty girl in the car in the dark?"

After a short hesitation, I said, "I don't know. What would you do?"

"Neck! You dumb *yabo!*"

"Neck? What's that?"

"Smooch, you understand?"

"Smooch?"

"Yeah, smooch! You kiss and kiss and feel each other all over! That's necking!"

"My god!" I gasped in amazement.

If I had played such a dating game in Korea, I would have scandalized my family, or worse, been ostracized by them. And the girl, if there were such a girl in Korea, would be in disgrace for life.

My own first date was with a Japanese girl! Not a native of Japan; she was born in Hawaii—a Japanese American. We arranged to meet in front of the popular movie house in town—the Hawaii Theatre. I got there early and bought two tickets—twenty-five cents each—with which we could sit anywhere in the theatre. I saw her coming, and all my nerves began tingling. But I had enough sense to notice how adorable she looked. I didn't know how to greet her; should I say something or should I just shake her hand? She solved the dilemma for me.

"Hello, there!" she said. It sounded so good.

"Hello," I said. I was so fearful that someone who knew me might see me side by side with a girl.

When the theatre doors opened, we were swept in with the crowd. We didn't go to the orchestra seats and we didn't go to the first or second balcony; we went farther, to the highest and darkest place near the ceiling. I don't remember the movie; I was so nervous sitting in the dark with a girl next to me. I didn't even dare touch her hand. It was sheer torture for two hours.

In this New World, women were not the creatures of home

drudgery. Girls competed on equal terms with boys in school, and there were almost as many women as men in colleges and universities. I was amazed to find women lawyers, doctors, and even politicians. My old ideas about women seemed almost feudal, but discarding them was not too easy; the old concepts and attitudes seemed to be ingrained in my veins. But helping with the dishwashing in the kitchen (unheard of in Korea), sweeping and mopping the floor on Saturdays (also never seen in Korea), and on occasion even ironing my own clothes (certain disgrace in Korea) helped me to shed some of my old misconceptions of women, slowly but surely.

Another startling change: I was becoming aware of my growing respect for money. In the beginning it seemed strange to hear everyone talking about money everywhere:

"How much?"

"How cheap?"

"How expensive!"

I was becoming conscious of what kind of clothes people wore, the cars they drove, and the houses they lived in. The variations and gradations were determined by money—the amount of money a person or a family had. "What do you do?" was the first question asked of people; it offered clues to their financial status. When I found myself feeling envious and covetous of material things, I felt alarmed. All through my childhood and adolescence, wasn't I taught to be disdainful of money and all material possessions? Wasn't I taught above all to respect and seek knowledge and wisdom?

But in my daily encounters, I couldn't help but breathe the air surrounding me. Besides, I was determined to master the English language as quickly as possible. And so I learned and tried to speak English like an American:

"What's it to you?"

"Mind your own business."

"I don't give a damn!"

These were not only expressions; they were weapons of attack and defense. I began to accumulate all such expressions as a means of fortifying myself as an American. I was also learning to say:

"Goddamn it!"

"Jesus Christ!"

not in prayer, but in cussing. However, I could not bring myself to utter the most popular one:

"Fuck you!"

Once I knocked my brother down for saying it in front of my sister Alice.

I finished the year at Iolani High School. With the help of my three Asian-English dictionaries and some American dollars in bribes, I received passing grades in all subjects. But I did not wish to return there for another year. Being with students from foreign countries, I felt, impeded my progress in English. Moreover, I did not enjoy being identified as a foreigner. So I enrolled at McKinley High School. It was the only public high school in Honolulu at that time, and all the students there were Hawaii-born Americans.

McKinley was a greater challenge and much more stimulating; it was good to have more reading and more book reports. My Korean-English, Chinese-English, and Japanese-English dictionaries were showing the effects of overwork. But I enjoyed the new associations, the endless jokes outside the classrooms, but most of all, being accepted as one of them.

To my dismay, my progress presented a new problem. Just when I thought I was speaking correct English, I would be ridiculed for doing just that outside the classroom. Correct English was for the classroom only; once outside, everyone spoke Hawaiian pidgin. When they heard me say, "What's the matter, don't you like it?" they would burst into laughter and put me in my place by saying, "Watsa matta you! You tink you *haole?*" That was Hawaiian pidgin for: "What's the matter with you—do you think you are a white man?" I had to learn and force myself to say, "Ya, me no like" instead of "No, I don't want it." "Me no care, him *pupule haole,*" meaning, "I don't care. He is a crazy white man."

They had nicknames for every nationality: *yabo* (Korean), *pake* (Chinese), *buddahead* (Japanese), *bayao* (Filipino), and *cashicong* (Portuguese). Mixing words from all these groups, as well as Hawaiian, the pidgin was colorful, but incomprehensible to all except Hawaii residents.

I discovered that the more vocal and glib I became with the pidgin, the more readily I was accepted by my newfound friends. So now I spoke two kinds of English, one in the classroom and one outside.

At McKinley I had another bonus: ROTC (Reserve Officers' Training Corps). I felt compensated for not having gone to Manchuria with the Korean guerrillas. Instead of drilling at night with smuggled guns, I had military drills on the athletic field fully dressed in an American military uniform. How strange! I tried out for the school rifle team. I spent an hour after school every day learning marksmanship. In practice, I could put three bullet holes so close together that they could be covered by a twenty-five-cent coin. I became a sharpshooter and a member of the team.

Not long after that, I found a "girlfriend." Really, it was not very difficult. I had traded my Model-T Ford for a 1921 Essex. And I had become a fairly good dancer. After school, I could choose my own girls and go for a joyride. And in the evening, especially on weekends, I would take a girl out to go dancing. That's how I found Haruko (daughter of spring), a Hawaii-born Japanese girl. My friends in Shanghai would not have forgiven me for consorting with a Japanese girl and would have branded me a traitor. But Haruko was slim and willowy with an impish face. And she was an excellent dancer. She worked as a maid for a *haole* family in the Punahou district. When the evening meal was finished, her work was done, and she had her separate living quarters. So we could go out almost every night to dance. In Honolulu, there was always a party or a wedding somewhere, and old Hawaiian hospitality welcomed all strangers to the party. When there was no private party, we would go to the public dance pavilion at Waikiki Beach. Here, even though it cost us money, the open-air pavilion with pounding surf, the swaying palm trees, and the haunting music of a big band made it all worthwhile and romantic. We would dance to our hearts' content until the dance's end at 2:00 A.M. We kept this dancing ritual for almost two months.

One evening, the dance ending with the strains of "Aloha-oe," I drove her home. This night, Haruko did not get out of the car to say goodnight. She stayed in the car—a long silence.

She broke the silence. "Let's go for a walk." A walk this late, I thought to myself; but to please her, I said, "Sure."

"It's so pretty," Haruko sighed, "look at that moon!" She held my hand and led me off the road.

Holy smoke! I said to myself, she's taking me to a cemetery. I braced myself as we walked among the shadowy graves.

Haruko laughed her infectious laugh and said, "You are not scared, are you?"

"Oh, no." It sounded louder than I meant it to.

Finally we came to an enclosed tomb. It was very fancy with an arched roof and wide stone steps and an imposing tombstone.

"Let's sit down," Haruko said as she sat on the stone step. I sat next to her. It was so silent around us, and in the distance we could see the Pacific Ocean shimmering in the golden moonlight. Haruko took my hand and pulled me closer to her. I put my arm around her; she shut her eyes and tilted her head. I kissed her lips. She threw her arms around my neck and kissed me passionately. I felt a thrill piercing my whole body, I didn't know for how long. I had to pull away so that I could catch my breath. It was repeated again and again. Finally, I marshalled enough courage and whispered, "Haruko, it's really very late. I'd better be going home."

Haruko shot up as though stricken by a bolt of lightning. I got up, completely baffled. Haruko was walking away in rapid strides. I followed her. At the entrance to her house, I said goodnight. Haruko didn't respond, didn't look back; she just walked away and disappeared. The next day in school Haruko didn't even notice me. When I saw her walking toward me at the end of school, I meekly said, "Hello." She walked past me as if I weren't there. I never talked to or danced with Haruko ever again.

Of course I experienced the normal sexual arousal. But without realizing it was old-fashioned, I had developed and adhered to an idea that I would not perform a physical union with a woman unless, and not until, I fancied I found someone with whom I would share my whole life. I knew such a woman when I was eight years old: Park In-Duk. She was one of the first women graduating from Ewa College in Seoul. She was so beautiful and was a brilliant orator. She also played the piano in the choir at my father's church. Inwardly, I swore my lifetime mate should be just like her.

This was the net result of the teachings of my parents throughout my childhood years. Not once did they deliver any lecture or prescribe any moral codes. I don't remember my father or mother ever bluntly discussing the relationship between a man and a woman. But they told me, especially my mother, innumerable stories, always with her merry laughter, of the unhappy wife and the foolish husband. Sometimes the stories were reversed to describe a faithful and happy wife and husband with beautiful children. Saturated with these living stories, I spent my formative years evolving my own moral codes.

Fortunately, my days at McKinley were abruptly terminated. By the decision of the Methodist Church Annual Conference, Father was transferred to the island of Kauai. Once again our family had to move. But this time it was not another traumatic upheaval. I was sorry to leave all my new friends and especially to have to sell my car, since it was too expensive to transport it to another island. However, I felt lured to Kauai, for it was my birthplace and was known as the "garden island," the most beautiful of the islands.

Father and Umma were both pleased and eager to move. Father was anxious to go back to the island where he had spent rewarding years as a traveling preacher. The little wooden church Father had built in 1905 was still standing there on the edge of a hill—unused and abandoned now in 1926. Father had it moved down to the valley of Kapaia and placed it next to the parsonage, our new home.

Our new home wasn't a modern house like the one we had in Honolulu, but all the rooms were spacious, and we all felt comfortable there. It was a barn-like two-story building built with rough lumber without any style or design. Father had put on a new coat of paint before we moved in—a muddy red color inside and out. The house stood a few feet off the ground to escape the tropical dampness and insects, and at each entrance there was a flight of wooden steps.

On the ground floor there was an L-shaped living room, which featured a player piano, some wicker chairs, and a sofa. At the end of the room was Father's library and office. It was also his sanctuary, where he could be alone undisturbed to read, study, and prepare his sermons.

A crooked stairway led upstairs to the two bedrooms—one for the boys and the other for the girls. These rooms opened to a wide porch that ran the whole length of the house. When wire screens were installed to keep out the insects, Brother Paul and I took our beds out to the porch and slept there. It was almost like camping outdoors. And the long stairway attached to the porch gave direct access to the outside, which afforded me complete freedom of movement.

The kitchen was separated from the house by a short wooden causeway. In the kitchen there was a long table of rough lumber with benches on either side. With a dim light bulb hanging on a wire from the ceiling, the table became the center of our family life. What wonderful meals and happy times we had around that table!

The bathroom was also under a separate roof and not connected to the house. It was made of flimsy wooden walls with a door left permanently open. Over the cement floor were a tub and faucet. Everyone went into this primitive bathroom to wash up in the mornings. For a bath, water was heated on the wood-burning stove in an old kerosene can, then carried to a large galvanized iron tub in the bathhouse. Except in the winter when the temperature would fall below sixty degrees, I always used the cold shower. The toilets were in yet another building. They were not modern; they called it an "outhouse." Fortunately, it was a little distance away from the house and, except in hot summer weather with an easterly wind, was not noticeable.

For the first time in our lives, we had a country home. Well, not exactly, but almost. It was one of only two houses in a little valley. Across an open space over which an old monkeypod tree spread its branches stood the other house, the home of a Japanese Buddhist priest and his temple.

The main road linking the north and south sides of the island ran through this valley, but because of the steep and curving road, traffic moved slowly. On the side of this road were two stores: one an old rickety house turned into a sad little grocery store run by a Japanese family, and the other a new building put up by a Portuguese family named Fernandez. It was meant to be a department store to compete with the plantation store owned and operated by the Lihue sugar plantation.

Sometime later, an old Chinese man called Tom Sui managed to rent a little room near the hill and opened a Chinese restaurant. Tom Sui was a jolly old man. We teased him and played with him, but we never ate in his restaurant.

That was the entire life in the valley, and except on Sundays when the Japanese people gathered to worship in their Buddhist temple and the Koreans gathered to worship in Father's Methodist church, life in the valley was serene and peaceful.

Father was always engaged in some program of study: different religions, science, psychology, and so on. In Kauai, he enrolled in the correspondence classes of LaSalle University of Chicago and began studying law. Oftentimes he would be engrossed in his study and stay awake in his office long after everyone had gone to sleep. I can still see him on the day his law books arrived by mail. He could hardly contain himself; caressing each book, flipping the pages, he was like a boy with a new toy.

When he was not studying, he worked outside digging, planting, watering, and weeding, and soon transformed the grounds around the house into a colorful and aromatic garden. All the plants seemed to respond to his humming and singing as he worked.

Despite all the shortcomings, Kauai was truly a garden island, and like Father with his books and garden, Umma, too, found a domain of her own where she was the sole mother and queen, where she could lavish her affection and care as much as she liked; a little world of pets and animals. In the house, she spent happy hours feeding and talking to the birds and fish and forever warning the cat to stay away from them. When she came out of the house she would be greeted by two puppies, each one jealous of the other. She would feed them in separate bowls and talk to them in Korean: "Don't behave like I've starved you! Don't eat so fast, you'll get indigestion!"

Next came the mother goat with two babies. Umma didn't have any special food for them; they were given special treats of cut grass when we boys came home from school. Just the same, they followed Umma around wherever she went, crying only as baby goats and a mother goat can cry. Umma would take some milk from the mother goat and give it to us to drink when we came home from school.

Next, Umma would enter the fenced-in compound. First came the Muscovy ducks quacking loudly at Umma's feet. "Don't make so much noise!" Umma would scold them as she poured out a bowl of rice mixed with some delectable chopped vegetables. Then she would enter the coop and face the impatient chickens. "Never mind all the chatter," she would chide them. "When are you going to give me some eggs?" She would toss some feed on the ground and pour the rest into a feeder. She would then clean out the coop and wash the bowl that held fresh water, all the while chatting with the chicks. "You are all so messy. You eat so much, but you are all so skinny," and on and on. . . . She would sit on a stool among the chickens and rest awhile before attending to the rest of her animal kingdom— the rabbits and pigeons. It was already nearing the time when her human brood would be coming home from school; time for her to bake some cookies or prepare some Korean snack for her starving children.

Once again, Father became a traveling preacher, but instead of riding horseback he now traveled in a Ford. I was his chauffeur. Every Sunday, after an early breakfast, the family would get in the car and head for the south, or the "dry side" of the island. Umma would have to be up at the crack of dawn to feed all the animals so she could join us on the Sunday travel.

We would stop at the sugar plantation camps and little towns wherever there were Koreans, conduct a brief service and a quick visit, and move on. This route usually had stops at Lihue, Koloa, Eleele, Makaweli, and finally ended at Kekaha. The two little towns of Koloa and Makaweli, had only one Korean family each, but Father wouldn't think of neglecting them.

All the services were held in the little plantation houses where the Korean laborers lived. The shiny wooden floors where we sat showed much wear from constant scrubbing and mopping. The services were very brief, but Father's deep feelings never failed to move me. Part of the time was devoted to the weekly news and listening to their problems. Father was especially happy to dispense news of the Korean independence movement that he had received from Kim Koo, the Korean patriot who maintained the one-man Provisional Government. They would respond to Papa's sermon by dropping a few coins into a little basket. Papa would save these for a month, then send the money to Kim Koo in Shanghai.

When the last service in Kekaha was over, we would be invited to lunch at one of the Korean homes: freshly cooked steaming white rice, a bowl of seaweed soup in broth made with meat bones discarded by the butcher, and slices of abalone, the family treasure, dipped in soy and vinegar sauce. All this out of their meager family provisions! We ate with much relish and gratitude.

The following Sunday, we would travel to the "wet side" of the island. The main stop was at Kapaa, about ten miles away, where Korean families lived because there was a pineapple cannery where Koreans could find work. With the help of the owners of the pineapple fields and cannery, Father had a church built for his flock. It was the only place where the bell in the belfry summoned the people to church on Sundays. Here the service was performed with the singing of many hymns and announcements of varied activities. Father's sermon, too, was more elaborate and lengthier. He followed it with his news of the week and of the Korean independence movement. Special collections for the movement from the entire island were sent to Kim Koo in Shanghai each month. Kim Koo was the only active leader preserving the name and carrying on the work of the Korean Provisional Government.

From Kapaa, we would travel to the north end of the island, Hanalei. On the way, we would stop at Kilauea and visit a Korean-Hawaiian family. We had to climb down a cliff to a little cove. The Korean was a fisherman married to a Hawaiian, and they had two handsome sons. He was always grateful for Father's visits and the recognition of his family as Koreans.

Hanalei was a little hamlet where the Chinese immigrants had settled and carried on the only remaining rice plantation in Hawaii. Winding down the road from a high cliff to Hanalei Valley were the beautiful patterns of rice fields, and little huts on stilts where old Chinese men pulled the network of strings with noisemaking cans to chase the sparrows. The sheer breathtaking cliffs circled the valley like a screen and caught the clouds for daily showers and so earned the name of Wet Side. The panorama was an immense, living, Chinese brush painting.

The road ended when we passed the town of Hanalei and approached the caves of Haena. We would walk over the jagged rocks and come to a clearing near the wet cave, so called because the enormous cave was filled with clear, fresh water. We would settle down and have our picnic lunch, always a surprise and a great treat. After the lunch, while we explored the mountainside, my younger brothers would strip and dive into the water for a swim. I never joined this adventure, for I had never learned to swim well or overcome my fear of deep water. Sometimes we would be caught by a sudden shower that came out of the blue sky; we would run into the cave and watch the rain until it passed over.

Father's church work was never finished on Sunday. He was always ready to help the Koreans whenever they needed him. Our telephone would ring at any time of day or night: Someone was very ill and needed to go to the hospital; someone was injured; some family needed more firewood and kerosene; some children were having trouble in school; and endless emergencies. I would drive Father and take him wherever the trouble was and wherever he was needed. I discovered that, for all his work, his monthly salary from the Methodist Mission was sixty dollars. With this paltry sum he was expected to carry on all of his work, pay the traveling expenses, and feed his six children (Alice had stayed in Honolulu), not to mention send them all to school.

Father's faith in his destiny once again came to his rescue. His work with the first Korean immigrants on Kauai in the early 1900s had left a lasting impression with some of the plantation owners. They were glad to have him back. The most prominent among them were George Wilcox, and after his death, his sister, Elsie Wilcox, and Dora Isenberg, whose late husband had been among the first to support Father's work. They bought the Ford for Father's travels and pledged monthly donations in support of his mission. Still, to help the family finances, during summer vacations all of us boys went to work—Paul and I at the pineapple cannery stacking cans, and Joshua and David in the cane fields. Stacking cans was backbreaking work, but working the cane fields with a hoe was much worse. First of all, they had to get up at 3:00 A.M., gulp down a quick breakfast, and walk up the hill in the dark to catch the little train. The narrow-gauge boxcars carried all the plantation workers up to the mountain foothills and dropped them off wherever there were patches of cane fields.

Joshua's and David's job was weeding and clearing irrigation ditches. They worked eight hours, with a short break for lunch. They would come home covered with the red volcanic dust and mud, looking like two red devils coming to avenge their cruel fate. David was ten years old, Joshua twelve. Each earned twenty-five cents a day. On payday, they would proudly hand their pay envelopes to Umma. She would reward them with a dollar each for their Saturday matinee movies and an ice cream cone.

I resumed my sophomore year at Kauai High School, the only high school on the island. Students from the far west and east of the island had to live in the boys' and girls' dormitories in Lihue. Compared to McKinley, this was a little school, with only a few hundred students. Many of them came from plantation families with ambitions to go to the university and become doctors or lawyers, or at the very least, dentists, and to become rich. I also wanted to go to college, not to make money, but to get an education and perhaps be able to follow in Father's footsteps as a minister.

The college preparatory course required that I study a foreign language; my three Asian languages didn't count. So I took up French. To my surprise, it was not half as difficult as English. I liked the masculine and feminine genders of nouns, verbs, and adjectives, and I liked the sounds of the language—they seemed so musical and affectionate. I also learned something more. My teacher was a Frenchman who had left his country, wandered around the world, and finally landed on Kauai. He lived alone in a tiny cottage on the beach and never mingled with other faculty members. All the other teachers were American men and women, a few of them married couples who came to Hawaii from the U.S. mainland. None of them showed any friendliness to the French teacher; they were not openly hostile, but neither did they acknowledge him.

Puzzled and curious, I asked my friends one day, "Say, why is our French teacher always alone?"

"Peter, don't you know?"

"No, tell me."

The friend lowered his voice and said, "He is a Jew!"

It only increased my puzzlement; why was a Jewish person isolated and shunned? I couldn't understand. My friends seemed appalled at my ignorance.

"Don't you know the Jews killed Jesus?"

"But Jesus was also a Jew, wasn't He?" My retort made little impression. This was my first flicker of awareness of anti-Semitism.

I had another teacher who influenced my life, but for a different reason: Mrs. Anderson was my English teacher and a great grammarian. For the first time I learned that the English language was built on sentences, and I learned what a sentence was. I learned how to analyze and diagram a sentence and understand the function of each word. Oh, what a wonderful feeling it gave me; English was not a mystery any more—there was an understandable reason and meaning for every word in a sentence.

Mrs. Anderson was also a mystic—not just a superstitious one, but a true believer and practitioner. Occasionally she would interrupt herself in class and tell us of her interesting experiences.

Quite casually, she would say, "Oh, I had a nice visit with my dead uncle last night."

"When did he die?" someone would ask.

"Oh, a long time ago—more than ten years."

Silence.

Other times, it was her dead mother who spoke to her, a dream she had of someone who died a thousand miles away, and the transmission of her thoughts to her dear friend living across the ocean. Though frightening to some, I was always fascinated by her stories. Perhaps because of my interest, Mrs. Anderson once invited me to visit her. Sitting in a darkened room, she showed me the rituals of concentration for communicating with a spirit, dead or alive. An hour's visit in her spiritual room was enough to satisfy all my curiosity! Nevertheless, I remained a good friend, and with her help I was beginning to discover the world of the English language.

The following year, my junior year, I tried out for the football team. Football in China was called soccer in America, and hardly anyone ever played it. American football seemed so farcical; stooping, jumping, throwing, kicking—it was a combination of all kinds of sports put together, including boxing and wrestling. But since I was learning everything American, I decided I should also learn how to play football. When the football season began, to my great surprise I was placed on the varsity team as a right tackle. With all the pads, the uniform, and the heavy cleated shoes, I weighed 140 pounds, still the lightest man on the team.

To survive, I used all my Korean fighting techniques—use of my legs and feet to trip and knock down the opponent. So the coach kept me as a guard and called the play on my side quite frequently. Then came a game against a team from Koloa. At the first lineup, I faced my opponent, a two hundred-pound Hawaiian left tackle. I had to do something at the very start so as not to be intimidated by the giant. At the snap, I beat him to the punch, tripped his leg, and let him fall. The next time I tripped his other leg and let him fall to the other side. I also varied this with a quick side step and let him fall on his face. I was having fun. I called for the off-tackle play on my side for consistent gains. Finally, before the half was over, the Hawaiian giant walked off the field. He quit!

The annual inter-island game was our big one, and that year we were to play Lahaina High School from the island of Maui. Lahaina was the school for children of Hawaiian ancestry, and their football team was always stacked with young giants. Naturally, they were heavily favored to beat us. We had a six-foot-tall German fullback and two other big fellows of Portuguese descent, but the rest were all Asians with slight and diminutive builds like mine. Our coach reminded us of this disparity and warned us not to get killed. We were inspired and ready. We held the big boys dead in their tracks, and I made several flying tackles to keep their runners from scoring. The townspeople, too, were excited. They whooped and hollered, "Beat the *Kanakas!* Beat the *Kanakas!*"

And we did beat them—6 to 0.

We still had to worry about the game for the following week. We had to travel to Maui and give Lahaina a rematch. They were ready and waiting for us. We knew we would have a fight on our hands that Saturday afternoon. What happened was not a football game; it was a war. The big fellows were out to avenge their defeat, and we were fighting for our pride. Every scrimmage was a fierce clash, and when the game had only ten minutes remaining, the score was 0 to 0. We had the ball, and the quarterback called an off-tackle play on my side. Then the snap, and we clashed once more. I was at the bottom of the pile. Suddenly someone grabbed my left foot with both hands and twisted it as though trying to break it off. I winced and writhed with pain, but I caught sight of the guy who did the twisting. It was their left tackle. The coach saw me hobbling and wanted to take me out of the game. I begged him to let me stay. The next play, when the ball was snapped, I threw a short right cross flush on the culprit's jaw. He went down. The referee didn't see it. The next play, same thing: The snap and the crack and the culprit went down again. This time he was taken out of the game, and I took myself out also. The final score was 6 to 0, Lahaina.

That evening there was a big school dance, and I didn't want to miss it. I bandaged my swollen ankle and, gritting my teeth, went to the dance. The auditorium was gaily decorated with colorful streamers, palm fronds, and flowers; a big band played sweet music, and all the girls were so pretty. I forgot all about my painful ankle and began to dance. Then I found this beautiful Hawaiian girl, slim and sparkling; named Leilani. She reminded me so much of Haruko, the Japanese girlfriend I had had for two months at McKinley. Leilani was also a wonderful dancer. We danced every dance, she turned down all the other boys. The music stopped for an intermission.

"It's so hot," Leilani said. "Let's go out for some fresh air." Outside, it was pitch-dark, with millions of stars sparkling in the sky. Leilani took my hand and led me through a path that went to the woods. We stopped among the tall trees, and Leilani faced me and lifted her face. I responded with a kiss, and she embraced and kissed me passionately.

The night in the cemetery with Haruko flashed through my mind. Oh, no, I thought to myself, and said, "Leilani, my ankle is really hurting me. Let's go back."

Yes, we went back to the auditorium, and she walked away without a word. Neither did we have another dance together.

Being on the football team taught me that an athlete could have special privileges and status in school, among which popularity with the girls was only one. Enjoying and wishing to expand my new-found honor, I also joined the basketball and baseball teams. I was becoming quite a hero in school, and I eagerly participated in other school activities, such as playing the violin in the school orchestra and joining the Hi-Y Club, the students' religious organization.

I also tried my hand at learning the secret of American "free enterprise." It was a small venture to win the ticket-selling contest. The school was promoting our annual play, in which I had the part of a silly detective. At the moment, however, I was more interested in becoming the best salesman in school. After school, I spent all my time in front of stores selling tickets. And in the evenings I went to the plantation camps and visited every house. There were many other students vying for the honor. I was confident I would win, for my sale of seventy-five dollars was far ahead of the others.

On the morning of the final day, when we were to report our sales and the winner was to be announced at the noon assembly, my friends brought me shocking news. A *haole* girl had one hundred dollars in total sales! How was it possible? The girl had never gone anywhere selling tickets. There could be only one answer: She had a rich aunt named Mrs. McIntyre. She must have purchased one hundred dollars worth of tickets and given it to her niece to win the contest. That was not fair; my anger mounted to a fury. But there was nothing I could do; there was no time. Oh, yes there was! I went to all the students who had participated in the contest and convinced them to let me have their sales results. Why not? They had no chance to win anyway. Besides, I asked, would they like to see some-one buy the contest?

The assembly bell rang, and the students were astir with excite-ment; no one was sure who the winner would be. Mr. Loper, our principal, began announcing the results of the contest. He began at the bottom with ten dollars in sales, then to the higher and higher sales. When he read, "McIntyre, one hundred dollars in sales," the students burst into applause. Mr. Loper held up his hand and said, "There is one more—Peter Hyun, one hundred fifty dollars! And the winner!" A deafening hurray and applause. I felt sorry for the crestfallen *haole* girl and her aunt, Mrs. McIntyre. But, in true American spirit, I said to myself, all's fair in love and business.

Not long after that, I learned a totally different kind of lesson about the power of money. Father let me drive his Ford to school, dropping off my brothers and sister at Lihue Elementary School on the way. Then there was a straight road for about a mile to the high school. Students from outlying towns like Koloa, Eleele, and Waimea on the south side and Kapaa and Kilauea on the north side all loved to step on the gas when they reached the straightaway and race to school. One morning, when school had hardly begun, I was called out of the classroom to report to the principal's office. I was surprised to find a Hawaiian deputy sheriff in Mr. Loper's office.

"Did you run over a dog on the way to school this morning?" Mr. Loper asked.

"No, I didn't," I answered, puzzled.

Well, Mr. Rice's dog, an Airedale, had been run over and killed, and he reported to the police that he saw my car speeding away. He demanded that I be arrested and punished. Impossible. I couldn't have; I saw no dog on the road. Mr. Loper advised me to go with the sheriff. At the county courthouse, the Hawaiian judge heard the sheriff's report; without even listening to my side, he pronounced his sentence: twenty dollars or two days in jail. He said I could go home and return with the money. I went back to Mr. Loper and told him of the unfair sentence.

"Pay the fine," Mr. Loper said.

"No, I won't," I said, "not even if I had the money. Twenty dollars! Why, that's one-third of my father's monthly salary! I will go to jail for two days."

Mr. Loper shut the office door, took me aside, and spoke to me frankly. "Look, Peter, Mr. Rice is one of the plantation owners, or married into the family, which is the same thing. You cannot buck the powers that own and run this island. And you and I have to get along with them."

I was touched by his frankness and concern. He pulled a twenty-dollar bill out of his wallet and handed it to me, saying, "This is a friendly loan. You may pay it back anytime you can."

Back at the courthouse, it pained me to hand over the money to the clerk. The Hawaiian deputy sheriff was standing by.

"You know I didn't kill that dog," I said to him, "but I am paying to make the *haole* happy."

At last, after having gone to school in three countries and having studied in three languages, I would soon receive a high school diploma in yet a different language, English, and in Hawaii. As the day of graduation approached, the question of going to college was no longer only a dream; it was a serious and immediate challenge. But where, and how? Financial help from Father was out of the question. The University of Hawaii seemed the most likely place; it was close to home, and I could find a part-time job and support myself.

For admission, I had to take a series of tests; the first one was called an "intelligence test," which determined the basic qualifications of an applicant. I couldn't even divine what the test was all about. Page after page, the questions asked were a big puzzle to me. How could I finish the line that followed "Hickory Dickory Dock"? Who said, "Give me liberty, or give me death?" Or, how many cylinders in a Cadillac? I thought all cars had four cylinders.

I left most of the pages blank, and the test result showed that I was a little below the level of a moron. Only years later did I learn that the so-called I.Q. test was based on studies of American children brought up in the Mid-west, and not for anyone brought up in Korea or China. I was discouraged. I thought, after all, that a higher education would always remain a dream for me.

One day, Father told me that Mrs. Isenberg, one of his benefactors, wished to see me. So one afternoon I drove up the hill to her mansion. Two German police dogs greeted me with ferocious barking. I almost jumped back in the car and went back home. Fortunately, a Japanese gardener appeared and called the dogs away.

The housemaid instructed me to wait in the living room. I sat in a huge chair and looked around the room. Rich tapestries and large paintings of men and women hung on the walls. Highly polished cabinets were filled with strange-looking silverware. Thick carpet covered the entire floor, and the room was filled with lush tropical plants in huge, beautiful pots. I was entranced by this strange world, when I heard the voice.

"Hello! You must be Peter, Reverend Soon Hyun's son."

"Yes," I said. I saw Mrs. Isenberg for the first time. She was a big, dignified lady with a broad, strong face and dark gray hair that settled on her head like an eagle's nest. She was warm and friendly. She came straight to the point.

"Tell me, Peter, what do you want to do when you graduate from high school?"

"I want to go to college, but I failed the test," I told her.

"I understand, Peter," she said, "you grew up in Korea and China." I felt comforted by her understanding. She continued, "If you did go to college, what would you study?"

"I want to study religion and become a minister like my father."

"All right, Peter," she said, "don't worry about the money. I'll pay for your college education. Think about where you might be admitted and let me know."*

I came home floating. When I broke the good news, Father and Umma cried out, "Oh!" and clapped like they were watching a performance in a theatre. Even Sister Elizabeth beamed with pride. But I noticed my brothers were silent and somber with envy. I went to the library and studied all the university catalogs. I also wrote to Dr. Fry, the Methodist superintendent, and asked for advice. He recommended DePauw University in Greencastle, Indiana; it was founded by the Methodist church, and they might welcome the son of a Korean Methodist minister. Indeed, they did. In reply to my application, they sent me a certificate of admission, together with the schedule of activities for the opening week. When I reported it to Mrs. Isenberg, she handed me a check for five hundred dollars: four hundred for the tuition, one hundred dollars for my travel expenses. She promised she would send money for my living expenses. I could hardly wait to announce this great news to all my fellow graduates.

Of course, I was excited and happy, but who would drive Father around the island for his work? I need not have worried; my three younger brothers came to the rescue and, taking turns as they grew older, more than filled my place. The week before leaving home, I went around the island with Father and Umma to say good-

---

*Miss Elsie Wilcox of Grove Farm also contributed to Peter's expenses. Letter from Peter to Miss Wilcox, dated October 18, 1928.

bye to all the Koreans. Without exception, their final words to me were: "Study hard! Stay well!"

I finally went to Mrs. Isenberg to again thank her and to repeat my pledge to become a minister. I waved goodbye to my family from the deck of a little boat that would take me to Honolulu. I was alone, on my way, finally, to fulfill my lifetime dream—to get a college education. In Honolulu, I boarded the SS *Monterey,* sailing away to the mystical city of Los Angeles. The Royal Hawaiian Band on the dock blared the farewell song, "Aloha-oe"; I waved at the elderly Koreans who had come out to see me off, and then the ship pulled out of the dock and headed for the open sea. I took all the flower leis I was wearing and tossed them into the water. Just as the leis would reach the shores, so the Hawaiian legend said, the wearer of the leis, too, would be sure to return to Hawaii.

# 3

## COLLEGE

Once again I was crossing the Pacific. It was February 1929, and, after a four-year interval, I was now completing the trip that had started in Shanghai, finally on my way to my ultimate destination—college. The "tourist class" in which I was traveling, though located in the hold in the stern of the ship, was quite luxurious compared to the steerage on the SS *President Wilson*. There was no stench, the two-tiered bunks were quite comfortable, and we even had a dining area with long tables and benches where our meals were served. The weather was warm and the sea calm, and all the passengers spent most of the time on deck.

There was a group of students from Hawaii, all traveling to the mainland to attend colleges. Among them were several Koreans: one a high school football player who wanted to become a doctor, another who planned to become a dentist. Both swore that they could make more money as a doctor and a dentist than in any other profession. There was also a Korean girl who was going to become a nurse. She was gentle and quiet and the only one to show some idealism associated with her planned career. I had to tell them about my own plans.

"Minister!" They all shouted, as though my idea to become a minister was too horrible to believe. Sitting under the warm sunshine, cooled by gentle trade winds, we spent many hours discussing and arguing about the purpose of education and missions in life. When the debate became too heated, someone would strum a guitar and start singing languorous Hawaiian songs, and soon everyone would join in. Oh, what concerts we had on the deck; Hawaiian songs, school songs, ribald and funny songs mingled with Korean and Japanese folk songs.

We had one other diversion—a game of poker. Someone started it in the hold. We sat on the floor and began playing. A gypsy man asked if he could join us, and we said of course. It was a penny-ante game—no one was to get rich or lose his shirt at this game. But very quickly we discovered all the money was going to the gypsy. One of us would win a hand, then the next several hands would go to the gypsy. After a while some of us lost interest and decided to quit. That's when the gypsy motioned us to stay.

"Sit down," he said. "Let me show you something." He picked up the deck of cards, shuffled, and asked for a cut. "I am going to deal one of you a pair of kings," he said, and began dealing. He asked us to turn up our cards. Sure enough, there was a pair of kings. Then he turned up his own hand—a pair of aces! He repeated this amazing demonstration while all of us watched to detect the trick. No one could. He would deal someone two pairs and three of a kind for himself. The last straw was to deal me a flush and deal himself a full house! We shook our heads in disbelief.

"Let that be a lesson to you," the gypsy said in a fatherly voice. "Never play cards with a gypsy."

For three days and nights we sailed eastward. On the morning of the fourth day, there was excitement afloat. None of us had ever been to the mainland, and each one harbored his own uneasy speculation. We expressed our hidden concern and fear by vocalizing and advising each other:

"Don't talk to strangers."

"Look out for the pickpockets!"

"Watch your money," and so on.

At mid-morning we caught sight of land—California. I had heard many fables about this land in my early childhood in Korea. In America, the streets were paved with gold, everyone was rich, and everyone believed in Jesus Christ. And there it was looming before me; I would soon set my feet on that land.

I could hardly suppress my disappointment as we approached the Los Angeles harbor. There was no grandeur of a big city; no scenic shoreline nor a forest of skyscrapers. We passed through a long and drab channel and reached the pier. What did impress me were the workmen on the dock—there were so many *haoles*. No Hawaiians, Filipinos, or Chinese. That was my first indication that not every white man was rich: some had to perform menial labor.

I picked up my suitcase and began walking down the gangplank. No newcomer to America could have walked with his head held higher or with more bounce in his steps. All of us got on a big red electric train, which took us to the city. It was a long and rather surprising ride. Except for a few structures of oil refineries seen in the distance, the entire thirty-mile ride passed through farmlands. It didn't seem possible that the great city of Los Angeles was really in the midst of all these farms.

The ride ended in a tunnel, and we didn't see the city until we walked out of the station to the street. The sight of the crowd of people moving on the sidewalks and the crammed automobile traffic indicated that, yes, this was a big city. On a taxi ride to the home of our family friend, I also glimpsed low stucco buildings, shops, and wooden bungalow homes with green lawns. The total appearance of the city, and the royal palms that lined some streets, resembled Honolulu, with a relaxed and leisurely atmosphere.

My next disappointment was the discovery of our family friend's home; it turned out to be a little basement apartment. Janet was the daughter of a deacon in Father's church in Honolulu. She had married a Korean stranger who had come to Hawaii from the mainland to find a wife. She had followed her husband to California where she was raising a son and two daughters. Park, Janet's husband, was hardly ever home; he traveled constantly and would not divulge what kind of work he did. When I met Janet in Los Angeles, she was practically destitute. Fortunately she was a registered nurse, and she worked a night shift in a hospital to feed and clothe her young children and saw that they went to school. I felt rather sad for her and wanted to go to a hotel, but she wouldn't hear of it. She was terribly glad to see me, to hear the news from Hawaii, and she said I was more than welcome to share whatever she had.

My major mission in Los Angeles was to locate and visit with Father's former colleagues. They were elated to meet the son of the Reverend Soon Hyun. These men were among the first Korean immigrants to Hawaii and among the few who had managed to escape from the sugar plantations and make their way to California. But their life had not been any easier; it was a never-ending struggle to provide for their families and send their children to school. But like

Korean patriots everywhere, they kept their faith and made necessary sacrifices to keep the flame of Korean independence burning. Their memory of Father as a dedicated and honest leader was very moving. With their meager resources, the Koreans in Los Angeles managed to maintain a Methodist church, a Korean language school for the children, and the Korean National Association, which published a weekly newspaper in Korean. It was distributed throughout the United States and even in Mexico and Puerto Rico—wherever there were Koreans. What proud and resourceful people the Koreans are!

I spent the afternoon of the second day in Los Angeles sightseeing. Together with the Korean students from Hawaii, I rode the big red electric car and went to a beach town called Venice. It was my introduction to the American amusement park. There were no trees or grass in the park; it was a long wooden pier that shot out of the beach toward the ocean. Both sides of the pier were lined with little stalls with garishly painted fronts, all designed to lure the customers. At some stalls men barked about the freaks, the belly dancers, and the world's greatest magician. Other stalls offered games of chance and skill with darts, rifles, rings, and baseballs and had displays of cheap dolls and stuffed animals for prizes. And over the din of the crowd and the barkers, the loudspeakers along the pier blared some unrecognizable marching music. I, too, got into the carnival mood and tried my hand at knocking down wooden milk bottles with baseballs and shooting rifles at moving targets. I didn't win any prizes.

The climax of the day at Venice was the roller coaster ride. At the suggestion of my friends, I got on one of the chairs without any idea of what I was about to experience. The row of metal chairs started moving with a noisy clatter. It proceeded slowly and harmlessly, then began climbing up an incline. There was a stir of excitement among the riders, which did not concern me; I was enjoying the view of the park as we rose higher and higher. Then it happened, the instant we reached the top—I was plunging into a bottomless pit to be dashed into eternity. What a foolish way to end my life! I didn't want to die. I was still alive, but we were climbing again to an even higher tower. I could not get off; I had to resign myself to my fate. After a series of such near-deaths, the car finally came to a stop. I got off in a daze, and needless to say, I have never gotten on another roller coaster.

In the evening I got on the Southern Pacific train to San Francisco. Again, my mission was to find and visit with Father's former colleagues. It was a tedious ride that consumed the whole night; I hardly had a glimpse of the country we passed through.

I walked out of the station in San Francisco, put my suitcase on the sidewalk, and stood there breathing the air of this storybook city. As I gazed at the stately buildings and the people hurrying to work, I remembered some of the legends I had heard about this city: the gold rush days, the clipper ships that sailed from here to China and brought back tea and silk, the first Chinese immigrants brought here to build the American railroad, and the holocaust of the great earthquake. Yes, I was here standing on a San Francisco street, breathing its air and contemplating its historical adventures.

San Francisco bore no resemblance to Los Angeles or Honolulu. A taxi taking me to the home of Father's old friend passed through streets that rose and fell like the roller coaster in Venice. Instead of bungalows, multistoried houses lined the streets with no space in between or in front. The colorful decorations on the front of every house made each block look like a giant stage backdrop. The driver found the address and let me off in front of a dry cleaning shop. I hesitantly walked down the steps and entered the basement. An elderly Asian couple dropped their work and stared at me with a blank look.

"Are you Mr. and Mrs. Min?" I asked.

"Yes," they said, still puzzled.

"My name is Peter Hyun—the son of Reverend Soon Hyun."

Their faces lit up instantly and both exclaimed simultaneously, "*Aigo-cham!* Not really!" Mr. Min rushed over and took my suitcase, and Mrs. Min came and squeezed my arm and patted me all over to be certain I was really there. They ushered me into the rear of the store to their living quarters. "How is Reverend Hyun? How is his health? And your mother, your brothers, and sisters?" They could hardly control the stream of inquiries. And what was I doing in San Francisco?

While giving them brief answers to all their questions, I looked at their animated faces. They were beautiful faces, unblemished and unwrinkled, smooth, white, and shiny. They hardly showed any marks of sixty or more years of life as immigrants. They were related to Queen Min, the last Korean Queen murdered by the Japanese.

They escaped somehow and joined the Korean immigrants going to Hawaii and from there journeyed to San Francisco. In Korea, as members of the nobility, they had never done any manual labor. Now they were making their living operating a dry cleaning shop. When Father was stationed in Washington, D.C., and was traveling around the United States to plead the cause of Korean independence, the Mins were among his staunchest supporters. They held their high personal respect and admiration for Father all through the difficult years. And now they were actually looking at and talking to Reverend Hyun's son, who was on his way to college.

As befitting time-honored Korean tradition, Mrs. Min repaired to the kitchen and prepared a sumptuous Korean lunch especially for me. They were elated to sit with me at the table and share the food, but they enjoyed even more hearing my account of our lives in China and Hawaii. Mr. Min made it a holiday for the afternoon and took me around to visit several other Korean men who had also been Father's coworkers in the independence movement. All of them received me with surprise and gladness, as though Father himself had dropped in to visit them.

At their urging, I spent the night at the Mins' and left early next morning on the Union Pacific to cross the American continent and head for DePauw University in Indiana. As a parting gift, Mr. and Mrs. Min presented me with a woolen top coat, saying, "It will be cold in Indiana."

I lived on the train for three days and nights, but compared with the three-day train ride through Manchuria, it was luxurious. The chair I slept on was not wooden; it was padded and upholstered. The bathroom had all the conveniences: flushing toilet, a wash basin with hot and cold running water, and even a large mirror on the wall. And I didn't have to carry bundles of food with me for the trip. For all my meals, I needed only to go to the dining car, sit at a table, and order whatever I wanted from the menu. I couldn't believe how it was possible to cook on a moving train and serve such delicious hot meals, from soup, roast beef, pie à la mode, and coffee. It was sheer magic, and I enjoyed every trip to the diner.

The ride was long but not tedious. I was fascinated by every bit of the passing scene. The entire first day the train traveled over mountains—rugged and wild rocky mountains. Some jagged peaks rose above us while other peaks pointed up from far below us. The train wound its way over the mountains and down, only to encounter another mountain range. In between the ranges we passed through dense forests of giant trees that shut out the sunlight and nearly turned day into night.

On the second day we traversed the desert country. Again, it took the entire day to cross it. Except for a few stops at dusty desert towns, there was no sign of life. Waves of sand dunes with shrubs and cacti rolled endlessly like an immense, dry ocean. Occasionally a hazy outline of mountains on the horizon indicated the boundaries of the desert.

On the third day, the train finally left the desert behind and entered the farmlands—a welcome change of scenery. But we were to discover the farmlands were as immense as the desert. All day long we sped past an endless patchwork of wheat fields, brown and heavy, ready for harvest. The vastness of the land and its crop would be inconceivable to a Korean farmer, and in the time the speeding train took to cross the farmlands, it could have crossed the entire Korean peninsula several times over. The legendary gold that I had been told paved the streets of American cities was really here—in those precipitous mountains, in the dark forests and the desert, and in these sprawling carpets of wheat fields.

Every morning, a vendor with a large basket hooked on his arm walked through the aisle and sold pastries, juice, candies, and the newspaper of the town we had just passed. These newspapers kept me in touch with the world—with news of the New York Yankees and the Boston Red Sox in the pennant race and the threat of a Japanese attack on Shanghai.

There was also a very special treat on the train. A young boy about eight years old was traveling with his mother or grandmother. In the morning, after breakfast, the guardian lady would take a violin out of its case and hand it to the young boy. After minutes of tuning, the boy would begin to play— first the scales and then some musical numbers. The boy was such an accomplished violinist that even the scales were played with complex variations, and he made it sound like a beautiful concerto. With only brief interruptions of comments by his guardian, the boy would continue playing for an hour. This truly beautiful concert was performed after lunch for an hour, and again he gave an hour-long concert after supper. I overheard some passengers whispering that he was a Jewish child prodigy. Many years later it would occur to me that the boy violinist was, or could have been, Yehudi Menuhin being taken to New York to launch his great musical career.

On the morning of the fourth day we were approaching Chicago. Everyone in the train began repacking their valises, and the bathroom was crowded with men shaving and grooming. The vendor entered the car and began hawking. But this morning his shouts sounded more excited; he was selling the Chicago morning newspaper. I bought one and read the headline, "Valentine's Day Massacre." I knew about Al Capone and his gangsters and their war with other rival gangs. But why this terrifying massacre just when I was coming to Chicago!

I got off the train and walked into the biggest railroad station I had ever seen. Someone wearing a red cap rushed over and grabbed my suitcase, but I was alert. I snatched it back and walked away from the first Chicago "gangster." I got in a taxi and directed him to the YMCA (Young Men's Christian Association) hotel; it had been recommended to me as the safest place in Chicago. When I was let off in front of a skyscraper, I was astounded—a fourteen-story YMCA! I got a room on the tenth floor for $1.50—a tiny room with a cot and the use of a common bathroom down the hallway. Anyway, I felt safe and secure.

After supper in the cafeteria, I sat in the lobby reading the afternoon paper; more about the massacre and the expected gang war. Just the same, my curiosity about Chicago and the urge to see it kept gnawing at me. "Just around the hotel," I promised myself, and ventured out. How was I to know that the YMCA hotel was located in the Loop next to the most notorious section of State Street. It was a very wide street but dimly lit. All the shops were closed, and in every doorway some figure stood leaning against the wall. I was sure their pockets bulged with guns and that they were were waiting for their prey. After passing a row of pawnshops, I found myself in front of a brightly lit theatre.

I had never seen such a theatre before. The sidewalk in front of it was littered with huge posters of young women wearing nothing but scanty panties. I thought they were the same as the ones I had seen at the amusement park in Venice—something to lure the customers. But they aroused my curiosity; I reluctantly paid the expensive admission price of fifty cents and went in. It was so dark inside, I had to stand there for a while to find my bearings. I could now discern the crouched figures in the seats. They seemed like old people, in shabby clothes—all men. The idea flashed in my mind that they might all be gangsters having their evening's entertainment. I found a seat and kept a careful watch on the men sitting at either side of me.

I saw movements in the orchestra pit, faint lights flickering, and finally the leader with a baton. There was a big and loud fanfare, followed by the most uninspired overture. The curtain parted on a dark stage, and a powerful spotlight shot down on a woman standing in the middle of the stage. The makeup on her face was so heavy, I couldn't tell whether she was a young girl of sixteen or an old lady of sixty. Keeping time with the music, she began to move, walking back and forth across the stage. I didn't see anything particularly entertaining until the girl deftly took off her blouse and tossed it off stage. Next, with equal deftness, she snapped her skirt, and off it went into the wings. She was practically naked, with only the token brassiere and the briefest possible panties covering her. The music quickened its tempo; the girl began shaking and shimmying, and the men began shouting, "Take it off! Take it off!" With her back toward the audience, she reached behind and snapped the brassiere off. The men began applauding.

When she turned around spinning the brassiere on her finger, she not only showed bare breasts, but she was shaking and rotating the tassels tied to her nipples. More applause. I felt embarrassed but fascinated. I also felt guilty: What would my family and friends in Hawaii think if they knew what I was watching in Chicago?

Encouraged by the burst of applause, the girl began to do a strange dance. It was mostly movements of her hips and buttocks; she crouched low, her knees bent, and rotated her hips like a Hawaiian hula dancer. But without wearing a skirt, the dance seemed vulgar and lewd. At the climax the girl loosened the string that held up her panties (I learned later it was called a G-string). The audience cheered wildly. She turned her back to them, pulled off the panties, and waved them in the air. With a coy backward glance and a kick with her heel, she strutted off stage. There erupted an uproar in the audience; I supposed they wanted to see the girl with her panties completely off. Condescendingly, the girl peeked out from the wings and in final acknowledgement gave a high kick with her bare leg.

After a brief interval another girl appeared on stage and performed the same routine, accompanied by more shouts of "Take it off! Take it off!" When a third girl appeared, I got up and left. It was enough of an introduction to American burlesque theatre.

Back at the "Y" hotel, before falling asleep, I reviewed my American adventure thus far: Los Angeles, the sprawling town with a handful of Koreans struggling for survival; San Francisco, a unique city, built on the ruins of an earthquake like a Roman city; the train ride through the American heartland; then Chicago, the gangsterland with Minsky's Burlesque Theatre, another view of American culture.

I did not sleep well, for I was eager to be on my way to Green-castle, Indiana, to college. I caught the morning train at the Dear-born station, which took me to Indianapolis. There, I got on a suburban train to Greencastle, a little college town. I checked in at the men's hall, the students' dormitory, and immediately went out to see the campus. This was my college, the final fulfillment of my life-time dream. I had read a little of the history of DePauw University. It was founded more than a hundred years ago by the Methodist church and was the first college to be established in the state of Indi-ana. Basically, DePauw was a liberal arts college, also offering basic studies in religion, philosophy, and the arts. Its student body was small, around fifteen hundred, and it maintained a very high scholas-tic reputation.

A few blocks from the dormitory was the center of the campus, where an old three-story, ivy-covered brick building presided over the rest of the surrounding college buildings, some very old and oth-ers comparatively new. All the grounds in between and around the buildings were filled with old maple and oak trees, and the ground, except for the narrow cement walks linking all the buildings together, was thickly carpeted with lush green grass. Oh, what a sight! Just the kind of image a college should bear—gracefully aged, peaceful, and somber. For a hundred years, young men and women had come here to acquire knowledge and wisdom and then had gone out into the world as missionaries, teachers, and artists. I, too, would be one of its sons, absorb all it had to offer, and become a useful citi-zen of the world.

The first week was spent on introductions—introductions to the school, its faculty, the courses I had chosen, and fellow students. I was highly impressed with my English instructor. First of all, it was my luck to have chosen a beautiful young woman named Miss

Hamilton as my teacher. And as an extra reward, she was completely dedicated to her calling, with an intense interest in her students. I was grateful for her attention to my efforts in her class. English was taught by having the students write a composition each week. By using the students' writings, she would show different kinds of sentences and the purpose of a paragraph. She showed the shadings and changes of meaning by the changes in the juxtaposition of words in a sentence and sentences in a paragraph. I was enthralled. For the first time in my struggle with the English language, I began to feel and appreciate the subtleties as well as the complexities of the language. At her suggestion, I often stayed after class so that she could analyze my composition more thoroughly.

"What did you really want to say?"

"This is too general. Be specific."

"Can't you say it more effectively?"

She drilled me on fundamentals until I developed my own creed in expressing myself in speech or in writing:

Be specific;

Be accurate;

Be effective.

The highest tribute I could offer Miss Hamilton for her accomplishment in teaching me English was that, for the first time since I had started studying English, I began to speak English in my dreams—not Korean or Chinese, but English! I knew then that English had indeed become my language.

Moreover, Miss Hamilton was so beautiful; it hurt me to be sitting beside her, alone together, discussing prepositional phrases and compound sentences. She was my teacher and I her pupil. How could I even intimate my personal feelings to her, natural and pleasurable though they seemed. Many, many years later, immediately following the Japanese surrender that ended World War II, while I was stationed in Seoul, Korea, I received a letter postmarked in Tokyo. It was from Miss Hamilton, now a Wac (member of the Women's Army Corps) stationed in Japan. She wanted to know what I had been doing, what my interests were, and what my plans were. These questions were not casual; they sprang out of unrevealed, deep feelings. How did she trace me, and how and what enabled her to keep such feelings for me for so many years! And I never knew!

Back to DePauw.

I earnestly began my studies in religion. As a first step toward becoming a minister, I enrolled in a class to study the history of the Bible. It was taught by a very warmhearted professor with an open mind, Dr. Hilderbrand. The course began with the Old Testament. As we began delving into the origin of various books, I felt something strange happening to me. I was learning for the first time that what was in the books were not the words of God as I had always believed, but actually words of men who recorded their experiences. Many of them were records of myths, legends, folklore; others, imaginations and fantasies. I raised this point with Dr. Hilderbrand, and we held many interesting discussions. His basic thesis was that most men who recorded the books were men with inspirations and deep religious experiences.

I began to ask questions: "Why were so many other records and books excluded from the Bible? Who decided what was holy and what was not?" Mortal men with personal tastes and prejudices, just like today's editors and censors, had decided what stories should be in the Holy Bible and what stories should be cast aside. Dr. Hilderbrand would then defend the judgments of those who assembled the Bible. But there were also many different versions of the Bible. Who decided one version to be the truth and worthy and another version false and not worthy?

Before the course was completed, I confided to Dr. Hilderbrand that I had decided not to become a minister. He was not unduly surprised but tried to salvage my religious fervor by directing it to other channels.

"You don't have to be a minister," he said. "There are many other fields of religious activities you could train yourself for. . . ."

I did not respond.

"There is a famous college in Springfield, Massachusetts," he said, "where men are trained to work in the field of religious education."

"Such as what?" I asked.

"Such as the YMCA, community service centers, and so on."

"Dr. Hilderbrand," I said, "I do not have the unquestioning blind faith I once had in the Christian God. I could not guide anyone to follow the path I was preparing myself to abandon."

Fortunately, there was another course I was taking that completely swept away the gloom of the Bible study. It was the introductory study of theatre in the School of Drama. Here at DePauw, my spiritual kinship with the theatre, which I thought had been forgotten and buried since leaving Shanghai, resurfaced alive and strong. And again, as my good fortune would have it, the instructor turned out to be a beautiful blond young woman fresh out of Northwestern University School of Theatre. She was buxom and pleasantly plump, but she was well proportioned, and her face, always glowing with fun and mischief, made her very magnetic and attractive. Her name was Clara Bell. Of course, at the first opportunity, I told her of my experiences in the theatre in Shanghai, which she thought was the most exciting thing she had ever heard. She directed us to read and study various types of plays, including Shakespeare.

She made the study and analysis interesting by having the students read the parts. We also studied the art of acting by doing scenes from plays before the class. I became rather ambitious and decided to do a whole play by myself. This was long before Cornelia Otis Skinner would appear as a one-woman theatre.

My love of the theatre also produced some unexpected income. Miss Bell thought so highly of my presentation, she helped to find bookings for my performance in schools, churches, and clubs in the outlying towns. I would travel to little towns by train and by bus, give my inspired performance, and return to Greencastle richer by at least five dollars.

Miss Bell became more than a drama teacher to me; she was my date and partner in all the men's hall proms. The Indiana hop was then the rage. It was the midwestern version of the lindy hop, a forerunner of the jitterbug. On the floor, Miss Bell would completely forget she was a faculty member dancing with a student. In addition, we drew a lot of attention with our wild dancing. It was such fun! After the dance, I would walk her home, and at the doorway she would give me a good-night kiss. Oh, how I looked forward to and treasured that moment!

Now all the trees turned their colors to rust, red, and gold, transforming the whole campus into a flaming inferno. Then they began to shed their leaves until nothing but bare branches pointed at the autumn sky. Busy with the semester examinations, I didn't even notice the change of the season. For the first time since I left Korea I was facing a freezing winter. I was very pleased with the results of the exams: all As, with one A-. Papa, Umma, and Mrs. Isenberg would be proud of me. Now, for the first time, I faced the prospect of spending the Christmas holidays away from home, alone! I conceived a brilliant idea; go to New York and visit and spend Christmas with Sister Elizabeth.

Sister Elizabeth had moved to New York in 1925 in pursuit of another kind of life. On Kauai, she had stopped going to school, which she had always hated. She was twenty years old, had no friends her age, and lived a terribly boring life staying home with Umma and her animals. One day, a Korean man appeared and introduced himself as the brother of Kim Chang Ho, one of Father's church friends in Honolulu. His name was Kim Byung Ho, his home was in New York, and he had come to Hawaii to visit relatives. He had checked in at the Lihue Hotel and had come to pay his respects to Father and Umma.

He quickly revealed his real mission: to ask for Sister Elizabeth's hand in marriage. He was not a youngster—perhaps between thirty five and forty, had lived and worked in the United States most of his life, and had decided it was time for him to get married (his story). He came to his brother's in Honolulu, who recommended that he go to Kauai and see if the Reverend Soon Hyun would approve of him marrying his daughter. Father and Umma told him it was up to Elizabeth. Kim gave Elizabeth a whirlwind courtship for two days. On the third day, Sister Elizabeth announced that she wanted to get married. They went to Honolulu, where the marriage ceremony was performed, and immediately left for New York.

As it turned out, after the marriage she led a tragicomic life for nearly twenty years, most of which were spent in New York's China-town. Kim was engaged in some sort of secret business operation that took him away from home for months at a time. Practically living alone, Sister Elizabeth reared two daughters and a son and supported them through college. Away from home, her husband was killed by a robber in a hold up. The oldest daughter, Doris, graduated from the University of California, Los Angeles (UCLA), and became a social worker. The second daughter, Eleanor, also went to UCLA and became a teacher. And the son, Chang-Nai, with the help of a bene-factor, graduated from Yale and became a highly successful structural engineer.

But how would I find a way to travel to New York and back at no cost? I went to the used car lot in town and made a small deposit on a 1924 Buick. It was a "touring" model with a convertible canvas top and detachable canvas sides over the four doors. What I liked was the price: one hundred dollars!

First, I signed up my roommate, whose home was near Boston, for a round-trip fare of fourty dollars. Next, it wasn't too difficult to convince three Asian students to join my Christmas tour to New York and back for forty dollars each. Together with my own share, I paid for the car and had one hundred dollars on hand for expenses. I gave instructions to my passengers: bring warm clothing and a blanket. We were all ready to start on a Saturday morning, the first day of our three-week Christmas vacation. I had never driven an automobile anywhere except in Hawaii. But with a collection of maps and advice from fellow students, I felt quite confident about driving across the country.

On Friday morning, the last day of school, the weather turned gloomy and cold, and it began to snow. By noon the snowstorm had developed into a blinding blizzard. The storm battered us through the night, and it was still snowing in the morning. I heard the news on the radio: fallen telephone poles and trees, snow drifts, and icy roads—very hazardous conditions. It was the worst snowstorm in twenty years in Indiana. Many highways were closed to traffic, and the repeated warning was, "Stay off the highway! Do not go on the highway!"

I called an emergency meeting with my passengers. I told them we could still go if we took the southern route. They trusted me; if I was willing to drive, they were willing to ride. Everyone dressed in sweaters and overcoats, piled in, and wrapped themselves in blankets. I started the car, drove out of Greencastle, and headed south toward Kentucky.

We passed by fallen trees, toppled telephone poles, and high snowdrifts. The road was icy and slippery; I had to drive very cautiously, especially around curves. After several hours of tense and nervous driving, we came out of the storm area. We were in Kentucky. I turned east toward Virginia and drove all day until dusk. This was a thrilling adventure in an automobile. On my train ride from San Francisco I had discovered the vastness of the mountains, the desert, and the prairie, and the rich pulsation of the American farmlands. Now, driving an automobile, I was discovering the chain of towns and cities that stretched across the other half of the country. I was also learning the intricate patterns of highways. By studying the road maps, charting the route, and following the road signs, I could find my way from city to city, state to state. I drove as though I had driven through this country all my life; crisscrossing, turning, and interchanging and keeping myself on the route. However, the highway system also had its hazards and pitfalls; a road sign misread, mistaken, or missed could lead one to a catastrophe.

By now I had driven for almost twelve hours traversing through Kentucky and Virginia. The sun had set. It was still cold and the road still icy on some stretches. Fatigue was beginning to overpower me. Only then did I discover that not one of my passengers knew how to drive. Then I heard my roommate, David Kingman, say, "I can drive a little." I was so exhausted, I didn't bother to ask what he meant by "a little." I stopped the car, changed seats with him, and gave him my last instruction: "Drive slowly and just keep the car on the road. I'll take only a short nap."

As the car began to move, I wrapped myself in a blanket and instantly fell asleep—I don't know for how long. I was shaken out of my deep sleep by the sensation of a strange motion. The car was spinning crazily.

"Take your foot off the brakes!" I yelled. The car spun once more and came to a stop in front of a railing. I jumped out and looked over the rail; we had stopped on the edge of a cliff, a bottomless pit. I was glad the three passengers in the rear seat, under the pile of blankets, had slept through the near tragedy.

That was enough. Again, I took over the wheel. I drove all night and the next day. We were fully out of the storm, having passed through Virginia and West Virginia. As darkness fell for the second evening on the road, we were in Pennsylvania. The scenery changed to rolling hills, lush valleys, and more frequent towns and cities. There was a feeling of relaxation among us; we all felt we were really going to make it to New York City. Except for brief stops at service stations and coffee shops for quick, inexpensive meals, and with the brief interval when Kingman nearly drove over the cliff, I had done all the driving for thirty-six hours. I fought off the fatigue and, worse, the overwhelming sleepiness, and kept driving until I felt I had reached the end of my endurance.

"David," I called out to Kingman, who was asleep next to me. "David," I begged, "do you think you can keep this car on the road for half an hour? I really need some rest."

"Sure," Kingman answered; he was such a willing, helpful guy.

We switched seats, and as Kingman drove off, I faded into oblivion, savoring the sweetness of a deep sleep. But again, I didn't know for how long. I was jolted out of my sleep by another strange sensation. The car was bucking like a wild horse, nearly throwing all of us out of the car.

"Stop! Stop, David!" I screamed. It was incredible; what could possibly have caused the car to behave like that! I got out of the car and surveyed the scene; we were in a freight railroad yard, bucking over the high rails. This time, even the three passengers in the back seat were awakened out of their sleep. They kept mumbling, "What happened? What happened?"

"How in the world did you get in here, David?"

"I don't know," he answered.

Yes, here indeed was the result of a misread road sign; perhaps making a right turn instead of left. How lucky no train was moving in or out of the yard just then! It dawned on me how this wondrous American highway system was fraught with hazards and pitfalls and innumerable potentials for human disasters. Of course, I took over the wheel once again, eased over the rails, and maneuvered out of the freight yard.

Resolving not to relinquish the driving to Kingman again, I drove on through lush Pennsylvania and then through the busy factory towns of New Jersey. As dawn ushered in our third day, I stopped at a gas station for a fill up.

"Hey, you got some bad tires!" the attendant called out. The wild ride bouncing and tossing across the freight yard had caused no injury to anyone, but it had caused some severe and ugly cuts in the walls of the tires.

"Where are you headed?" the attendant asked.

"New York."

"You can't make it with those tires."

"But we can't afford new tires."

The attendant scratched his head and said, "We got some good recaps—cheap."

"Okay, please replace the two worst ones and mount them in

the rear." The cost of even used tires was not part of my travel budget.

I drove through the Hudson Tube. Once out of the long tunnel, we were in New York. Yes, we were really driving on the streets of New York—the five of us; one Caucasian from Boston, one Korean from Seoul, two Japanese from Tokyo, and one Chinese from some remote Chinese village. For the first time since we had left Greencastle three days ago, everyone was fully awake, alert, and excited. We were really in New York—the name we had heard in Korea, Japan, and China and had visited in our dreams.

My first impressions of New York City were quite disappointing. Instead of glitter and grandeur, I saw only dirty buildings, dirty streets, and people in shabby overcoats shuffling along. They reminded me of Shanghai.

The city map showed, except at the tip of Manhattan Island, that all the streets and avenues were laid out in a systematic rectangular pattern. So it didn't take long to locate the apartment building on West Twenty-eighth Street where Sister Elizabeth lived. I placed the three Asian students in a taxi and directed the driver to take them to the YMCA. I then handed the car key to Kingman, and without any word of advice or warning, simply reminded him to come back in a week and meet us at the same place. I didn't stop to question what prompted me to trust Kingman to drive to Boston and back alone. Could it be that I was allowing him to go and get himself killed?

Sister Elizabeth opened the door and let out a scream. "Pedroya!" She didn't really believe my letter telling her I was coming to see her on Christmas. Neither could she believe the story of my motor trip from Indiana to New York. When we recovered sufficiently, she began to prod me with more reasonable queries about my college, about my life living alone, and about what kind of food I had in school. While drawing a picture of satisfaction and contentment in college, I watched Sister's face and scanned the apartment to find out if she was happy here with her married life.

She began showing me around the apartment. The living room was furnished with a comfortable sofa, an armchair, a console radio, and a handsome mahogany cupboard with a large mirror. She took me into the bedroom—a neatly made-up double bed, a maple dresser, and two old fashioned straight-backed chairs. In the bathroom there was a shower over the tub, a large washbasin, and over it a medicine chest. I was impressed with the special rose-colored cover over the toilet seat. She was obviously proud of all her possessions, but most of all of her kitchen. Everything in it shone and sparkled—the new refrigerator, the new stove, all the pots and pans, and the dishes on the shelves. Yes, I was convinced she was happy. Here, at last, was her kingdom, where she did what she enjoyed the most in life—making a spotlessly clean, shining, and comfortable home.

She then took me upstairs and showed me the spare bedroom with another bathroom. Her stranger-husband about whom Father and Umma had such misgivings had, after all, provided well for her. The only thing lacking was human contact. Kim, her husband, was away from home most of the time. Her first child, a son, had been entrusted to Umma in Kauai, and she knew no one in the big city. The only relief came on Sundays, when she rode the subway to West One Fifteenth Street. There she would join a handful of Koreans who gathered at the Korean Christian Church for services and a Korean dinner afterward. Her loneliness was the price she had paid and accepted for her marriage and her own home.

However, I had decided that my visit to New York was not to be lonely. I arranged to have Cynthia Kim meet me to explore the city together. Cynthia was from Honolulu, had graduated from McKinley High School with honors, and was attending Harvard Law School on a scholarship. She was a Hawaii-born Korean. She admired my father and had attended his church in Honolulu regularly. That's how I met her and became her admirer. Needless to say, she had to be awfully bright, not only for the scholarship, but to be the only woman admitted to the Harvard Law School. In contrast to her high intellect, her physical endowments were rather meager. In fact, she would be considered rather homely by most. But to me, she was beautiful. Her brilliant intellect and her rich sense of humor made her whole personality radiant; she was the only person from Hawaii with whom I could discuss politics and religion, as well as music and the theatre. When she arrived at Sister Elizabeth's from Boston, we gave her the upstairs guest room; then she and I began our exploration of the city.

Of course, Times Square was our first target; it only cost a nickel each to go there on the subway. Our first sight at night was breathtaking. The entire Square lit up with bright, dazzling lights seemed like a gigantic amusement park. We held hands and walked through the crowds of people, some just standing and gawking, others jostling and shoving as they milled around. There were so many theatres whose marquees were lit with blinding lights! We stopped at some to look at their billboards and to peer at the enormous and glittering lobbies inside. We passed by restaurant after restaurant, each offering some special national food: Greek, Italian, Chinese, Indian, and others I had never heard of. Then we saw a doughnut shop. We stood at the window watching the doughnut machine in operation. We saw souvenir shops with strange and odd things from around the world.

The billboards at Loew's Theatre attracted us: Cab Calloway and his band, and Helen Morgan. The admission, at fifty cents each, was not too expensive. We went in and found two seats in the cavernous house and sat through a movie starring Ramon Novarro—in what picture, I have forgotten. After two hours of the movies, including the Movietone and Paramount News, rosy lights slowly lit up the immense proscenium for the vaudeville show. We saw five or six acts: some comedian talking through the side of his mouth, trying so hard to make people laugh; a magician who did amazing tricks with cards and coins; a juggler who tossed four wooden pins in the air and kept them there as though he had three or four hands to do the trick. Then the curtain parted on a darkened stage. Helen Morgan, sitting atop a grand piano, began singing with an ovation from the audience. She hardly moved or gestured, and her round face with short-cropped hair didn't seem too beautiful, but her entire personality and her sultry singing were magnetic. After several encores, the curtain closed.

Then we heard the music of a big band as the curtain parted—it was Cab Calloway. He was singing his famous gibberish: "Hidey, hidey, hidey ho! Hodi, hodi, hodi, hey!" The audience broke into wild applause. They yelled out for their favorite songs, and Calloway obliged. The band played and Calloway sang without stopping— song after song. The finale was everybody's favorite: "I went down to St. James infirmary, to see my baby there. . . ." Oh, how wildly the people cheered.

Cynthia and I spent the next two days riding the subway, going everywhere. At The Battery, we got on a little boat that took us to Liberty Island. We climbed to the top of the Statue of Liberty. From there, we surveyed the New York harbor and the incredible sight of New York City—a man-made fairyland. Before we left the inspiring site, I read the inscription on the base of the statue; I had never read or heard of it. The most inspiring part:

> *Give me your tired, your poor,*
> *Your huddled masses yearning to breathe free,*
> *The wretched refuse of your teeming shore,*
> *Send these, the homeless, tempest-tossed, to me:*
> *I lift my lamp beside the golden door.*

Back in Manhattan, we spent the rest of that day and all of the next at museums. First we went to the Museum of Natural History and then to the Metropolitan Museum. We marveled at the work of the curators, the amount of knowledge gathered, and the painstaking work of mounting each exhibit. The Metropolitan was too big even to pass through in one day. So we settled for two exhibits: the Egyptian and the Chinese. Cynthia was enchanted. To me, the Egyptian collections were so remote and strange; but we were both thrilled with the Chinese exhibit, which also included some paintings, ceremonial screens, and celadon porcelain from Korea.

The climax of our exploits was our evening at the theatre. We saw Walter Hampton in *Cyrano de Bergerac*. This was my first visit to an American theatre. The cheapest seat we could afford put us in the highest balcony, where our heads almost touched the ceiling. It didn't matter; we had a wonderful view of the stage, as seen through a telescope. What impressed me was the smooth flow of the dialogue and the movements. The entire play had the quality of a dream. Everything flowed from one scene to another like a river, sometimes rushing and cascading and sometimes just floating in languid stillness. At the final curtain, Cynthia and I stood and applauded with fervor. It was an evening at the theatre that I would remember for the rest of my life.

The next morning, Cynthia had to return to Boston. We didn't even kiss good-bye because we were both too shy. And that was the last time I saw her until many years later in Los Angeles in 1940. I was on my way to Honolulu and she was on her way to San Francisco. Our accidental meeting in Los Angeles after so many years seemed like a belated revival of New York all over again. But not quite. She was now a practicing lawyer and deeply engrossed in the theatre. She confided to me that she was pregnant and that the father of her child, a doctor, would not marry her.

A shock of pain swelled inside me and without hesitation I said, "Cynthia, I will marry you, and we'll give the baby a name, a fine name."

She thanked me, in tears, and said, "No, Peter. I am going to try to have the doctor marry me." That was the last conversation I had with Cynthia. I never saw or heard from her again.

My vacation was now over; we had to return to Greencastle and school. On the morning of the appointed day, the doorbell rang. When I opened the door, I was met by the most unbelievable sight: Kingman was standing there at the door, and behind him the Buick, apparently intact. I was afraid to ask him how he had managed to drive to Boston and back. I had a faint suspicion he had picked up some hitchhiker on the road who did the driving.

Our three Asian student-passengers also showed up on time. No time to talk about our New York experiences. A thankful good-bye to Sister Elizabeth—and her husband, who had just shown up for the holidays—and we were off! I felt elated; I was now a veteran cross-country driver, the weather was fine, and by taking a direct route, I calculated that we should be in Greencastle in two days, the day before the opening day of school. The only thing that worried me were those two used tires we had put on.

We had a late start, and by the time we passed through New Jersey and started to cross the Allegheny Mountains, the beautiful scenes of forests and valleys and winding roads faded into pitch-darkness. Near the mountain crest we encountered fog, which became heavier and thicker with every mile. When we began our descent, the fog was so dense, the visibility was zero. We could not stop and wait for the fog to lift—it might take all night. The only way I could avoid going over the cliff was to hold the door open with one hand while steering with the other, looking straight down at the white divider line. The fate of the three students from Japan and China and another from Boston were in my hands—one on the car door and the other on the steering wheel. Except for brief, intermittent clearings, the fog would not lift. The harrowing drive lasted through the whole night.

The awakening dawn was the most welcome sight. The fog

floated away, and I began to see the road ahead. We were passing through a lush, green country, and at last we wound around the last mountain curve onto a straight and wide highway that pointed directly to the city of Pittsburgh. I had been driving for over twelve hours. That peculiar fatigue from driving began to creep over me. But the memories of spinning on icy roads and the expedition across railroad tracks were still too vivid to think of turning the driving over to Kingman. Yet when my eyelids became too heavy to keep open and my head began to nod, once again I weakened and lost my sense of caution. Besides, I said to myself, didn't he drive all the way to Boston and back to New York? "Dave," I called, "can you take over the wheel for a while?"

"Oh, sure," he answered, as readily as ever.

"Just keep the car on the road," I repeated the instructions. We changed seats, and I promptly fell asleep.

Again, I didn't know for how long, but once again I was jolted out of my sleep to see the car going off the road, lurching over a bank, and heading for a deep gulch. Fortunately, Kingman kept his nerve and held on to the steering wheel until he found a telephone pole in the way. The car stopped, firmly wrapping itself around the telephone pole. We got out and helped the three passengers out of the back seat. They held their heads in apparent pain, but, thank God, no serious injury. What's the sense of asking Kingman how it happened! I thought. What's the use of saying anything!

I hailed passing cars and asked the driver of one car that stopped to send a tow truck from the first town he reached. We wrapped ourselves in blankets and huddled together in a heap by the roadside. And we waited in silence. To all the people rushing by in their cars, we must have presented a most puzzling sight. An hour passed, and a tow truck finally did show up and stopped at the scene. The driver looked at my Buick and shook his head.

"What will it cost to repair it?" I asked.

"That's beyond repair, mister," the driver said.

"Well, I'll sell it to you," I said, and added, "cheap."

"No, thanks."

"Well, I guess I just have to leave it here then."

"If you do, you will get a ticket and it will cost you a fortune for abandoning a wreck on the road."

"Well, tow it away and keep the car. I give it to you," I said.

"No, thanks. If you want me to tow it away, it will cost you ten bucks."

"Ten bucks to get rid of it!"

The driver just shrugged. I gave him the precious ten dollars and all the papers on the car.

Now we faced a real dilemma: how do we get back to school in Indiana? None of us had enough money to ride the bus; the only solution was to hitchhike. The three Asian students and I had never tried it. We were too shy to raise our thumbs at passing cars. I suggested that we split into smaller groups—we would have a better chance of being picked up. Kingman was to take the student from China with him, and I took the two students from Japan. Kingman got the first ride; he waved at us as he disappeared. I soon discovered no one would or could give all three of us a ride. I explained this to the two students from Japan, gave them a map, and at the first opportunity put them in a car heading for Pittsburgh. My last words to them were, "Don't be afraid." Not too long afterward, I, too, got a ride.

Normally it would have taken twenty-four hours to reach Greencastle from Pittsburgh, but I found very quickly that one can't follow a schedule while hitchhiking. The university authorities, two days after school reopened, became concerned and sent out a missing persons bulletin. On the morning of the third day of school, Kingman and the Chinese student showed up on the campus, and that evening I straggled in. But no sign of the Japanese students! I was really worried and imagined all kinds of possible disasters. Oh, what a happy sight to see them walking up the dormitory steps with silly grins on their faces. They apologized profusely; they had taken rides from whomever stopped for them, and they had made a long and roundabout tour of Ohio. They finally landed in Indianapolis, where they spent their last dollar for the suburban train ride to Greencastle. Some Christmas vacation!

The second semester passed swiftly. The only memorable events: being appointed, on the strength of my boxing experiences in Shanghai, an assistant boxing coach for the freshman class; a guided tour of an American whorehouse in Indianapolis; and the delightful men's hall proms with Miss Clara Bell, my drama teacher. Incidentally, the American whore had nothing in common with her counterpart in Soochow, China, where I was initiated into manhood. In

America I can describe the experience with only three words: business, business, business.

The final year-end exam. I had developed a studying technique, and I faced the exams with full confidence. Yet I was surprised to get As in all subjects, with one A-. More than the grades, I was elated with the award of a full scholarship for my remaining years at DePauw. It meant my tuition would be paid for; I needed only to pay for my room and board and other incidentals. I was determined to earn the money to free myself from all obligations.

The three-month summer vacation gave me my chance. I traveled back to New York, on the Greyhound bus this time, and after a few days' stay with Sister Elizabeth, I found a job at Rye Beach, New York. Rye Beach was a high-class Coney Island, but because the trip to Rye Beach was more expensive, its visitors were limited to fairly well-to-do New Yorkers. One of the attractions was a huge saltwater swimming pool where Gertrude Ederle, the first woman to swim the English Channel, supervised and performed.

My job was at a hot dog stand, the concession that belonged to a Korean. All the workers at the stand were Koreans, and we lived together in a loft in town, making my rent minimal. Mr. Lim, the concessionaire, invented a new way of serving hot dogs. (Of course, it would take a Korean to make improvements on the American hot dog.) The buns were roasted on the grill, making them just as hot as the dogs. Then they were smothered with mustard and catsup. The juicy dog was then covered with relish and chopped onions. In the amusement park, word spread like wildfire, and from mid-morning until midnight a crowd of people stood before our stand to buy our hot dogs. My job was to roast the buns and turn the dogs over and over on the grill. The next worker wrapped the dog in the hot bun, smeared it with mustard and catsup, and passed it to the next worker, who filled it with relish and chopped onions and passed it to the next one. That was the last stop; this worker took the money and handed out the famous hot dog. I never counted how many dogs we sold in one day; I could only guess by the number of empty cartons we threw out at the end of the day. Each carton contained three hundred dogs, and some nights we threw out as many as fifteen empty cartons. My arms and legs would be so sore when we closed the shop at 1:00 A.M., I would barely have time for a shower before flopping onto my cot and instantly falling into a deep sleep.

The summer season at the beach lasted three months, and because our job was so taxing and required fifteen long hours of work each day, we were paid the unheard of high wage of $1.50 per hour. Besides the rent, I spent very little on food because I could eat all the hot dogs I wanted. The only other meals I bought were breakfasts and an occasional dinner at a restaurant in the park. When the season ended, I was the first one to be relieved, and I returned to Sister Elizabeth in New York. I had saved over one thousand dollars—enough to pay for all my living expenses for my second year in school.

Before leaving New York, I wrote to Father and Umma and to Mrs. Isenberg, my benefactress. It was not an easy letter to compose, but I conveyed my decision not to pursue a religious career. I hadn't yet decided what my major studies would be. I also thanked Mrs. Isenberg for her interest and help, but since I was not following my promise to become a minister, she didn't have to give me any further financial help. I told her of my scholarship and my summer job. I assured her I would be able to get along without her help. I also assured her that whatever field of work I undertook, I would always devote myself to the freedom and advancement of the human spirit. I also added, "In truth, the church and the theatre are not so far apart." It must have been a terrible disappointment to her; I never again heard from her.

I was now a sophomore and began enjoying college life to the fullest. I was at home with the surroundings, the entire student body, and especially all the professors and instructors. This was college life as I had envisioned it, until the day I encountered the professor of philosophy. In place of the study of the Bible, I enrolled in the introductory course in philosophy, which was taught by Professor Eckhardt, the head of the department. In his very first lecture, Professor Eckhardt expounded on the differences between scientific and philosophical methods. He was consulting and reciting from his timeworn notebook. I guessed the notebook dated back to his college days at Boston University, many years past.

"The scientific method," he expounded in a deep, sonorous voice, "is the method of analysis. But the philosophical method—" he paused and looked at his notebook,—"the philosophical method is the method of synthesis." He then elaborated. "The scientific method breaks down and identifies the parts. But the philosophical method synthesizes the parts and interprets the whole." He made it clear that the philosophical method was superior to the scientific method.

After listening to further elucidation, I raised my hand.

"Yes, Mr. Hyun?" Professor Eckhardt gave me the floor.

"Professor Eckhardt," I addressed him politely, "the scientific and the philosophical methods—aren't they both indispensable to each other?"

The class lapsed into a stunned silence.

"Without the analysis by the scientific method and breaking down into parts," I continued, "what does the philosophical method have to synthesize?"

I had no idea my hypothetical question would provoke such agitation in Professor Eckhardt. His face turned pale, and he was speechless for a full minute. When he regained his composure sufficiently to speak, he fumed and sputtered. "Anyone whose mind is set and closed is not fit to study philosophy. And anyone who comes here with preconceived ideas and beliefs will gain nothing by studying philosophy!"

He harangued in this vein for some time, straining to swallow the overflowing foam in his mouth. The bell rang, but the professor of philosophy kept us in class because he couldn't quite bring his indignation and agitation under control.

That was my first lesson in philosophy, and for the rest of the year I didn't raise my hand again. While he read from his battered notebook, I took faithful notes. And for the final exam I memorized all his quotations and answered all the questions with his own words. My papers were returned without a single red line, but the grade I got was a B—the only one below an A in my whole second year of courses.

Some years later I decided to visit the DePauw campus. At the men's hall, my old dormitory, I was introduced to some young students.

"Are you really Peter Hyun?" one of them asked.

"Yes; why are you surprised?"

"Because," he said, "you are famous around here."

"Is that so?" Now it was I who was surprised. "But I don't understand. Tell me why."

"You are famous in Professor Eckhardt's philosophy class," he said. "Every year he begins his opening lecture by telling the story of Peter Hyun."

"Really! What does he say?"

"Well, it runs something like this: 'We had a student here named Peter Hyun. He was full of prejudice and preconceived ideas. His mind was totally unfit for philosophical studies.' "

So, I had become a famous student, unfit to study philosophy.

There were times in school when I felt alone and lonely. I had friends among the faculty, like Professor Hilderbrand of religious studies, Miss Hamilton of the English department, and, of course, Miss Bell in the drama department. But except for my roommate, Kingman, I had no other close friends with whom I could share my personal feelings—the feelings of frustration and resentment at being pointed and stared at as an "Oriental." Some of them would even ask me if my family was in the laundry business. In town or in the city of Indianapolis, as I walked on the streets, I could feel the surreptitious stares of people around me; stares of curiosity, sneers of scorn, and even of hate. Once at a meeting of the Metropolitan Club—a social campus club of foreign students, plus interested American students—I was asked if we had ice cream in Korea.

"Of course," I replied, and added, "except ice cream in Korea is made differently."

"Really? How is it made?"

"Well, they make it with boiling water."

No comment. After a long pause, another student asked boldly, "But why do the Chinese people always do things upside down?"

"Upside down? What do you mean?" I asked.

"Well, for instance, . . ." the bold one hesitated.

"Come on, tell me," I encouraged him.

"Well, I saw in the movies, when the Chinese men greet each other, they shake their own hands, not each other's. And on the street, the men walk in front and the women follow behind."

"That's not upside down," I said. "That's the proper way."

"They seem cockeyed to me!"

"Look, in China and Korea there are many dangerous germs, so they don't go around shaking people's hands; they shake their own— it's more sanitary and safe. Also, in China and Korea there are tigers everywhere. So men walk ahead of the women to protect them from tigers." Taking advantage of my critic's momentary befuddlement, I continued, "I thought it was the Americans who really did things upside down."

"Americans? Upside down?" The American student bellowed with laughter.

"Yes, Americans," I repeated.

"Well, how?"

"Well, for instance, about drinking tea," I said slowly, to allow the idea to sink in. "Chinese and Koreans have been drinking tea for thousands of years, so they should know how to drink tea, don't you agree?"

"Yeah, okay, go on . . ."

"But you Americans do it all upside down."

"How?"

"Well, you boil the tea to make it hot . . ."

"Yeah . . ."

"Then you put ice in it to make it cold . . ."

"Yeah . . ."

"Then you put sugar in it to make it sweet . . ."

"Yeah . . ."

"Then you squeeze lemon into it to make it sour."

Silence.

"Then you say, 'Here's to you,' and drink it yourself."

Silence.

It was Thanksgiving time and we "foreign students," as usual on holidays, became very homesick. All the students would be going home, and we would be left alone in the dormitory. Just when we were beginning to feel sorry for ourselves, we received a collective invitation; it was addressed to all four of us. The invitation came from Dr. G. Bromley Oxham, the president of DePauw, and Mrs. Oxham. We were invited to their home on Thanksgiving day to share their family Thanksgiving dinner. I knew Dr. Oxham was an unusual university president, but I began to discover he was also a very unusual man.

He left the faculty of the University of Southern California to accept the presidency at DePauw in the same year I became one of its four hundred freshmen. I was deeply impressed with his first address to the student body. In his extraordinary rapid-fire speech, he said that he was opening the classroom doors to the students to discover the thrills and the beauty of knowledge that would set them free—free to develop their own values and judgments. One of his first official acts as new president was to abolish the ROTC. He declared that college was not for the military training of the young. For this bold action, he was attacked by the American Legion and the Daughters of the American Revolution, and the board of directors sounded a serious alarm. How wonderful to have been invited by such a great man to share with him his home and his holiday celebration!

It was my first visit to an American home as a guest, and the home of such a distinguished university president. Together with the three other Asian students, I entered the house and found myself in a strange world; the thick carpet under my feet, the shiny tables and chairs, plants and flowers around the room, a large mirror and tapestry on the wall—I had never been in such a room. I couldn't help feeling I was an intruder. And when we were led to the spacious living room, I must have seemed like a country boy in a big city, staring and gawking at the plaques and paintings on the walls and running my hand over the velvet coverings of the upholstered furniture.

A young woman, the housemaid perhaps, brought a tray and set it down on a low table. Then Mrs. Oxham, a handsome and distinguished-looking lady, stepped into the room. As we were introduced, she gave each one of us a warm handshake. She then poured from the pitcher on the tray and introduced us to warm apple cider with cinnamon sticks. "An American Thanksgiving drink," she said, "to help warm our bodies and souls." She asked where our homes were and what would it be like at Thanksgiving season. We didn't have Thanksgiving in the Orient, but most countries had Autumn Harvest Festivals, we told her, and we described such festivities celebrated in Japan, Korea, and China. Mrs. Oxham seemed delighted with our stories and asked about what the men and women wore and what special foods they ate.

I described the Autumn Harvest Festival in Korea. In villages, hamlets, and even cities, they would use strong rope to rig up long swings tied to the tallest trees. And usually in pairs, girls with long braided hair, dressed in colorful skirts and blouses, would get on the swing and push it high up to the sky, to the delight of the crowd watching and applauding. The boys, too, would be dressed in new pantaloons, blouses, and straw sandals, and, standing in a circle, would kick a bird made of a coin wrapped in rice paper. The one who missed the kick would have to drop out, until the contest was decided between two remaining boys, who would kick the bird to each other with amazing skill. Among the many kinds of cakes, the ladies always baked cakes with strips of newly harvested pumpkin.

"Just like our Halloween!" Mrs. Oxham exclaimed, "except instead of making cakes, we make goblins with ours to frighten the witches away."

We were then ushered into the dining room and seated around a large, long oak table laden with silver candelabra, vases of flowers, and platters of food. We no longer felt like strangers; we felt at home and at ease. Dr. Oxham carved the turkey as precisely as he delivered his address at the weekly student body assembly. Mrs. Oxham loaded the plates with sweet potatoes, vegetables, and cranberry sauce and passed them to us. I had never used such a heavy silver knife and fork nor a starched linen napkin, but I was no longer awed by anything; Dr. and Mrs. Oxham had made us all feel so completely at home. I enjoyed every morsel and was soon passing my plate for second helpings. So did the other three "foreign" students.

Throughout this sumptuous dinner, Dr. Oxham kept the conversation running, asking us questions about our school experiences. What were our major studies? How do we like our professors? What plans do we have after graduation? His genuine and eager interest inspired us to tell him some of our personal thoughts and feelings.

"I want to teach," one student from Japan said, "but not so that I could make money. I want to teach Japanese people to think for themselves, not just imitate the Western ways." Dr. Oxham was impressed with every word and kept asking the same questions of the rest of us.

"I believe in a strong, healthy body," said the student from China. "The British forced opium on the Chinese people and poisoned their bodies. I am studying physical education so that I can go back and teach people how to build healthy and strong bodies."

"Opium was not the only poison we, the Westerners, brought to China," Dr. Oxham commented. "We also brought gunboats and warships to extract profits from China. We will have to pay for all these crimes someday," he continued.

During my turn I said I had come to DePauw to prepare myself for the ministry, but I became disillusioned and changed my mind after studying the history of the Bible.

"How?" Dr. Oxham asked.

"By shedding my blind faith," I said.

"I would like to hear more about it someday," Dr. Oxham said.

The young maid cleared the table and then brought in the dessert.

"Here's our American pumpkin cake—we call it pumpkin pie."

It, too, was delicious, and I wasn't ashamed to ask if I might have another piece. The Japanese and the Chinese students gladly followed my example.

With heart-felt thanks, we bade the Oxhams good night, and as we walked back to our dormitory, breathing the fresh, brisk Greencastle air, we all agreed it was the most memorable evening at DePauw.

The end of the Thanksgiving holiday meant the approach of the final semester exams. This was the time all students became frantic and burned the midnight oil to catch up with their studies. I wasn't too concerned, for I had developed a technique of taking proper notes in every class, then memorizing those notes for the exams. What I did worry about was what I should choose as my major study: religion or theatre? In addition, I also worried about the approaching Christmas vacation. I couldn't repeat the disastrous auto trip to New York. Fortunately, before I became totally depressed, I received an invitation from a fellow student, Bob Ellis, to spend Christmas at his home. I also felt relieved to learn that the three other Asian students had also received invitations from American students to go to their homes for Christmas.

On our ride on the electric train, I learned that Bob's home was on a farm some fifty miles away. This was an extraordinary bit of luck, for I had dreamed of visiting an American farmer's home. At a tiny wayside station, Bob's sister, Mary Ellis, met us with her family car. She was an impressive sight. I never saw such a tall young woman. Her erect carriage and measured strides made her appear even taller than she really was. But she didn't seem conscious of her unusual height, which I guessed was at least seven feet. She spoke in an animated, soft voice, much like a little girl. She drove us over the country road that wove around vast snow-covered fields on either side. Dark shadows of woods rose in the distance like a protective screen, and streams of smoke rose from the farmhouse chimneys. Each house was surrounded by a great expanse of snow-covered fields. Invariably a large red barn stood at the side of each house. The whole panorama made a beautiful picture postcard.

Mary drove off the main road onto a private path and finally stopped in front of the Ellis' home. I was surprised to find the house that had looked so stately in the distance was so old and weather-beaten. The front door opened, and out came a young boy and girl, and then Bob's father and mother, who looked solid and strong.

Finally, I found myself inside an American farmer's home. My first impressions were of the roominess and the sparse furnishings, but with much warmth and comfort. The young ones kept quiet and watched while Bob's father and mother spoke only occasionally and in a few brief words. Of course, having a Korean in their home must have caused quite a stir in the family, but they appeared calm and reserved; only Mary spoke with unconcealed animation.

For my first meal with the American farmer's family we all sat at a very large round table. I quickly learned the meaning of a farmer's dinner: Mr. Ellis loaded each plate with heaps of meat, potatoes, and vegetables and passed it around. It was the most sumptuous and delicious dinner.

Mr. Ellis lit the fire in the big stone fireplace, and all of us joined him around the fire. Now, all the Ellises took turns plying me with questions about life in Hawaii, Korea, and China. They were enchanted with my descriptions of the indolent, romantic life in Hawaii; the Korean traditions of respect between the young and the elderly, between parents and children and between teacher and pupil. Mary took the opportunity to chastise her younger brother and sister for their lack of respect toward their parents and teachers, to which they protested loudly. All joined the fray, losing their manners and reserve for the moment; they teased and bantered with each other in great fun. The quiet American farmer's family suddenly erupted and was almost like a Korean family.

It was now my turn to ask questions about the Ellises and their farm. I learned the Ellises had been farmers for generations. They owned several hundred acres of land. Luckily, they were able to send Mary to college, and she was the teacher in the village school. Now supporting Bob at DePauw and with two more children growing up, Mr. Ellis expected to keep on farming for at least ten more years. His whole life was concerned with the farm and his children, and he was worried about what would happen to the farm when his working days were over.

Mrs. Ellis was quick to change the subject by asking, "Peter, would you like to see my work? Come, let me show you." She stood up and led me down a stairway to the basement. Stopping before a row of shelves loaded with jars of all sizes and shapes, she said proudly: "This is my handiwork."

"What are they?" I asked.

"Oh, some jam, jelly, and preserves."

"Really? What kind?"

"They are from all the fruits around the farm—apricots, peaches, apples, and strawberries."

"That must be an awful lot of work."

"A little bit," she said, smiling, "but they taste better than the ones bought at the store. Besides, they help to ease our family budget."

I asked about sacks piled high against a wall.

"Oh, those are some potatoes and onions," she said.

We went back to the living room to find everyone leaving for their beds. Reluctantly we ended the warm, pleasant evening, and I followed Bob to his bedroom, where I was to occupy the spare bed. There was no heating in this room, and I found the bed icy cold. But the heavy quilt and the fluffy comforter soon warmed me and put me to sleep.

The next day we made a tour of the village. First, Mary drove us to the schoolhouse where she taught. It was a tiny one-room building that looked like a little church. Inside there were twenty school desk-chairs and a blackboard on the wall. Mary taught all twenty pupils, from the first grade to the eighth, in the same room. Mary was the principal, teacher, and administrator, and she reveled in her work.

Next we dropped in at the general store, which also served as the post office. From the sight of men and women gathered there to talk about all the happenings, it was obvious that the store also served as the village news center. The biggest news, of course, was my visit. Bob introduced me to all the farmers and their ladies, and they greeted me with warm and vigorous handshakes.

The tour ended with stops at the homes of a few of their family friends. It was interesting to find that every home appeared so similar; the furniture, the curtains, and even the colors of the rugs. More vigorous handshakes, more questions about China, and invariably more refreshments of hot cider with cinnamon or hot chocolate with cookies. I was delighted to meet the American farmers. They were all real people; they were so warm and open. Of course, they had hours of worries, but also hours of fun and enjoyment. After all, except for their language and food, the American farmers were not too different from Korean farmers.

One evening before we went to bed, Bob asked me if I would like to go rabbit hunting in the morning. I told him I had never gone hunting, and that I didn't know anything about it.

"Oh, it's simple," he said. He had a spare gun I could use, and he would show me what to do.

Early next morning, we went out trudging through ankle-deep snow. "The rabbit will jump out from anywhere," Bob said. "Just point your shotgun and fire."

Oh, how I hoped no rabbit would jump out in my path! I heard Bob firing his gun a few times, and each time I cringed and hoped the rabbit got away. Fortunately, he missed them all.

After a while I suggested we return home; my feet were frozen, I told him. Sitting before a fire in the living room, I felt relieved that we didn't kill any rabbits.

Bob's mind, too, must have been on rabbits because he asked, "Do you like rabbits?"

"Yes, why?"

"I mean, do you like to eat rabbits?"

"No," I said, "I have never eaten a rabbit."

"Why not?"

"I don't know," I said. "I guess I never had the opportunity. Besides, I don't think I could eat a little soft, fluffy animal like a rabbit."

"We eat soft, fluffy animals all the time," he said, laughing, "like chickens, ducks, and sometimes geese and pheasants." Abruptly, I changed the subject.

That evening Mrs. Ellis treated us to another sumptuous farm dinner. All of us sat around the round table and watched and drooled as she loaded the table: a huge platter of baked potatoes, another platter loaded with steamed cabbage, a big bowl of creamed corn, and an even bigger platter full of fried chicken. She topped them all with rich gravy and cranberry sauce. Oh, what a meal; I stuffed myself shamelessly.

In the middle of after-dinner conversation, Bob asked, "So, you really liked the fried chicken, eh, Peter?"

"I certainly did." I said, "I have never eaten such delicious, tender chicken."

"Well, Peter," he said, grinning, "now you know what rabbit tastes like. I didn't catch any today so I bought them at the store," Bob explained.

The whole family burst into laughter, Mr. Ellis most loudly, and I had to join them, laughing more loudly than the rest. And that was how I was initiated into the Farmers' Order of American Rabbit Eaters.

It was springtime in Greencastle. With the appearance of pale green leaves on trees, the soft carpet of new grass on the lawn, and the sprinkles of white, pink, and yellow wildflowers, the whole DePauw campus transformed into budding exuberance. Boys walked around with more bounce, and the girls came out wearing shapely dresses of bright colors. As for me, all my revived energy was spent wrestling with the problems of my future: Should I follow the path to a religious career or the road to a lifetime of work in the theatre? It was strange that my love of the theatre in Shanghai days, which I had believed forgotten, was alive and growing in importance to me.

Besides the encouragement of Miss Clara Bell, the drama teacher, a theatre event at DePauw further increased my leaning toward the theatre. For the annual homecoming production, the theatre fraternity chose *Seventh Heaven,* and I was cast in a nonspeaking bit part as a "sewer rat." In a surprising review of the show in the school press, my name was mentioned prominently: "Peter Hyun, as the sewer rat, without speaking a word, created a true atmosphere of a cul-de-sac with his scurrying and pantomime." It was the push I needed to do something about finding a school of theatre.

There were three universities with established reputations for their schools of theatre: Northwestern, Carnegie Tech, and Yale, all very difficult to get in and expensive. Then, by chance I came across an ad in *Theatre Magazine* for the Gloucester School of Little Theatre, open for three summer months. Locating Gloucester, Massachusetts, on the map, I became doubly intrigued by the idea of seeing New England. The brochure I received outlined the summer program: classes in acting, speech, and dance, and participation in productions of three major plays. The tuition was moderate, which included meals but no facilities for rooming. I sent my application with a brief sketch of my background, and in a letter I expressed my eagerness to attend but that I could come only with a full scholarship including room and board. Of course, I would be glad to do any work to repay the costs.

I was surprised by a prompt reply from Miss Florence Cunningham, the school director. Even more surprising was her offer of a scholarship including room and board. They had no living facilities for men, but she promised to rent a room for me. The only stipulation was that I arrive as early as possible in June and help with preparations for the school opening.

I could hardly wait for the close of school in the first week of June. I spent my last dollar on a bus ride to Chicago, and from there to Boston. The Greyhound fare was about twelve dollars. I pawned my watch for fifteen dollars; it was a seventeen-jewel Bulova pocket watch and chain Papa and Umma had given me when I left home for college.

I ate very little on that forty-eight-hour ride to Boston, where I got on a suburban train to Gloucester. There, I was greeted by a strange odor; the whole town smelled like a decaying animal. Later I learned the obnoxious odor came from the town glue factory. Before the summer was over I became fond of this smell, and in later visits to Gloucester I always felt at home as soon as I got a whiff of that pungent odor.

The school was located outside of the town at water's edge, overlooking the Gloucester harbor. The one hundred-seat theatre was a rustic structure, half of which jutted out over the water. In a little room under the stage, Mrs. Evans presided over the acting classes. She was a proponent of human "body language"—long before the term became commonly known. She used it not only in class but in directing all the school productions.

A little court separated the theatre from a spacious red loft where classes in diction and dance were conducted. Lester (I don't recall his full name), a faculty member at Vassar College, taught stage design. Under his supervision, the students built and painted the scenery. On the other side of the court a little cottage housed the kitchen and office, and a narrow, long arbor provided shade for the dining tables where the students ate all their meals. A handsome Canadian lady came to Gloucester every summer to take charge of the kitchen at the school. She produced three meals a day for fifty people and managed to please everyone.

There was one extracurricular activity: a class in puppetry under Norman Bel-Geddes. Students made puppets and performed every Saturday for the town's children. I offered an old Korean folk-tale about a swallow who brought pumpkin seeds of good or ill for-tune to people, depending on what the people deserved. Norman built it into a puppet show that became a favorite of the Gloucester children.

I attended all the classes, worked with the stage designer build-ing and painting sets, and stage-managed some shows. But the most exciting thing that happened to me was meeting a young actress, May Sarton, from Cambridge. In great measure, she was to change the course of my life.

May Sarton, at seventeen or eighteen, was endowed with a sparkling mind and great beauty. Not the kind of beauty to grace the Chesterfield cigarette ads, but that rare variety that had to be nur-tured and discovered. That's what I did whenever a group of us gath-ered under the shade of a tree and carried on our serious discussions of the theatre. I discovered May's brilliant mind, unshackled imagina-tion, and childlike sense of humor. She was a good listener as well and was easily delighted by any good story, and just as easily broke into infectious laughter. I sought her company, and we spent many an hour sitting on a rock by the water's edge immersing ourselves in dis-cussions and exchanging our ideas for the theatre.

"What are you going to do after Gloucester, Peter?" she asked one day.

"Go back to college, I suppose," I said.

"Why?"

"Well, I have less than two years until I graduate," I said.

"But why waste two years if you could get into theatre work right now?"

"What would I do and how could I get in the theatre?"

May told me about Eva LeGallienne and her Civic Repertory Theatre in New York. "She interviews all the aspiring young actors and actresses from all over the country, nearly five hundred in the course of a year, and selects a dozen or so to join the Apprentice Group of her Civic Repertory Theatre." May said she had been accepted the previous year.

"What do you do in the Apprentice Group?" I asked.

"Well, we are given training in voice, speech, and body devel-opment; we get to play bit parts in the company productions, and we work on our own plays for presentation to the members of the com-pany for their critique."

"It sounds fabulous," I said, "but my main interest in the theatre is in directing. How will I be able to do that?"

"Well, have an interview and discuss it with Eva." May was positive Miss LeGallienne would understand and suggest something. That was the high point of my season at Gloucester.

When I called Miss LeGallienne on the phone, she sounded warm and friendly and granted me an interview the same afternoon. Of course, with the mention of May Sarton, how could she refuse?

Miss LeGallienne was dramatic even in her casual personal appearance. She was beautiful and totally disarming. She asked about my experience and special interest in the theatre. I drew a quick sketch of my life and told her that my main interest in the theatre was directing. She suggested that I work as an assistant stage manager for her company, which would give me technical as well as directorial experience. She also suggested that I work with her Apprentice Group and direct some of its work. She sealed it all by offering a weekly salary of fifty dollars.

I came out of the interview on a cloud. It just didn't seem real that the direction of my life had changed in the course of less than half an hour's conversation. First, I wanted to share this happiness with May, but she was in Cambridge. I managed to carry my suitcase on the subway and find my way to Sister Elizabeth, now living in the Bronx. She couldn't quite grasp the turn of events, but she offered her home for me to stay until I could afford my own place. How wonderful to have a sister nearby at such a time!

Now I had to sit down and write the dreaded letters. First to DePauw, informing them I would not return to school and that I would donate the trunk full of books I had left at the dormitory, including Havelock Ellis' *History of Sex* and Kraft Ebings' *Sexualis Abnormalis* to the library. That was not so difficult a letter to write. The next one to Papa and Umma required more time and thought. I was to have been the first college graduate in the family. How could I tell them I was not finishing college without breaking their hearts? In the end, I trusted their infinite capacity to face the unexpected and to allow their hearts and minds to understand and accept all the whims of life.

That was how I closed one chapter of my life in America and opened another.

# 4

# THE

# THEATRE

In the fall of 1930 I entered another new world—the world of the theatre in New York City. It was my first working day at the Civic Repertory Theatre, only a stone's throw from the elevated train stop at Fourteenth and Sixth avenues (Avenue of the Americas). The opera house–like theatre, flanked by nondescript little shops, must have been built in the days when Fourteenth Street was "uptown" for the dwellers of the Lower East Side and Greenwich Village. I entered through a tiny stage door and walked through a narrow basement passage, on either side of which there were rows of little dressing rooms. It was dark and gloomy, and I could smell the mustiness that comes with age. At the end of the hallway I turned, walked up a flight of steps, and entered the stage.

It was immense, more so since the stage was dark except for a single bare light bulb on a stand in the center of the stage. The only other person on stage was Norma Chandler, one of two stage managers with whom I would be working. She switched on the border lights and took me on a quick tour of the backstage of a professional theatre. I was awed by its immensity. Overhead, in back of the giant proscenium, hung multiple borders of lights of all colors and huge spotlights pointing in all directions. Off the back wall of the deep stage another passage was filled with all kinds of props imaginable. But the most impressive sight of all was the great height of the stage galleys rising over the stage where sceneries and backdrops were hung.

People began to saunter in—members of the Repertory company coming to attend the first meeting of the new season. Among others, I met Jacob Ben-Ami, the distinguished actor from the Hebrew Theatre, who would play the lead in Chekhov's *Cherry Orchard;* Richard Waring, a young, almost boyish British actor, who would play Romeo to Eva LeGallienne's Juliet; and Egon Brecher, a master of comedy whose performance in Molière's *Would-Be Gentleman* would rock the old theatre.

Suddenly the babble of conversation stopped as Eva LeGallienne, accompanied by her companion Josephine Hutchinson, appeared on stage. In typical theatrical fashion, we all applauded her entrance. She was dressed in a simple skirt and blouse of delicate lavender, her flaming hair brushed back in wild waves. She had penetrating eyes, and her square, open face was adorned with only a tiny pair of earrings. She smiled and greeted everyone, embracing and exchanging some rapid-fire queries and quips. She took her seat, welcomed them all for a new season, and introduced the new members, among them, Peter Hyun, "our new assistant stage manager. Did I pronounce the name correctly?" she asked.

"Close enough," I assured her.

She briefly outlined her plans for the season: *Master Builder, Romeo and Juliet, Cherry Orchard* as the mainstay, with *Peter Pan* for Saturday matinees. They would also add Ibsen's *Hedda Gabler* and Chekhov's *Three Sisters* along with Molière's *Bourgeois Gentilhomme* and the little-known *Cradle Song* by Spanish playwrights Gregorio and Maria Martinez Sierra. The plan also envisaged work on one or two new plays—an ambitious program that represented LeGallienne's dream of a true repertory theatre in America, where theatregoers could come to see the classics performed in professional productions.

In the afternoon, I attended the first meeting of the Apprentice Group. The members of this group, twelve in all, had been chosen from interviews conducted by LeGallienne. Young aspiring actors and actresses came for interviews throughout the year from all over the country, and out of nearly five hundred interviews she chose twelve. It was indeed my good fortune and an honor to have been among the chosen.

That season the Apprentice Group included John Garfield, a fiery young actor from the Lower East Side; Burgess Meredith, moody and brooding and suffering with asthma; and Howard daSilva, an audacious young actor hiding behind British manners. There were others: Charles Martin, a fast-talking New Yorker who would eventually talk himself into directing radio shows; Mark Lawrence, even then a slinking, shadowy figure who would later perpetuate that image in the movies; and Beverly Roberts, the perfect "American beauty" who would go to Hollywood and be instantly plucked by a mogul for himself.

This was an impressive group of young talents. Without exception, everyone in the group eventually made an impact on the theatre world; some in little theatres and others on Broadway and in the movies. Personally, my eyes were on Jane Kim, a tall, willowy beauty who was not only unconscious of her magnetic personality but extremely shy. When on stage, her chiseled face resting on her long graceful neck, and the flowing movement of her statuesque figure painted a dramatic picture, highlighted by her husky, breathy voice. Everyone, including the members of the company, admired her, but she was too shy to push herself in the theatre.

May Sarton, the second-year member of the group who had inspired me to give up my college education and come to the Civic, was now my daily companion and confidant. She was the most sensitive person I had ever known, always attuned to every living thing, and insatiably curious. Her whole personality and appearance were very pointed—her nose, mouth, and chin, and especially the glint in her eyes. With such natural weapons, she easily disarmed everyone she met, resulting in instant acceptance and communication.

Without any effort, she and I became inseparable friends. After the end of the day, which was usually midnight, we would meet at a nearby cafeteria, and over cups of coffee (thank God it only cost five cents a cup) we would review the day's events, especially what happened in the classes and in rehearsals. We exchanged our critiques of the acting and directing and our ideas about improving them. These nightly sessions gradually evolved into discussions of our ideas for the ideal theatre we would build. She lived in a professional girls home on McDougal Street, and each night I would escort her safely home. I would then take the long subway ride to West One Sixty-seventh Street and get to bed at two or three in the morning.

At this period, in order to make ends meet, I took another job between 6:00 and 10:00 A.M., which enabled me to be at the theatre by 11:00. The most difficult part of the job was getting up in the morning after a few hours of sleep. I would be only half awake when I reported for work at the wholesale chop suey house. Gallons of paper cartons filled with chop suey and chow mein would be ready for delivery to the drug stores around Manhattan. I was the delivery man. I would load up the orders in a taxi, which was hired by the month, and start off. We drove through uptown, downtown, crossing and recrossing the West Side and the East Side, until the last order was delivered. I would turn in all the money collected, together with new orders for the next day. By then it would be ten in the morning, and I would rush to the subway for my trip to the theatre downtown. The daily half-hour subway ride to Fourteenth Street afforded me a chance to read the *New York Times* to keep up with national and world events: politics, sports, and the theatre.

Fortunately, the first class of the Apprentice Group was fencing, taught by Signor Santelli, the famous Italian Olympic saber champion. Going through the paces, I would quickly shed all lingering drowsiness. Moreover, I enjoyed its subtle rhythm, intense concentration, and the degree of mental and physical coordination. I progressed rather quickly and soon earned the privilege of fencing with the master. Santelli had his own fencing studio, where John Garfield and others did more intensive work.

One day Signor Santelli took me aside and said, "Peter, come and fence at my studio."

"Gee, thanks." I was pleasantly surprised.

Then he quickly added, "Why don't you give up theatre and concentrate on fencing. I'll make you an Olympic champion." By his serious tone of voice, I could tell he was not tossing me idle flattery; he was serious.

So I answered seriously, "No, thanks, Signor Santelli," I said. "I have already chosen my lifetime work."

Ballet was our next class; Peter Hyun, twenty-four years old, from Korea, studying ballet! It was really alien and strange, and I tried for a few weeks but then gave it up. I didn't learn to appreciate the ballet until some years later when I watched the Ballet Russe perform. I could see how the rigorous and regimented forms of movements could be assembled and released to create the most beautiful human movements. On the other hand, modern dance prompted my immediate response. Its movements were more akin to the industrialized culture, identifiable in feelings and images. I became acquainted with a few young dancers belonging to the Martha Graham Group, who took me to watch their rehearsals.

I was fascinated by Martha Graham, a slight, frail figure who painted the most heroic images on stage with her dance. In this respect, I thought there was a kinship between modern dance and the classic Chinese opera forms in which the actors were trained to perform breathtaking acrobatic leaps and somersaults and fantastic dances with swords and spears. Then I saw Mary Wigman from Germany in a dance recital. She exuded supreme confidence in all her movements; she was in complete control of her body, and every movement, small and large, seemed to express deep human emotions. I learned much from modern dance, and in later years, when I was directing, I borrowed much from modern dance as well as Chinese opera in stylizing the movements of the actors on stage.

My day at the Civic would continue with classes in diction and improvisation. The speech class was taught by a retired actress whose immaculate speech I admired. She taught us how to breathe, how to enunciate, and how to project. Just as an athlete needs training to be able to compete, so does an actor need rigorous physical training to be able to perform on stage. An inspiring performance was never an accident, but the reward of immeasurable hard work.

An elderly man who spoke with a German accent taught the class on improvisation. He firmly believed that through improvisation the actor could dig into his personal experiences and discover his real emotions. "Improvisation," he said, "helps to ignite the actor's creative impulse." Improvisation, he lectured us, was a method by which an actor could explore and expand his emotions. This was some years before the Group Theatre under Lee Strasberg, Harold Clurman, and Cheryl Crawford discovered Stanislavsky and the so-called "method acting." In his class, the German teacher would pick one or two of us and put us in an imaginary situation: a new visitor to the city being held up by a robber in a park. The actors were given a few minutes to think through the situation and then live it on stage. The most surprising and interesting aspects of the actors' personalities would be revealed in improvisations. When it was finished, we would conduct a critique to evaluate how truthful the improvisation was.

I still remember one of the improvisations I did. I chose my own subject, "In Search of God." The stage is empty except for a chair. I sit in it and begin to read; it's the Bible, and I am reading about God's creation of the world and Adam and Eve in seven days. I am entranced; I lift my head and look around. I stand up and hurl the book away; I don't believe it. I wander around like a lost soul. Then I notice a temple and enter. I see a monk sitting on the floor meditating. I join him. In a lotus position with eyes closed, I hold my hands together under my chin and meditate. I find peace and serenity. When I open my eyes, there is no monk, no temple. I am disillusioned, and again I wander around. I hear people singing; it's coming from a basement. I go down and enter a little room. There I see people singing an old hymn, some swaying and some rolling on the floor. I join them. I see them waving their arms and screaming, "Hallelujah! Hallelujah! Amen! Amen!" The air is charged with emotion and hallucination; it is depressing. I run out of the basement and wander around the street. I am lost, I am lost—I have lost my mind.

The critique that followed expressed mixed and varied reactions, but they agreed that whatever it was I did it was honest and believable.

Besides these classes, I also learned another vital art—music. My knowledge of Western music had been limited and superficial until May Sarton took me under her wing and introduced me to the symphony. Every Sunday afternoon I would meet her at her dormitory; she would bring her record player and albums of symphonies into a little room. We would listen to Beethoven, Bach, and Brahms. I learned to listen to various instruments, each evoking distinct moods and feelings. I began to recognize the thematic melodies, their infinite variations, the climactic heights, and the depths of silence.

"Do you hear the oboe?" May would ask, and then whisper, "Here's that haunting melody."

I became a serious student not only of the classics, but also of jazz and American folk music. Sometimes, whenever our budget allowed, May and I would spend our Sundays at great concerts.

The most exciting and inspiring part of the day at the Civic was the company rehearsals in the afternoon. To watch the professional actors at work and to be close enough to see a great actress directing —it was a rare privilege given to all Apprentice Group members. It was interesting to listen to LeGallienne's direction—always in a warm, intimate voice. I never heard her raise her voice in anger. Her most extreme measure was humorous ridicule, such as: "Take the hot potato out of your mouth so we can understand what you are saying."

At any critical and serious moment, she would take the actor aside and go offstage. When they returned and the actor repeated the scene, I could almost feel the new inspiration of the actor infused by LeGallienne.

For the first time in my life I came to understand and appreciate the subtleties of Shakespeare, Ibsen, and Chekhov. I also discovered the plays of Molière, the Quintero brothers, Susan Gladspell, and Gregorio and Maria Martinez Sierra. Working behind the stage and watching the performances at close range was richly rewarding. It was from the wings that I experienced the most memorable moments in the theatre: Jacob Ben-Ami in Ibsen's *Master Builder* lamenting, ". . . the youth is knocking at my door . . ."; Nazimova in the closing scene of Chekhov's *Cherry Orchard,* sitting on a stool in enveloping darkness, listening to the sounds of an axe chopping down her beloved cherry trees; and Eva LeGallienne as Juliet in the tomb scene when she awakens to find her Romeo beside her, dead. One evening, during the entire tomb scene, I stood in the wings and watched the audience. The air was tense throughout the house.

Juliet awakens and discovers Romeo dead. She tears the vial out of Romeo's hand and prepares to drink the remaining potion. The suspense mounts, and I heard a man in the audience groaning loudly, "I can't stand it! I can't stand it!"

These were the precious moments in the theatre that I would treasure all my life.

May Sarton was absolutely right; I couldn't possibly have obtained such a study of the theatre in college, especially not this insight into all the intricacies of a production. As an assistant stage manager I was fortunate enough to attend most of the planning sessions with scenic designer Mordecai Gorelic; costume designer Irene Sheariff; lighting technicians, composers and choreographers, and makeup consultants. Listening to LeGallienne's animated discussions with all the specialists was like observing a group of artists jointly creating a production; a process possible in no other form of art. Each actor was a distinct personality, with his own complex and sensitive makeup, with his own unique talents and shortcomings. How to reach and explore these potentials, how to mold them into a dramatic pattern—that was the task and the challenge of a director. They work and suffer in their rehearsals to capture the magical moment when emotion, spoken word, and action converge in the moment of truth; that is what the director strives for.

There were also some painful experiences at the Civic. Most of them arose out of my dealings as a stage manager with the stage crew. They were mostly old-timers who had worked all their lives as stagehands—prop men, electricians, and scenery handlers. It was part of my job to give them instructions and cues. They would respond quite curtly, and sometimes they even ignored me. I knew what the problem was; an "Oriental" was giving them orders! Behind my back, they would say to each other (loudly for my benefit), "What's a Chinaman doing here?" Of course it hurt me, but I refused to give them the satisfaction of showing my pain. Instead, I would deliberately approach the slanderer and slowly repeat my orders.

But after all, this was 1930; a live Asian working on the stage of a New York theatre was unheard of, not to mention as a stage manager. It wasn't only that I was a foreigner; I was an "Oriental," a "Chinaman," an inferior.

Not infrequently some stranger loitering on the street would call out to me, "Hey, Chinaman!" The ignorance and the deeply ingrained racial prejudice were not confined to street scenes; even some friends in school and later in the theatre would ask me if my family was in the laundry business. When I walked down the street with May or we were seated together in the theatre, I had to ward off all the hostile glances and muffled whispers.

I refused to be distracted, least of all by bigots and the ignorant. Every day I worked and learned, and soon I was rewarded with a wonderful opportunity. John Garfield, of the Apprentice Group, came and confided his plan to me; he wanted to do *The Last Mile.* He asked me if I would direct. This would be his major project and would be performed before LeGallienne and the company for their critique. I welcomed the opportunity. I could now test all that I had learned—my ideas and theories about acting and directing.

There was only one character in the one-act play—a condemned prisoner awaiting his execution. He sees his entire life filled with shame, remorse, and even humor. There's no time left to repent or do it over. He wishes only for his last moment in life to be honest and brave. I found John a very sensitive and intense person, with great pride. However, he was too young to conceive death. I had to direct him to identify it with the most precious possession he had and imagine its destruction and loss. John's response was most remarkable. For a very young actor to understand and feel such human cruelty, defiance, and pathos—it had a humbling effect on me as a director. John's last line in his performance, as he walked to his execution, ". . . cowards die many times, but the brave die only once. . . ." rang out ·with an absolute truth. LeGallienne and the company broke into applause, a most unusual compliment. The critique that followed pointed to all the highlights in praise. Only LeGallienne had a word of criticism: "John, you must learn to keep your emotions under control."

Years later, a stranger came to see me at my place of work in Los Angeles. I was managing the First Grand Liquor Store, so named for its location on Bunker Hill. This prize location has since become the elegant entrance to the Los Angeles Music Center. The stranger said that he had been sent by John Garfield to invite me to visit him. This was quite an honor, for John Garfield was now not only a big movie star, but he was producing his own pictures in his own studio— Enterprise Studio. Curious and somewhat excited to see John again after nearly fifteen years, I dropped in at the studio one afternoon. I was ushered to the set where John was working.

He recognized me, came over and greeted me warmly, and, dismissing the shooting, took me to his office upstairs. He was eager to know what I had been doing. He asked if I had been in touch with any of the Civic gang. I gave him a quick sketch of my life and told him that I hadn't worked in the theatre for a number of years.

"How would you like to work here with me?" he asked.

I didn't know what to answer. "Doing what?" I asked.

"Anything you want."

"But I don't know anything about pictures," I said.

"That's okay," he said. "You are the best director I ever had. Just hang around and give me any ideas you might have."

That was a most generous and tempting offer; I was flattered and moved. But I couldn't accept it. I had left the theatre some years before, never to look back. Accepting John's offer would mean traveling backward and becoming involved in the theatre all over again.

"Thanks, John," I said, "but I really can't." That was the last time I saw him before his untimely death at the height of his career.

Back to the Civic—winter of 1930. After several months, for reasons of health, I had to give up the delivery job; the load at the Civic was heavy enough. I also rented a room in an apartment of one of the actors in Greenwich Village and saved myself the two-hour subway ride each day. Still, I spent twelve to fourteen hours a day at the theatre.

Each day, I looked forward to the final curtain of the evening performance and the last curtain call. Then, the set struck, new scenery put in place for the next day, we would hold our rehearsals for the Apprentice Group. This was the most exciting part of the day; to create and carry out our own ideas on stage. After that, May and I would go to Child's Cafeteria around the corner and review our day. May was always breathless recounting all the little happenings; some incidents in class, a marvelous discovery at the company rehearsal. Over countless cups of coffee I would go over my own notes of the day. These exchanges always led us to the discussion of our dream theatre; what a theatre should and could be. There was no question we would someday have such a theatre of our own.

About this time, stories were being circulated in theatre circles about the exciting Russian Theatre, the Moscow Art Theatre in particular. All the stories spoke of the wondrous and magical happenings on and off the stage in Russia. There were no publications except a rather superficial account of the Russian Theatre by Norris Haughton, a Princeton graduate who had spent a summer at the Gloucester School of Little Theatre. Sometime later, a book by the director of the Moscow Art Theatre, Stanislavsky's *An Actor Prepares* appeared in America and made a profound impact. May and I followed these developments and finally decided that we should go to Russia and study their theatre firsthand. This was the beginning of our dream for a journey to the Soviet Union.

We read *Humanity Uprooted* by Maurice Hindus, the only book then available on the Russian Revolution and the founding of the first socialist state in the world. We also read of the onslaught of the Western powers to destroy the Bolsheviks, the successful repulsion of this attack and the suppression of counterrevolution from within, and the emergence of an industrialized society out of the ashes of near-total destruction. It was the miracle of modern-day history. In 1930, the Russian people were still struggling for self-sufficiency in all basic necessities: food, shelter, and clothing. One of the weapons they utilized in that struggle was what they called the Shock Brigades. These were brigades of volunteers, from all of the performing arts—actors, singers, and dancers. Each brigade would be sent to critical areas throughout the country where production lagged—the mines, farms, and factories. The Shock Brigade would appear with fresh material and perform to inspire and exhort the people to new heights of production.

Why not an American Shock Brigade? The idea flashed like a thunderbolt in our nightly session at Child's Cafeteria. May and I toyed with the idea and began laying concrete plans. We decided to add two others to the brigade: a beautiful young woman of Norwegian parentage named Renee, who worked as a secretary in an office; and for the fourth member, a college friend of mine from the Midwest, John, who was studying to become a minister. Together with May and me, of Belgian and Korean ancestry, respectively, the first American Shock Brigade would be truly as American as apple pie. Wherever we might be sent, we would present scenes from American plays and harmonize some American folk songs. At the end of each day, before going to bed, we would review our experiences and impressions, and Renee would record our conversations in shorthand. And when we returned to the United States we would publish the documented diary of the American Shock Brigade. We could already visualize the whole experience and the book; we could hardly wait to embark on our journey.

But wait—where was the money? Where could we find the money to finance our trip? It was a formidable challenge, but not enough to discourage us. Our first inspiration took us to the only office of the Soviet government in America—Intourist. We found it in a semi-basement in uptown Sixth Avenue. Its staff consisted of one white-haired American lady. We explained our mission to her; we wished to take the first American Shock Brigade and place it at the service of the Soviet Union. The white-haired lady was highly impressed and believed we would be welcomed by the Soviet people. But she wasn't sure if the Soviet government would be willing or able to pay the expenses. She was sorry she could not give us an answer and asked us to come back in a week; she might have an answer then.

Yes, she did have an answer when we returned. She had received official approval for the American Shock Brigade, and the Soviet Union would pay all expenses while we were there. All we had to do was pay our fare to and from the Soviet Union. The estimated round-trip steamship fare for each came to five hundred dollars. We needed two thousand dollars to launch our grand project. There certainly would be two thousand dollars somewhere—such little money for such a great undertaking!

Jane Kim, the willowy beauty of the Apprentice Group, had a father, James Imbrie, once known as the "white-haired boy of Wall Street"—everything he touched turned to gold. He had been a very, very rich man. But then came the stock market crash, and he lost everything. When Jane took May and me to meet him, we found him living in a tiny mid-Manhattan apartment with his beautiful Irish wife. Jane's father was fascinated and excited by our projected trip to Russia. He was heartbroken that he could not finance the whole project himself; it would have been so simple before the crash. After much searching, Mr. Imbrie said that our best bet would be Howard McCann, the publisher, who was a very close friend. He said, "Go see him and tell him I sent you. Tell him everything, offer him the rights to the book, and ask for a two thousand dollar advance."

Oh, we were so encouraged, and our hopes soared to new heights. May and I were at McCann's office the very next day. He, too, listened to our plans for an American Shock Brigade with keen interest. We then told him that he could have the full rights to publish our diary if he could only give us a two thousand dollar advance. There was a long pause. We couldn't tell whether he was counting his potential loss or profits.

He broke the silence with a deep sigh.

"Let me tell you a story," he said. "Just the other day, Maurice Hindus came to see me and offered me the rights to his second book on the Soviet Union and asked for a five hundred dollar advance." He sighed again and said, "I couldn't give it to him."

We left his office in dead silence.

Next evening at Child's, May and I assessed the situation; we were near the end of our rope. Two thousand dollars! Was it really so much and beyond our reach? No! I swore. And I swore again I would find the money. Of all the people I had ever known, I was convinced Dr. Oxham, president of DePauw University, would understand and appreciate my audacious project. A few days leave from the theatre was all I needed, and a kind of collective fund financed my trip to Indiana.

On the long train ride to Indianapolis, I mulled over and over again all the details of our impossible journey. It was already spring. In two months the theatre season would end; we had to be prepared to leave for the Soviet Union immediately thereafter. We could spend three months there and return to New York in time for the opening of a new season at the Civic.

The spring sun was setting over old DePauw when I arrived at Greencastle. Mrs. Oxham, who had answered my telephone call, greeted me at the door, and fortunately Dr. Oxham was also at home. They were both surprised but not shocked to see me dropping in so unceremoniously. They suggested that we all have dinner first and talk afterward. Through the dinner, I gave them an account of myself; the reason for my leaving school, my job at the Civic Repertory Theatre, the interesting people I had met, and the work I was doing in the Apprentice Group. They both congratulated me on my bold move.

Now seated comfortably in the living room, I told them of the purpose of my mission. They seemed fascinated by our idea of a young American group offering its services to the Soviet Union. I told them that we already had obtained the approval of the Soviet government, which would subsidize all our expenses once we arrived there. The only cost for us would be the round-trip fare to and from Russia; two thousand dollars for four people. We needed the money as soon as possible so that we could depart when our theatre season ended. We would repay the money when we returned and had our book published.

Dr. Oxham was visibly sorry he couldn't underwrite the project himself. "You know, Peter," he said morosely, "a college president's life is like a minister's—he lives by the grace of God." He then raised our spirits—his and mine—by saying, "But we must find a way— there must be a way." He began to think out loud, going over name after name as a possible angle, then suddenly he stopped. "Do you have enough money to travel to Gary, Indiana?" he asked.

"Yes, I do." I answered.

"Then you must go there and see the president of the Studebaker Corporation. He's a good friend of mine who has given money to many worthwhile causes." He then added, "I'll give you a letter of recommendation."

I spent the night at the men's hall, the dormitory where I used to live. The housemother was still there, as well as a few old classmates with whom I relived some old memories, and we exchanged our experiences. I also met a group of new students—freshmen and sophomores. One of them related the story about my fame on campus due to Professor Eckhardt's story to his philosophy classes about a former student named Peter Hyun who had come to DePauw with a mind filled with preconceived ideas, thus totally unfit for the study of philosophy. He warned his students not to become another Peter Hyun. My encounter with Professor Eckhardt in class flashed through my mind. The one challenging question I had raised in his class evidently had inflicted such a deep and lasting wound. What a pity!

With great trepidation I arrived in Gary, Indiana, near Chicago, at the offices of the Studebaker Corporation. By flashing the envelope with Dr. Oxham's letterhead, I passed the gate. At the main office I was screened past several more offices before reaching the president's office. I was halted there by the secretary. She asked me what I wanted to see the president about. I told her I had a letter from the president of DePauw University to be given to the president of the Studebaker Corporation. She took the letter and asked me to wait, then disappeared. A few minutes later she emerged and said, "The president will communicate with you by mail."

I left the office without another word. Drained and empty-handed, I had a lonely bus ride back to New York. Of course, I didn't expect to ever hear from the president of the Studebaker Corporation.

The most dreadful part of my unsuccessful mission was facing May and telling her I had failed. Her reaction to my report was typical of May; she felt more painful about my pains. She comforted me by reiterating her faith in me. "You'll get the money, Peter," she said, "I know you will."

Like magic, May's few words revived my own faith, and I said, "May, I'll find the money. I swear I will."

The theatre season ended, much too soon. All the members of the Civic and the Apprentice Group instantly scattered to the four corners of the country, some to visit their families, some to join summer stock companies, and a few just to enjoy the break. To the members of the American Shock Brigade I gave notice to be prepared to leave at a moment's notice; they would be contacted the minute I got the money.

Alas! Life had a way of setting its own course. Only a short time after the Civic closed, I was struck dumb by a headline in the morning paper: "Eva LeGallienne in a Fire Accident." I read the account with a trembling heart. It happened in her Woodstock home. She had gone to the basement to light the heater, and it exploded and burned her badly. The hospital bulletin said that her face was severely burned. In shock, all the Civic members waited for the prognosis. It came in stages; her face was burned most severely, and even with plastic surgery the scars would always remain. When released from the hospital, she made a public announcement: the Civic Repertory Theatre would be closed for a year. She planned to spend a year recuperating in Europe.

Soon afterward I heard from May. She said that she was going to Europe for a year and that she would have to withdraw from the Shock Brigade project. I knew how attached and devoted May was to LeGallienne, and I could understand her desire to be near Eva while she recovered from the accident. May also said that she would spend the time writing. She wrote poetry, some of which she let me read—the most beautiful poems I had ever read. In my mind, I could understand and appreciate all this. But my heart was in turmoil and wouldn't stop throbbing. I had lost May, and with her, our dream of the impossible journey.

Suddenly, my whole life seemed to lose all its meaning. The fire that burned inside me so fiercely was snuffed out. I had no more energy, no desire, no ambition. The only thing moving relentlessly was time. Summer was approaching, and I had to go somewhere, do something.

I found my way back to Gloucester, where May and I had first met. Everyone was happy to see me and welcomed me with open arms—the sweet and kind owner-manager of the school, Miss Cunningham; the ever-serious director, Mrs. Evans; the lovely lady from Canada, and everyone else. There were a few students who had been there before, but the new group was mostly bright, pretty young girls from Boston's high society. But no one and nothing could bring me out of my depression, not even the chance to assist in the summer's first production. I passed the time in the day somehow, but the nights were hellish; I could not sleep. Miss Cunningham gave me a box full of pulp magazines—*True Detective Stories*. She asked me to read them; if nothing else, those stories would put me to sleep. It didn't work. I broke out in hives, which kept me scratching all night. Finally, I was taken to a doctor who diagnosed the outbreak as  shingles.

Only I knew what brought on the breakdown—the loss of May Sarton. It was painful to remember our year at the Civic; yet all the thrilling, fun moments we shared kept reeling through my mind: our midnight rehearsals, our nightly sessions at Child's, our Sunday concerts, our plans for our own theatre, and so many other precious moments that drew us together so closely. If that was love, then it was a pure and utterly unselfish kind of love. How strange; I had never even kissed her.

During the long nights when sleep would not come, I would go for a walk and usually come to the water near the theatre. A part of the theatre jutted out over the water, and sitting at the water's edge, I could see the blinking lights of the town of Gloucester across the harbor. Occasional lonely rings of the bell on a bobbing buoy kept vigil over the restless sea. Suddenly I would be gripped with a thought of ending all the pain. I needed only to walk a few steps into the water until I could be swallowed up. In a very short time all the pain would end; no more brooding, no more suffering. It would be such an easy and simple solution. Life and death are really close allies, separated only by a minute or two.

But in the dark recesses of my mind, there still was a spark of sanity and hope. My thoughts turned away from death to life; to live, to create, and to work. Yes, only work could be my salvation. Instead of a watery grave, I plunged into all the work I could find in the theatre. I found new life and new interest in working with Mrs. Evans on a new production. I began working closely with Lester, the scenic designer who taught at Vassar College, to learn and experiment on the technical aspects of the theatre. I spent Saturdays staging the puppet shows with Bel-Geddes.

Overnight, the shingles disappeared. I could hardly wait to get in bed and fall fast asleep. I needed all the sleep to revive my strength

and fortify my sanity. The only worry now was where to go and
what to do when the summer theatre closed. Even then, my spirits
were high, and soon I found a job in Cambridge, Massachusetts. Yes,
I was alive. I helped to put away all the scenery and props, closed all
the doors and shutters, and battened down everything for the winter.
With only a few dollars in my pocket, but with fantastic plans in my
head, I left Gloucester, Cambridge bound.

# 5

# THE

# STUDIO

# PLAYERS

Yes, work was my only salvation—physical and spiritual. Work kept my body and soul together. That summer, at the Gloucester School of Little Theatre, I met Margaret Bouten, whose mother happened to be the director of the American Red Cross in Cambridge. It was she, this charming, indefatigable, young old lady who found a job for me. I moved into the home of the Blackwells on Blaisedell Street. I was given a little room in the attic where I parked my suitcase and began dreaming the implausible dream of founding a theatre of my own in the Boston area. Meanwhile, I was the "houseboy" of the Blackwell family. Mr. Blackwell was a retired Harvard professor, and Mrs. Blackwell a kind and gracious lady. Their son had left home to teach in a nearby town, and they lived alone in the old, spacious home. I was hired to help Mrs. Blackwell with her cooking chores.

I quickly discovered how a New England family was distinguished from other American families I had known, such as those in Indiana and New York. The New Englander, I found, was extremely tidy, orderly, and systematic. They were proud and cherished their family traditions. The close-knit family, the customary gathering of the clan for the holidays, and the sharing of kinship among the members were almost like those of a Korean family. They were punctilious in observing the established schedule of their daily routine; time for awakening, breakfasting, shopping, sitting down to supper, socializing, and finally going to bed. Even their diet was maintained by schedule. Thus, despite its inevitable effects, I learned to eat and even enjoy the regular Saturday evening diet of baked beans. I also learned New England table manners from Mrs. Black-well, and much more. I learned to prepare vegetables, meat, and fish, but the most important lesson was not to throw away anything that was usable. A piece of string was tied to a ball, wound, and placed in the proper niche where balls of strings were kept. Likewise, pieces of paper, not to mention paper bags, were carefully pressed, folded, and placed in the proper compartment according to their size and color. There was a time-honored method for saving each item, and all the work and effort seemed perfectly painless.

The job for which I received free room and board was menial but not hard. As soon as I had learned, I cooked the family breakfast, which I served and then shared at the family table. Then I would clear the table, wash the dishes, and clean up the kitchen. I was free until midafternoon, when I had to assist Mrs. Blackwell with the dinner. During the free hours, I could be theatre designer, organizer, and director until I became the houseboy again. Then I helped to clean and cook the vegetables while Mrs. Blackwell prepared the main course of meat or fish. When all was ready, Mrs. Blackwell joined her husband at the table, and I served the dinner, properly, as I had been taught. I would then join them at the table, and interrupt my dinner only when it was time to serve coffee and dessert. With the dinner over, I had to clear the table and set it for the next morn-ing's breakfast, wash the dishes and put them away, clean the sink and polish the faucets, and sweep and mop the kitchen floor. I was through for the day and the rest of the evening.

Then I would plan my future as a theatre director. I spent hours in my room in the attic reviewing and revising my plans for the the-atre. I searched out and met all the people of the theatre in the Bos-ton area: designers of sets and costumes, publicists, and business managers. The basic idea of my master plan was rather simple: to test my ideas for an ideal theatre. They were the ideas that May Sarton and I had developed over countless cups of coffee at Child's during the early morning hours. In our own way, we analyzed the theatre experience and tried to discover the basic ingredients of theatre art. Quite distinct from other art forms, it was the product of the creative work of a collective—writers, composers, painters, actors, and direc-tors, as well as technicians and craftsmen. The degree of artistic suc-cess in the theatre, therefore, depended greatly on the close and intimate collaboration of the participating artists.

While such grand designs for a theatre of my own were brewing in my head, my meager capital was shrinking fast. I was in dire need of some cash just to make the phone calls and to pay for the subway rides to and from Boston. When I came to Cambridge, one of the first things I did was register for a couple of courses in Harvard Night School. It dawned on me that I might find a job through the student employment service. I rushed there to apply. The manager asked me, "What can you do?"

"Anything," I said, meaning my willingness, not my qualifications.

"Can you cook?" he asked.

"Yes! No!. . . no, . . . not really. I can cook a simple breakfast."

"That's fine," the manager said, and concluded, "I'll call you when we have a job." To my amazement, he called me the very next day. "We have a job for you, Mr. Hyun;" he sounded quite pleased.

"What kind of job is it?" I asked.

"Oh, just a simple job to cook the Sunday dinner for one of our professors."

"But I told you I wasn't a cook," I protested.

"But this would be a simple meal. I tell you, why don't you go on over there and find out?"

"Oh, all right," I answered reluctantly. At the moment, my doubt and fear were overshadowed by the prospect of earning some money. It was a Friday afternoon, and I trudged over to the professor's home to learn the details of the job.

I came back in a state of nervous prostration. Mrs. Blackwell saw me and asked with alarm, "What's the matter, Peter?"

"I got a job," I said tragically.

"But what's so terrible about that? You wanted a job so badly."

"But, Mrs. Blackwell, this is a job as a cook. I am supposed to cook a Sunday dinner for eight people. I have never cooked a dinner in my whole life."

"That is a predicament, isn't it?" Mrs. Blackwell agreed. "But don't panic, Peter; maybe you can manage it somehow. Did they give you the menu?"

"Yes. Soup, roast beef with two vegetables, dessert, and coffee."

Mrs. Blackwell was positive that I could do it, and spent a couple of hours for two days tutoring me. For the soup, the simplest way would be to use Campbell's canned vegetable soup; four cans should be enough for eight people. For the vegetables, I would bake eight potatoes.

"How do I bake potatoes?" I asked.

"Why, you just throw them in the oven at the same time as the meat, and by the time the meat is done, the potatoes will be done also."

Simple enough, I thought. For the second vegetable, I would serve string beans. She showed me how I should wash, French-cut, and boil them for ten minutes, then drain them and serve. Yes, simple enough, I wanted to convince myself. And as for the dessert, everybody would like a Washington layer cake. I could buy it at the store, along with a carton of whipping cream to spread between the layers and on top of the cake before serving. Yes, it really is simple, I thought again.

The most important part of the dinner, of course, was the roast beef. First, I would need to find out how heavy the roast was, set the oven at 350 degrees, and allow fifteen minutes to the pound. It was that simple!

Mrs. Blackwell drilled and quizzed me over and over again until she was quite sure I had the dinner well under control. "You see, Peter, cooking is really not all that hard," Mrs. Blackwell concluded in triumph.

"I'll find out on Sunday," I said ominously. "Anyway, Mrs. Blackwell, thank you so much for all the help."

I had nightmares for two nights before the fateful Sunday. I went to the professor's home early so that I would have enough time for that roast. It was a ten pounder, and by Mrs. Blackwell's instructions, I should cook it for two and one-half hours at 350 degrees. I didn't have a watch, so I was glad to see an old clock on the kitchen wall. It showed ten o'clock—lots of time before cooking the roast. I had rehearsed the whole routine dozens of times in my mind and felt I had it pretty well mastered. First the vegetables. I washed eight good-looking russet potatoes (I didn't know that such a lowly vegetable had a special name) ready to go in the oven with the meat. Next, I cleaned the string beans, snapped off the ends, and French-cut them; I thought they looked rather pretty. For the dessert I had bought a large-size Washington layer cake and a carton of whipping cream. What puzzled me was that the cream was liquid, not at all like the fluffy stuff I found in cream puffs.

How do I transform this liquid cream into whipped cream? It was too late to call Mrs. Blackwell; she would already have gone to church. Just then, the housemaid who was to serve the dinner came into the kitchen to ask how everything was. I said fine, and then casually asked if she would make the whipped cream for me, and I pointed at the carton of cream on the table. Sure, she said, and I watched her pour the cream into a large bowl. She took out a strange gadget, put it in the bowl, and began cranking it. In no time she stopped cranking and said, "Here's your whipped cream." Lo and, behold! There it was—white, fluffy whipped cream.

The last problem having been solved, and feeling greatly relieved, I went out of the kitchen to relax a bit. I sat on the doorstep and contemplated the quirks of man's destiny. I didn't know how long I had been lost in my thoughts, but I was jolted out of my reverie by the housemaid who poked her head out the door and asked, "Aren't you going to cook the meat?" I jumped and ran into the kitchen to look at the clock.

"How can this be? . . . It's still ten o'clock . . ." I muttered to myself.

"Oh, that old clock! It doesn't work!" the housemaid said.

"Do you know what time it is?" I asked.

"It's almost twelve o'clock," she said, and walked out of the kitchen.

I was nearly in a panic, but I kept telling myself be calm . . . be calm . . . don't lose your head . . . don't lose your head. . . . To make up for the time lost, I lit the oven and turned it up to 500 degrees. Then I threw in the ugly-looking hunk of meat together with the eight russet potatoes. Next, I dumped the pretty French-cut string beans into a pot of water and put it on the stove to boil. Now, there was nothing more to do but wait; less than an hour to cook the ten-pound roast! Suddenly, I noticed some smoke drifting out of the oven, and when I opened it, a puff of black smoke engulfed my face. The 500-degree heat must have been too much, I guessed, so I turned the heat down to 350 as Mrs. Blackwell had instructed me. But the damage was done, and I had to take the meat out and scrape off the burnt crusts.

"What's burning?" the housemaid rushed into the kitchen to inquire.

"Everything is fine," I answered, and sent her away.

In a matter of minutes she returned and asked if the dinner was ready; it was one o'clock, she said. I told her to give me ten minutes and shooed her away again.

Oh, my God! I had forgotten all about the soup, but thank goodness I knew how to open cans. I opened all four cans of Campbell's vegetable soup, poured them into a large pot, added four cans of water—remembering Mrs. Blackwell's lesson—and lit the fire under the pot.

Too soon, I heard the housemaid's voice again.

"May I serve the dinner now? It's a quarter past one."

"All right, you may start with the soup," I said, pointing to the pot on the stove.

"What's in this other pot? It's boiling."

"Oh!" Only then did I remember the pretty French-cut string beans. "Please, turn the fire off," I said. They must have turned into soup by now, I thought. Anyway, it pleased me to see the housemaid carrying a beautiful porcelain bowl with my soup in it.

In a few minutes, she returned carrying the soup dishes, which she dumped into the sink.

"Well," she said, "they are ready for the main course." She sounded rather hostile, but I was in no position to be concerned with the manners of a housemaid.

"Please, serve the vegetables first," my voice didn't sound any too friendly either.

When I drained the bit of water still left in the pot and emptied the French-cut string beans into a bowl, I noticed they weren't so pretty; in fact, they were sad and dead. I fished the russet potatoes, which had some ugly burnt scars, out of the oven and put them on a beautiful platter the housemaid was holding. Then she brought out a very large and even more beautiful platter for the meat. I dug out the badly abused piece of meat and put it on the platter. The sight of the burnt meat on the beautiful platter struck me as quite ludicrous. No wonder the housemaid raised her nose in the air as she carried the meat platter out of the kitchen. Well, it was almost over; only the dessert and coffee remained to be served. The Washington layer-cake and the beautifully whipped cream were ready. Little did I realize just then that the climax of the drama was yet to come.

It appeared like a horrible apparition. The housemaid carried the meat platter back into the kitchen. Without a word, she dropped it on the table and walked out. I didn't have to ask what had happened. Only a single slice had been cut off the roast, and the dripping fresh blood nearly filled the platter. The russet potatoes were untouched. I stuck a fork into one and it felt as hard as when I brought them from the store. My impulse was to run out of there and disappear, but the housemaid stomped back in and held her arm out straight at me.

"Here, this is for you," she said. She was holding out a ten-dollar bill.

"What about the dessert?" I asked meekly.

"Never mind the dessert," she said icily. "The Missus just wants you to take this and go." I couldn't bring myself to take the money, but the housemaid kept waving it at me, saying, "Here! Here! You'd better hurry up and take this and leave."

Yes, I took the money and walked out of the house, numb with such mortification as I had never known before. Back at home, Mrs. Blackwell greeted me and asked how the dinner went. I had neither the strength nor the nerve to recount the horrors.

Next morning, the student employment manager telephoned and asked what happened at the Sunday dinner. He said the professor's wife called early in the morning to harangue about the cook we had sent, who was a total fake and who had ruined the whole dinner, and that they had had to take their guests out to a restaurant. "Furthermore," the manager continued, "she made all kinds of threats if we should ever send this fake cook out again on another job."

"I told you I wasn't a cook, but you insisted I should take the job." The reminder was futile and meaningless. Needless to say, the manager never called me again for another job.

Well, life had to go on, and I took some comfort in the old wise saying that every evil has its good. And the good that resulted from my evil experience was my resolve to learn to cook. I read books, studied recipes, and begged Mrs. Blackwell to teach me how to cook. In a short time I became quite a confident cook, being able sometimes to relieve Mrs. Blackwell and prepare the entire family dinner. I was particularly pleased with my prize dish, which, of course, was roast beef.

The cooking-for-pay episode, however, did not deter me from carrying on with my plans for the theatre. Following my plan, I began assembling my company of actors—actors whose talent and love of the theatre I had discovered at the Civic Repertory Theatre. I contacted Jane Kim and Howard daSilva in New York. Yes, they would be only too happy to join my theatre in Cambridge. Two others, David Kerman and Sala Stow, were also enthusiastic about joining us. In Boston, I found Lester, the scenic designer who used to teach at Vassar College. He liked my concept of the theatre and agreed to work with our group. And I met a rather conservative but bright young woman, a recent graduate of Radcliffe in theatre arts, who "would do anything" to be a part of our theatre. I put her in charge of promotion and public relations. And to complete the company, I found a pretty young woman with considerable experience to take care of the business end of the theatre.

But what about the theatre itself? Where could we stage our show and have people come to see it? My search ended in the center of Cambridge. Brattle Hall was a mellow, time-stained building that must have seen some gala happenings of the town, but which had been left forgotten and grown decrepit. It was a dear structure, nevertheless, whose design inside and out oozed charm. It suited us perfectly, for it had a surprisingly large stage and a seating capacity of almost two hundred. Without any hesitation, I took an option for a six-month lease.

Now all I needed was money. Again, my search for sponsors and financial backing met its first success in the heart of Cambridge. Harry Wadsworth Longfellow Dana, the grandnephew of the beloved poet, became our first sponsor. I heard that he had conducted two theatre tours to the Soviet Union. I introduced myself over the phone and was given an appointment. From the beginning, he was enthusiastic about my theatre idea. He was particularly glad to know that the theatre would be located in Cambridge. He bemoaned the fact that there had never been a permanent theatre in Cambridge, the so-called cultural center of the country. I told him of my plans for three major productions and the budget of five thousand dollars for the season. His response was to underwrite five hundred dollars. It was the first concrete confirmation of my faith. With this initial capital, I not only closed my lease on Brattle Hall but also leased a three-story brick building to house the acting company.

The plan to have the group live together under the same roof was one of the basic theories I wanted to test. Theatre art, I believed, is a collective art, and it would be achieved to the degree of integration of the members of the collective. Living together and knowing each other intimately would offer rare insight into each other's hidden feelings and talents. The final fruition of harmonious interplay of the characters on stage could be achieved with such a collective group.

Now, armed with the name of our first sponsor, it was easier to contact other prospective patrons. My presentation was simple but quite appealing: a permanent professional theatre in the Boston area with a resident company whose members would come out of the Apprentice Group of Eva LeGallienne's Civic Repertory Theatre. We would present a minimum of three plays for the season for a subscription price of five dollars. Five hundred subscriptions would pay for half of our total budget; we needed patrons who would sponsor and guarantee the other half. Each sponsor, I suggested, would underwrite five hundred dollars as Professor Dana had done.

My approach in the search for sponsors was quite direct and cut and dried: I wished to have none but the best known and most famous names of Boston society as my sponsors. I was able to reach such a circle through my contacts and acquaintances with the daughters of the famous Boston families in the Gloucester School of Little Theatre.

The responses were beyond all expectations. In a short time, five new sponsors were added to the list. Their patronage not only assured the financial feasibility, but even more important, rendered great prestige, for their names included Mrs. Richardson, whose husband was to become a state senator; and Mrs. Bancroft, whose husband was an important stockholder of the *Wall Street Journal*.

The first company meeting of our new theatre was held in Cambridge early in September. The founding members were, beside myself, Jane Kim, Howard daSilva, Sala Stow, and David Kerman. Later, Elaine Basil joined the company. It was really a dream; no one dared ask how I managed to bring it all about. I had to reassure them that everything was real; we had the sponsors, the money, the theatre, and a house to live and work in. All we had to do was test our collective talent, our ideas, and our ideals for a theatre. To symbolize such an approach, I decided to call our theatre group the Studio Players.

As for financial remuneration, except for the business personnel, there was to be no regular salary. Instead, the company would pay for all the living expenses and limited personal expenses. Yes, I had obtained the Actor's Equity Association approval. I also reported that the initial endowment of three thousand dollars would carry us through our first production, and if we could generate enough of a following, we should be able to complete the season with two more productions. Once the initial shock was over, the members asked the most pertinent question: What do we do for our first play?

I chose Henrik Ibsen's *When We Dead Awaken*. They were somewhat baffled. They were familiar with Ibsen; they knew *The Master Builder, Hedda Gabler, A Doll's House,* and *Ghosts* but not *When We Dead Awaken*. Small wonder. It was Ibsen's last play, written just before his stroke and subsequent death, and was practically unknown to American theatregoers. Except for an obscure production in New York in the early 1900s, it had never been done. Why? I guess the lack of a conventional dramatic plot held little commercial value. These were precisely the reasons for its challenge to the Studio Players. Moreover, this was Ibsen's most personal and subjective play, and there was some debate as to when he lost his mind—before, during, or after writing *When We Dead Awaken*. My personal fascination was with Ibsen's almost extradimensional dialogue with love and death. Only recently I, too, had engaged in a similar encounter. I handed out the working script and asked them to study it before we began our rehearsals.

We held our first rehearsal in the living room of our dormitory. We spent considerable time in informal discussions of the play and the characters, with occasional interjections of passages from the play for clarity and emphasis. I had asked the cast first to memorize and master the lines, and by so doing, become free of the external and superficial confines of acting. This was essential before we could delve into the inner works of the drama. We moved on to reading the parts and groping for the thoughts and feelings of the characters. Ibsen's characters spoke not an ordinary but a symbolic language, and very often they uttered simple words while thinking complex thoughts. Only when the actors began to think those thoughts and feel the impact of their emotion could they begin to breathe life into the characters. My job was to lead and guide the actors to strive and reach this point of self-identity.

Then came the exciting phase of our work. I would set the actors free on stage and let them improvise movements both large and small to accompany their words. The improvisations produced marvelous movements and gestures of which I never would have thought. As the director, my job was to select, modify, and weave them into a dramatic pattern. Once the pattern was drawn, the difficulty was in finding the underlying motivations so as to be able to repeat their actions at every performance. One of the drawbacks of commercial productions was the hectic and maddening dress rehearsals that invariably took place only a night or two before opening night. To avoid this, I worked with the designer to have the set ready for rehearsals. I also had the costumes fitted so that the actors could live in them long before the opening. It was just as important to have the smallest of props for the actors to touch and handle all through their rehearsals.

Thanks to our collective living, which allowed our day and night rehearsals, we completed our work in a month and a half and opened for a two-week run in the middle of October. Thanks also to our method of work, the opening night atmosphere was not the usual nervous prostration; it was one of calm and confidence. The only one suffering was Miss Thompson, the one who took care of promotion; she was fearful we would not fill the two hundred-seat auditorium. We filled it that night and for all subsequent performances as well. Miss Thompson was also successful in enrolling life-sustaining new subscribers. The opening night performance was quite professional. The curtain went up on time, the scenery, lights, and props moved and performed smoothly, without any mishap. The actors were inspired. Their performances demonstrated the validity of all our ideas, and the audience response was more than gratifying.

We could hardly wait for the morning to see the review in the Boston papers, though we were not sure if the critics had been at the opening. I personally did not subscribe to the institution of theatre reviews as the ultimate judge of theatre arts. Its power to determine the life and death of all theatre productions was too awesome. To avoid such sentencing, the Broadway producers would first try their show away from New York, usually in Washington, D.C., Philadelphia, or Boston. But there were critics in these hinterlands as well, some of them as entrenched and powerful. These were the men whose words and judgment we were awaiting.

The *Boston Globe* gave a rather superficial but friendly and warm review. But the more revered critic from the *Boston Transcript* offered a serious in-depth review. It took note of the fact that the Cambridge production of Ibsen's *When We Dead Awaken* was the second time it had been offered to American theatregoers. It expressed surprise in the creditable performance of such a serious drama by a group of actors so young. The "old man" of the *Boston Transcript* applauded the Studio Players for their plans to settle in the Boston area permanently and urged the support of all theatre lovers.

I offered my own review and evaluation to the company. Without question, the opening night performance was extraordinary. From the moment the curtain rose until it came down at the end, the actors, performing as an ensemble, sustained a high dramatic quality of intellectual and emotional upheaval. Individually, Howard daSilva portrayed the role of Professor Rubek with his own brooding temperament, his childish idealism, and his insatiable ambition. Jane Kim as Irene, with her statuesque figure, her sculptured face, and her deep, resonant voice, was an enigma of introspection, fascination, and mystery. In contrast, Elaine Basil, with her petite and compact body, her red hair, and sparkling, darting eyes, was, as the professor's wife, Maia, as she was in life—totally physical and materialistic. She was a perfect counterpoint of sunshine to Jane Kim's overshadowing darkness. David Kerman's Ulfheim, the bear hunter, was exhilarating. He was a virile, physical man, scornful of intellectual frills and social restraints. Sala Stow played the part of Irene's shadow, the nun. Though without words, she was eloquent in creating the feeling of the inevitable fate. I congratulated and thanked them all for their creative work.

I didn't know the financial gains resulting from the encouraging newspaper reviews, but I knew that the Studio Players were no longer strangers in Cambridge. We became somewhat like celebrities, and the requests for one of us to speak at various meetings around town became more frequent. Our Miss Thompson was very much occupied with promoting social and cultural affairs to raise funds. Even then, the number of subscribers did not come up to our hopes and expectations, which meant our precious capital was shrinking. Undaunted, even before the two-week run was over, we began to discuss our next production. We were going to do George Bernard Shaw's *Great Catherine*.

Why Shaw and why *Great Catherine*? To me, Shaw was the extension of Ibsen. Just as Ibsen was concerned with the social problems of his time, Shaw applied his sharp wit to produce barbed commentaries of his era. I was particularly attracted to *Great Catherine* for its uproarious farcical form. After Ibsen, it was naturally tempting to test ourselves with a comedy. The members liked the idea, and we plunged into work eagerly. Here was the chance to experiment with my ideas of how to create humor on stage. Basically, it was the actors' absolute preoccupation with the ludicrous while the audience watched, listened, and laughed. The clashes of logic and absurdity, beauty and ugliness, polish and awkwardness, were the elements that ignited the audience to laughter. Of course, the fabric of comedy was a lot more complex and fragile. The rhythm and tempo, and the lighting, hand props, and movements all had to be meshed and woven into a harmonious pattern of discord. As opposed to Broadway's preoccupation with the spoken word, I tried to construct a flow of movements to accentuate and complement the flow of voices. Besides, it was a great deal more fun working this way.

Howard daSilva began blooming as Patiomkin, a buffoon of many dimensions. Jane Kim as Catherine was developing her own grotesque, queenly manners; she was beautiful and haughty and ridiculous all at the same time. Sala Stow loved the part of Varinka, Patiomkin's favorite niece. She was a perfectly spoiled pet who took liberties with everyone except the empress. David Kerman began weakly as the English Captain Edstaston; he lacked the polish and the imperturbability of an Englishman. However, he learned to suppress his emotions and emerged as a credible English captain. Elaine Basil, on the other hand, easily understood the part of Claire, the proper and humorless English lady and wife of Captain Edstaston. She was delightful in her matter-of-fact dispensation of all international crises.

Our sponsors gave us more than money. They allowed their beautiful daughters, some of them recent debutantes of Boston society, to be in our show as extras. In eighteenth-century costumes, they not only brightened Catherine's court but also drew a whole set of young people to the theatre. I found enough talented young students from Harvard to fill the rest of the cast.

The real problem still was money. Because of the more elaborate sets and costumes, the production cost of *Great Catherine* rose much higher. The only way we could meet the cost was by cutting our living expenses. The meals that were prepared by the members in rotation were at best dismal, but now, with a tighter budget, they were becoming downright unhealthy. To rescue us from this predicament, my sister Alice left her job in New York and joined us in Cambridge; she offered to take over all the cooking chores. Our diet made an immediate improvement, and our morale soared. Dear Sister Alice! She had been supportive of all my dreams and ventures throughout my life, and now she appeared on the scene again to help me in my most serious undertaking.

Unfortunately, our revived morale and the domestic peace did not endure. The constantly shrinking budget forced Sister Alice to feed the brood a rather meager fare, mostly vegetables and spaghetti, and only occasionally hamburger. All the little complaints, though unintentional, affected innocent Sister Alice. She felt hurt; not only were her efforts not appreciated, but she felt abused despite all her valiant efforts. She begged to be freed and left us.

Now the New England winter was settling in Cambridge just as our coal supply for the furnace was dwindling rapidly. Then the dreadful thing happened. The coal supply gone, the house was without heat for several days just as the arctic blast dipped the temperature to near zero. One day, in the dead of night, I was awakened by a low, moaning cry. I listened and traced it to Sala Stow's room. The moaning continued intermittently. I got up and went to her.

"What's the matter, Sala?" I asked.

"I'm cold!" her voice was quivering.

I was at a loss. "Wait, Sala," I said. "I'll bring one of my blankets."

"No," she moaned, "you need it yourself . . ."

I really didn't know what to do.

Finally I said, "Well, then . . . let me come in your bed and warm you up."

"No! No! Peter!" She let a little laughter mix with her groans. "Thanks anyway, Peter," she said. "I'll be all right." With that, she stopped moaning.

I went back to bed but could not resume my sleep; the specter of more freezing nights without heat in the house haunted me the rest of the night. I had to get some coal before another night passed.

The strain of collective living with a limited budget was affecting our work. Little progress was being made in our rehearsals, and temperamental clashes flared on stage more frequently. Our concentration wavered, and we wasted a lot of time. Something had to be done. Of course, a little more money would have helped, but more than money, we needed to reaffirm our purpose and goals and assess our capacity and strength to go on. I proposed a series of meetings. They were held in the evenings over cups of coffee and cinnamon toast. Everyone was encouraged to freely express his or her grievances, ideas, and suggestions for restoring our morale. This was another of our creative approaches to a collective problem—long before I would hear the term "group therapy." In the beginning, everyone seemed reluctant to speak for fear of hurting each other's feelings. Miss Thompson, our publicity and promotion director, seemed almost distressed to be present at such a confessional. Slowly, the walls of ice began to melt, and trickles of honest words built up to a veritable torrent. At last, we were able to objectify all the criticisms and complaints. Only then could we discuss our problems on a group level and accept some of the proposals and ideas.

This was how we managed to overcome what seemed at the time formidable obstacles and direct our concentration and energy to the task at hand—stage *Great Catherine* as it had never been done before. And once again we accomplished what no one thought possible; we completed the production and opened it in less than two months. Everyone shared in the reward: that indescribable feeling of satisfaction that comes only with a creative accomplishment. The audience response was most vocal and volatile, and the cast reciprocated more expansively with each performance. Every morning we held a brief meeting of evaluation of the performance the night before. We studied the varied and unpredictable moods of the audience at each performance. The timing, intensity, and character of their laughter were not always the same. They were rich lessons for the actors never to "play for laughs"; to be ever so truthful to the characters.

The *Boston Transcript, Herald,* and *Globe* all gave warm praise to our *Great Catherine,* while again expressing their surprise at the youth of the Studio Players. What pleased me personally was that the reviews were directed at the work of the group rather than at individual actors. Of course, Howard daSilva and Jane Kim were mentioned for their "outstanding" portrayals of the principal roles, but not out of context of the whole group's work. The critics were especially delighted to see local young people on stage with the professionals. The presence of the Harvard students and the daughters of

Boston society brought a totally unexpected reward: the turn-out in droves of a new group of admirers. Our dwindling treasury was replenished, and we began to eat better and to sleep in warm, heated rooms again. With the improvement of physical well-being, our collective spirit rose to new heights.

The spell of prosperity in 1931 offered us an even greater luxury—a week's vacation for the holidays with travel expenses so that everyone could go home to New York and visit their families. For me it was a God-sent break to be alone, to have the time to think and evaluate my work thus far. The two seemingly successful productions had tested and had even confirmed some of my formative ideas on theatre. At the same time, the experience produced serious questions. I did much soul searching and wrestled with the doubts and questions.

Would I always be a stranger in the American theatre?

How solid was my work as a director?

Was I prepared to direct a permanent theatre?

Would I always have to face and battle the insufferable racial slurs?

These and other serious questions rose in my mind and gnawed at me without rest. These pains, however, did not diminish my elation at our accomplishments, and in spite of the inner turmoil, I launched yet another undertaking: the production of Chekhov's *Uncle Vanya*. I suffered some fears of extending myself to such a grave challenge, but they were overshadowed by the bountiful confidence of my youth.

Moreover, to me, the Russian Chekhov was no more remote than the American Eugene O'Neill. In fact, by geography and history, the Russians and the Koreans were neighbors, and I grew up thinking of the Russians as less foreign than the Americans. Also, there was Leo Tolstoy's *Anna Karenina*. I was about ten when that sad story swept over Korea like a summer storm. It was translated into Korean from the Japanese translation, and even though I never read it, like most Koreans I knew the story by heart and shed my share of tears over Anna's tragic end. We even had a popular song about Anna, and everyone sang it over and over again all over the country. When I finally found my way to America, so engrossed and determined was I to learn the English language and become an American that I forsook all my childhood friends, including Tolstoy and all the

Russians. It was not until I went to DePauw University that my interest in Russian literature resurfaced.

Now I could read Tolstoy in English. Of course, first I read *Anna Karenina* and after that, *War and Peace.* I discovered Dostoyevski and his *Idiot, Crime and Punishment,* and *The Brothers Karamazov,* which helped to revive my childhood feelings of kinship with the Russian people. Maxim Gorki's *University Days* and *Lower Depths,* I found, were filled with characters who so resembled Koreans. However, it was not until I joined the Civic Repertory Theatre in 1930 that I was introduced to Anton Chekhov's plays. LeGallienne's production of *Three Sisters* and *The Cherry Orchard* marked the most cherished moments of my life in the theatre. I was not alone. The early thirties also ushered in the era when the American theatre workers became enamored of the Russian theatre, the Moscow Art Theatre in particular.

The book *An Actor Prepares,* by Stanislavsky, the director of the Moscow Art Theatre, became the bible for all young actors, and its thesis was the topic of heated debates wherever the actors gathered. The birth of Group Theatre was one of the crowning glories of this era. Under the direction of Lee Strasberg, Cheryl Crawford, and Harold Clurman, many looked upon Group Theatre as the American counterpart of the Moscow Art Theatre. And it was largely through the group's conscientious study and application of Stanislavsky's approach to acting that the term "method acting" was introduced to American theatre. Chekhov himself was not only a modest man, but he was actually doubtful of his talent to write for the theatre. Chekhov could hardly have dreamed that his plays would have such a profound influence on the American theatre and produce countless numbers of playwrights who would pattern their work after his style—among them Irwin Shaw and Clifford Odets.

With the holidays over, the Studio Players reassembled in Cambridge to live and work in our old collective in a building that was now heated regularly and kept warm. We began rehearsals of *Uncle Vanya.* I noticed that everyone was aglow with the success of our two productions. There was also a warm feeling of mutual respect and acceptance; a priceless asset seldom found in a commercial company. We were free of the usual suspicion, mistrust, and heartless rivalry that wreck most theatre ventures; we could direct all our time and energy to our common goal—to bring Chekhov's characters to life, and by so doing, to share their pain and pathos with the American audience.

Of course, this was not easy. *Uncle Vanya* on the surface seemed so simple, but its inner fabric was so complex. In the beginning, it was difficult for American actors to perceive and appreciate the Russian characters. Their oblique language was so simple and childish, but once its true meaning and feeling were understood, it became insidious and devastating. To the extent that we could penetrate such paradoxicality, we would come close to touching the Russian soul. The challenge was formidable, but with each step of growth in the perception, the actors became more enthusiastic. In the end, they were able to free themselves from the constrictions of their own American culture and relish the taste of another culture and another historical period. The dress rehearsals were filled with joy, pride, and enjoyment.

The audience received us with unrestrained enthusiasm. The press reviews, again, noted the youth of our group and applauded our remarkable accomplishment. They were amazed and pleased that we fulfilled our promise to present three major productions for the season. No one had believed us, and few thought it possible. But in the midst of the lingering economic depression of 1932 and accompanying cynical surroundings, we managed to establish and sustain a theatre in Cambridge for an entire season. When the excitement subsided, it was time for our own appraisal.

Financially, we were in much better shape than when we launched our project; we were solvent, with a surplus to boot. Artistically, we succeeded in large measure in what we attempted to do— to create a new dimension of theatre art through a collective approach. We overcame all the unexpected obstacles and doggedly pursued our ideals. Everyone made great personal sacrifices, but all were rewarded with precious experience and development as artists. Our pride and elation were justly earned. But now we were at the crossroads; we had to decide whether or not we would return for a second season and so notify our followers. After much soul searching, the thought flashed through my mind: No, we would not come back for another season.

To dispel such a horrible thought, we needed a celebration—a grand celebration. We would offer a bonus production for our precious patrons and fans and at the same time wind up our season with a surprise finale. That evening, I called Burgess Meredith in New York and asked if he would join us and do a play. He was elated. I called a company meeting in the morning and announced we would close the season with a production of the Quintero brothers' *Fortunato*. I informed them that Burgess Meredith had promised to come and play the Chaplinesque character of Fortunato. The company burst out with prolonged hurrahs.

I said this would be our thank-you present to our followers in Cambridge and Boston and a grand finale for the Studio Players. It would be a complete surprise not only to our followers but to the critics of the Boston press as well. To begin with, the Spanish playwrights, the Quintero brothers, Serafin and Joaquin, were unknown in America, and the appearance of Burgess Meredith with the Studio Players would be a double treat to our patrons. Also, as befitted the occasion, there would be a curtain raiser, *Swan Song,* a gem of a one-act play by Chekhov.

*Fortunato* is a cruelly misnamed, unfortunate man. Misfortune follows all of his efforts to earn a living in a big city and feed his children. He is too honest; all the food for his children is literally taken from their mouths by the dishonest and the cheaters. In desperation Fortunato tries to steal from a blind beggar's cup. Clutching the precious coins, he discovers the blind man, too, has children to feed. Ashamed, he puts the coins in the blind man's hands. The man thanks him profusely. Fortunato shrugs and says, "Not at all . . . not at all! I can spare it . . . I can spare it."

Fortunato walks across the city to answer an ad for a helper. A woman with a gun hires him with only one question: "Are you afraid of gunfire?"

"Me, gunfire? Oh, no!" Fortunato answers.

The woman takes Fortunato to a standing target and shows him how to stand against it spread-eagled. The woman, a sharpshooter, takes her position in front of Fortunato and orders, "Steady, now!" and begins firing at the target. Fortunato shuts his eyes and freezes. The sharpshooter keeps firing and draws a figure around Fortunato with bullets.

Fortunato screams, "My children will eat! My children will eat!" as the curtain falls.

The *Boston Post, Herald,* and *Transcript* all gave warm and gratifying reviews.

"Burgess Meredith . . . made the spectator laugh at and pity the man at the same time," said the *Boston Herald*.

"As an artistic achievement . . . really fine acting . . . it deserves a high place in the annals of the contemporary theatre," from the *Boston Post*.

In his review, George Brinton Beal somehow got wind of our plans not to return for another season. He wrote: "It is to be regretted that conditions prevented carrying out their promised repertory. Not in many years has such fine, sensitive acting been brought to a contemporary stage by any similar group."★

It was time for me to let the group know of my decision: We would not come back for another season. When I announced it to the company, everyone was stunned. They could not fathom any reason for my discarding what we had built with so much love and pain. Miss Thompson, our business director, was particularly perturbed. She said that our financial position was good and the prospects for a new season even better. Why should we throw all this away? Professor H. W. L. Dana, our first sponsor, seriously urged me to return, saying that we had earned the support of the community. It was very flattering, and yet my answer was still no. I could not offer any satisfactory answer to all the queries of "Why?" I could only give the most superficial of reasons: The job was too taxing and I was too exhausted.

In the end, everyone resignedly accepted my decision. The money on hand was used to pay off all outstanding bills, the remainder was divided equally among the members, and the group dispersed. I visited and thanked our sponsors and bade farewell to Cambridge and to all the many good people I had found there.

One of our patrons gave us a farewell party. It was a warm spring evening, and the enormous grounds of the house were strung up with lanterns like at a gay festival. All the patrons and a large number of fans were there. I knew only a few people by sight, but I made the tour to shake hands and thank everyone. There was a lavish spread of food on a long table, and all kinds of wine and liquor flowed in streams. But I hadn't yet learned to drink and turned down all the drinks being passed around. But I didn't miss the conversation. Everyone was overwhelmed and loved the Studio Players dearly.

---

★For additional information on Studio Players productions, see Appendix, page 285.

"Why? Why aren't you coming back?" was on the lips of everyone. For me, it was the final memorable evening of the Studio Players.

At that moment, I couldn't articulate the real reasons for my decision not to return. I was convinced, however, that I couldn't and that I shouldn't go on. In truth, I guess, I was afraid to admit or to spell out the underlying reasons for the decision. Only when I had left the scene and allowed some time to lapse was I able to put the whole experience of the Studio Players into proper perspective. I tried to evaluate and determine how I was able to go to a strange town and start a theatre movement. From where such audacity? Such courage? The driving force was my complete belief in myself and in my ideas. I had no doubt that if people would only listen, they would share my beliefs. And they did. I had no fear of tackling the production of works of the world's foremost dramatists. I believed my dramatic perceptions to be sound and true. I also knew that I could work with actors, that I could discover, explore, and expand their talents. These beliefs generated the strength that could move the mountains and the people.

But in the process, I encountered invisible but powerful roadblocks; I was never allowed to feel completely at home in America. Time and time again I was reminded that I was not just a foreigner, but an "Oriental." For me to rise from the accorded level of servitude, such as a "houseboy" or "laundryman," to the unheard of level of theatre director was inconceivable and unacceptable to most Americans. Perhaps it was my own personal inadequacy, I sometimes thought. But even if it were, why was it compounded and perpetuated by the people surrounding me? These were the people I had to live and work with daily: the shopkeepers who looked askance, the people on the street who stared, and the stagehands and electricians who ignored me. Without any spoken word, they would remind me that I was an outsider, an intruder. I could ignore or excuse their blatant prejudices, but I could not make them disappear. The worst aspect of these encounters was that I had to endure it all in silence. Had I mentioned such sufferings to the Studio Players, no one would have believed me.

But there appeared an even more serious crack in the armor of my self-confidence. The apparently successful work also made me conscious of my limitations and weaknesses; there was much too much for me to learn before I could carry on such an undertaking as the Studio Players. I believe this truthful self-evaluation and the resulting humiliation were the signs of a maturing process. As nearly as I could formulate, these were the underlying reasons for my decision not to attempt a second season in Cambridge. At the time I was unable to share these thoughts with my fellow members or with our benefactors, because my thoughts had not crystalized; and even if they had, I didn't have the courage to reveal such inner thoughts.

With such newfound awareness, then, how could I continue to direct a permanent theatre? With my share of the financial gains, I bought a one-way ticket on Greyhound to San Francisco, and from there to Honolulu on the Matson liner *Lurline,* in the tourist class—a highfalutin' name for steerage. I had just enough money left to go on from Honolulu to the island of Kauai on an interisland steamer. And as it had been throughout the ages for a tired and exhausted son, I returned home for rest, solace, and comfort.

# 6

## INTERLUDE

It was 1932 and I had been gone from home for only four years, but the impact of rediscovery was tremendous. After New York and Boston, the old parsonage in Kapaia Valley seemed shrunken drastically. It not only looked small, but so old and tired. And most of the animals Umma so loved and cared for were gone. Only an old dog and a lazy, fat cat were around; no birds, fishes, ducks, goats, or rabbits.

But inside the house, though the paint had long faded and peeled, it was still warm and friendly; the player piano, the soft couch and stuffed chair, and Papa's office with loaded bookcases were all still there. And upstairs, they had moved my bed from the balcony into the bedroom. The first thing I did was to move it back out to the balcony.

Outside, the neighborhood remained exactly as I had left it, except it, too, seemed to have shrunk considerably. True, the trees had grown bigger and taller, but everything else looked like miniature hovels: the Japanese market, Tom Sui's Chop Suey House, and even Fernandez' Department Store and the Buddhist temple. There was one new two-story building built by the Cavalho family. I never knew what Mr. Cavalho did for a living, but on weekends he played a hell of a good saxophone with a band. The only time I saw him was at the dance in the Lihue Armory; Cavalho's sax was a big hit. I understood that he traveled with the band and played in other towns around the island.

I dropped in at every store and paid my respects. They all remembered me and were glad to see me. And they all said the same things:

"How was the big city, New York?"

"Understand you were a big shot in the theatre there."

Father and I, as with all parents and children in a Korean family, never had an open personal relationship. We accepted and respected each other's family status: father and son, brothers and sisters, older or younger. I don't remember ever having spoken to my father as a person: "How are you, Papa?" or "Did you have a good day?" Nor did he ever express his personal concern for me by saying, "What's wrong, Pedro-ya?" or "What did you do in school today?" It didn't mean there was any animosity between us, nor that we had no feelings for each other. My heart was always filled with pride and admiration for my father. What it did mean, however, was that, despite Father's modern education and his rebellion against the old world, he was still a child of the ancient and feudal social system. A father did not share his personal feelings with his offspring—only with his peers. And the child did not intrude into the world of his father. Should the necessity ever arise for a father to communicate with his son, it was always conveyed through an intermediary—the mother. Father and I were victims of that social system, and whatever feelings we had for each other, they were expressed only indirectly, at a distance, to avoid the embarrassment of personal contact. Tragic? Of course! But for us, at the time, it was as natural as an American father and son who called each other by their first names. But my return home after four years broke down some of the centuries-old traditional barriers. Papa was really interested in knowing how my college life had been. At first, rather hesitantly, he asked; "Was there any discrimination?" "How did the professors treat you?" And the most ominous question: "Tell me why you changed your mind about studying for the ministry."

I found it terribly hard to answer. But once I began talking to my father as a friend, it felt strange, but good, to talk to him as an equal. I was able to tell him in detail about my study of the history of the Bible, Old and New Testaments; the revelation of the true sources of the words in the Bible—highly spiritual and religious but not directly from God as I had believed.

Papa listened with a heavy heart, I am sure, and finally said, "Well, Pedro-ya, you must follow your own conscience and convictions." Then he added; "You know the theatre is like a temple. They also deliver sermons for people to follow the right path."

And for the first time in my life I was able to tell him, "Papa, you are a great man."

Umma was as tactful as ever. She would wait until everyone went to bed. She would draw me to sit close by her side in a quiet corner of the living room. She would casually set down a dish of some special snack—boiled chestnuts, my favorite, or freshly baked cookies—and begin our conversation. The questions most important to her: "Did you have enough to eat in college?" "What kind of food did they give you?" And many other questions, all dealing with my well-being. Satisfied with my answers, she would then switch to another subject: "Were you very lonesome living alone away from home?" "How did the *haoles* treat you?" "Did you meet any nice *haole* girl? Go on, you can tell me, Pedro-ya."

"Oh, Umma!" I laughed and protested. "Don't worry. When I find the right girl, you will be the first one to know."

Such were the most unusual sessions held between a Korean mother and her son. The intimate late-evening sessions opened the door between Umma and me, and we kept it open for free exchange and communication with each other. I don't believe there ever were a Korean mother and son who chatted with each other in such an open and friendly fashion. That alone was worth my four-year sojourn from home.

Papa was still the traveling preacher. I let my brother Paul do the driving and accompanied Papa and Umma around the island, stopping at the same little towns, holding Sunday services in the aging plantation houses, and partaking in the special lunch prepared for us. The menu was still the same: Abalone out of a can, sliced and dipped in soy sauce; rice and *kim chee* with a very special Korean favorite, *bul-go-gee* or broiled beef.

I couldn't help but notice everyone, both men and women, had aged so much in such a short time. The years of back-breaking toil in the cane fields had taken their toll. Moreover, the families had been depleted; the second generation couldn't wait to leave the plantations. When they finished high school—and some even before graduation—the young ones left the plantations behind for the big city, Honolulu, in search of jobs and a better life.

My own dilemma remained: What about my career in the theatre? What about my future as a director? How could I face and resolve the formidable wall of discrimination and bigotry?

Seeking to meditate in solitude, I packed some groceries and books and went up to the highest mountain retreat on Kauai— Kokee. A Korean man looking after the irrigation gates for the cane fields had to take a month of leave. I gladly took his post and his cabin and spent a month in complete solitude.

I would have an early breakfast, pack a simple lunch, saddle the horse, and take off. I would follow a new trail every day, which would always end at the top of the cliff, overlooking the pounding sea far below. After tying up the horse, I would spread a blanket and settle down among the tropical fern for the day. All my senses became as alive as the warm breeze. I could read and think with no distractions. Every thought and memory became alive and clear. Scenes of the past years paraded before me: DePauw University, Mary Hamilton, Clara Bell, and Professor Eckhardt. And President Oxham and the Thanksgiving dinner. Rye Beach and millions of hot dogs. The Gloucester School of Little Theatre, Florence Cunningham, Mrs. Evans, Lester, and Norman Bel-Geddes. The Civic Repertory Theatre and Eva LeGallienne. The most persistent and brilliant vision, however, was May Sarton—her chiseled face, her sparkling eyes, her penetrating voice, so warm and comforting.

In the main, the Studio Players group was a triumph of a collective spirit. All of our work underscored my convictions, my faith, and my basic concepts of theatre art. Why did I turn down all the pleadings to continue? Why didn't I go on?

The question gnawed at me all through my sojourn on the mountain. I was thankful to be completely alone. Without any distraction, without any interjection of others' influences, now with a clear mind I could look at the termination of the Studio Players at the height of its achievements. I was awed and at the same time fearful of success. I was afraid of facing possible failure. With such doubts, I was not prepared to direct a permanent repertory theatre. I needed to gain more confidence through experience, with more tests in the crucible of trial by fire. I could not reveal such feelings to anyone, not even to the loyal members of the Studio Players. I feigned exhaustion and the need for rest.

In comforting solitude, I reviewed every production; Ibsen, George Bernard Shaw, Chekhov, the Quintero brothers. All of the scenes appeared more vividly on the mountaintop of a remote island thousands of miles away from the theatre world of New York and

Boston. I would shudder at Irene's contemplation of death, chuckle at the buffoonery of Patiomkin and moan at the soul-searching encounters of Uncle Vanya. And the memorable performances of Burgess Meredith and Jane Kim in *Fortunato*—mixing laughter and tears was truly a projection of the classic concept of a comedy.

How could I forsake all this? The flattering reviews, the grateful sponsors who gave all moral and physical support besides money, the loyal fans who followed our work with burning enthusiasm. It was not easy, but it had to be. Continuing with another season and yet another would have brought only less and less satisfaction and more and more deterioration of the collective. It was indeed wise of me to have refused to go on with the Studio Players. However, this was not to be the end of my work in the theatre. I would go on seeking new vistas, new challenges, and new experiences.

With peace in my heart, I came down from the mountain. I had found peace with the world. I was really at home again. I was filled with love and gratitude for Papa, my hero; for Umma, my guiding spirit of courage and fun; and for all my brothers and my baby sister, Mary. I was proud and grateful to be a part of such a wonderful family. I even loved the lazy, fat cat and the homely dog. And as if they understood and appreciated my affection, all of them responded with warm snuggles.

Suddenly, without warning, I was seized with the urge to be with women. They are such a tempting breed. True, from my earliest childhood I preferred to be near women rather than men. Now, my urging was not only to be near them, but to touch and feel as well. Just then two Korean ladies from Honolulu came to visit us. They were both considerably older than I. One was the mother of one of the girls who took me out to Waikiki Beach, and the other a student at the University of Hawaii. Never mind the age difference; they were both so beautiful and desirable. I was anxious to take them up to my mountain sanctuary.

There on top of what was my sacred mountain we spent two evenings in the cabin, and I made love to both; not sexual love, but something more precious. The first evening, I took the mother for a walk. Of course, there was a full moon. Listening to the soft wind floating through the jungle, we settled on a rock overlooking the deepest darkness of Waimea Canyon. I held her in my arms and whispered the most moving sweet nothings. Both of us, drunk with spiritual love, came back to the cabin and went to bed, separately.

The next evening I took the beautiful college student for the same walk. We listened to the same soft wind whispering through the jungle, and we settled on the same rock, looking down at the limitless pit of darkness. The full moon also showed up to brighten our moment of love. She was at least ten years younger than the mother. Sitting so close, I was bolder than the night before. I touched and caressed her breasts. They were ripe and full. My whispers of sweet nothings were real, sprung out of my heart. She responded with soft caresses. Sadly, we came back to the cabin and went to bed, again separately.

There was one other encounter—with a schoolteacher. A tiny bundle of a woman, she was not pretty, but beautiful. She was my baby sister Mary's teacher, Lily, and I met her by chance when I went to pick up my sister after school. She was a Hawaii-born Chinese. She was petite, compact, and alert.

"Which way do you go, Mr. Hyun?" She sounded open and friendly.

"To Kapaia," I answered.

"Could you drop me off at the Lihue dormitory?"

"Sure thing," I said. I was trying to figure her situation; a teacher living in the girl's dormitory. During the short ride, we covered a lot of ground.

"How come you live in the girls' dormitory?"

"Well, my home is in Hanalei. I can't travel that distance to school every day." I liked her voice and her frank manners. "By the way, Mr. Hyun, are you free tomorrow?" Tomorrow would be Saturday.

"Yes, why?"

"Well, how would you like to drive to Hanalei? It would be a lovely drive. Besides, I haven't seen my family for quite a while. I could give them a surprise visit." Her manner was so direct and innocent and her ringing voice so pleasant, I was completely enthralled.

"Yes, that's a wonderful idea. I'll drive you to Hanalei." Without hesitation I offered to take her on an eighty-mile round trip.

Lily was ready when I drove up to the girls' dormitory. We started off with the sunrise. We both felt strange but exhilarated. In appreciative silence we drove the first ten miles.

"This is really good of you, Peter," Lily broke the silence. "And it's a lovely day."

"I'm very glad to be with you, Lily," I assured her. "It's not often we have any exciting things happen on the island." That helped to break the ice and open up the floodgate. She confided that she was almost thirty years old and had been married since her graduation from high school. She had been attending the Normal School in Honolulu when she met her husband-to-be. Soon after their marriage she discovered that she had had no idea what she was getting into.

Her husband, David, was a good, honest man. But beyond the business of making money, he had no interest in anything else. Lily's intense intellectual curiosity, her interest in literature and art, held no particular interest or meaning for her husband. As time passed, the chasm between them grew wider and communication more and more distant. Nonetheless, she was grateful for David's financial support to see her through graduation from the Normal School.

"My first appointment for a teaching job was on Kauai." Lily continued, "In a way, I was glad, because I could escape from the impossible 'married life.'"

"Why was it impossible?"

"Because we shared no common interests. He's not interested in music, he doesn't read, he doesn't even go to the movies. So you see, we have very little to talk about with each other."

"That's too bad," I said. "What does he do with his time?"

"He putters with his business in the garage."

"Doing what?"

"Fixing old radios—that's his business."

Our conversation, going over Lily's life, took our minds off the distance we were traveling, and we were already entering the village of Hanalei. We pulled up at her parents' home. They didn't hide their surprise at seeing me with their married daughter. Lily broke into a merry laugh and admonished them by saying, "Peter is a minister's son in Lihue; he was good enough to drive me all the way here so I could visit you." To make amends, Lily's mother prepared an elaborate lunch for us.

Lily's parents were first-generation immigrants from China. They had worked in the rice fields all their lives and were now retired with the meager fruits of their back-breaking labor. At least they had their own home, and their children, all educated, helped provide their sustenance.

The sunset over Hanalei valley was incredibly beautiful. A giant brush was painting over the rice fields, the rooftops of little houses, and the beach and sea in the distance. It was almost dark when we started on our trip back to Lihue. Now our conversation turned to my life. Lily was intensely curious. To make light of it I said, "Well, I worked in the theatre in New York."

Lily refused to be put off so easily. "What kind of theatre? What kind of work?" And a continuing stream of questions.

So I had to tell her the whole story, with as many details as she demanded. Time and distance flew by, and we crossed the Waialei River bridge, only five miles from Lihue.

"Let's go look at the beach," I suggested casually.

"Sure, let's go." No hesitation whatsoever.

I drove off the road and followed a winding dirt road to the beach. I pulled up near the beach and, of course, the moonlight was shimmering on the waves. Without a word, I drew Lily close to me and kissed her. I felt her warm lips and a perceptible tremble.

"Oh, Peter!" she moaned, and embraced me tightly.

"Oh, Lily!" I echoed.

Our kisses grew more and more passionate. We were reaching the point of complete surrender—when the lightning bolt struck. Lily pushed me away and sat up as though she had seen a ghost.

"What's the matter, Lily?" I was stunned.

"Peter," she said tearfully, "I want you so much, but I must stop."

"Why?"

"Because I'm still a married woman. I have a husband. And as long as I am married, I can't be unfaithful."

I had no words in response. I, too, withdrew and sat up. After a long silence I said, "Lily, I respect your moral integrity." Then I added, "I also admire your spiritual strength."

The moonlight was still shimmering in the waves, but it suddenly turned cold and impersonal. After some moments of deep breathing, I started the car. In dead silence, we left the beach, drove the short distance to Lihue and stopped at the girls' dormitory. She warmly held my cheeks in her hands, planted a perfunctory kiss on my lips, and got out of the car. She turned and said, "Peter, thanks for everything," and disappeared into the night. I would never see her again.

My next adventure was of a totally different nature; I joined a road construction gang. Someone from the Kauai Construction Company called and informed me that they had an opening for a timekeeper on their road construction project; they needed someone immediately. Could I take the job? Yes, but I had never worked on any construction projects, and I didn't know anything about time-keeping. That's okay, they assured me, they would give me all the training necessary. I was told to report to their office in Lihue at eight in the morning, and bring my lunch.

How should I dress? What does a road construction timekeeper look like? I put on a pair of khaki pants and shirt and an old pair of shoes and reported for work. The head bookkeeper took charge of me and showed me all the material for keeping the time records of every laborer. There were several sections of roads scheduled either for repair or widening.

The work stretched from Kapaa, ten miles north of Lihue, to the south—Koloa, Waimea, Kekaha, and Kokee up the mountain—a total distance of sixty miles. I had to cover the areas twice a day: once in the morning to check the men at work and once in the afternoon to record the time they quit. This was very vital both to the workers and the company because the workers' pay and the company's cost of labor completely depended on the timekeeper's record. I hadn't real-ized the job had so much responsiblity and was so important.

An assistant bookkeeper took me out for the road training. Beginning at Kapaa, I was introduced to the foreman and to a few of the laborers. I made entries of their time started from the notes of the foreman. We traveled on and repeated the procedure at each area. When we reached the top of the mountain, it was almost 11:00 A.M. It was noon when we returned to the office. I joined the office staff, opened my tin lunch box, and ate the sandwich and hard-boiled egg. I washed it down with water from the tap. After a short break during which everyone asked me how I liked my job, one of them approached and confided, "Say, Peter, I saw you play football against Lahaina High School. You were great!"

The bookkeeper showed me how to make the entries in the master time sheet. Then he said, "We'll have to go for the check-out in an hour." That would be around 2:30 P.M. The bookkeeper and I took off and repeated our rounds. At each location I was taught how to check out everyone still working. I was surprised to discover that one worker was missing. The foreman gave me the time when the worker left the job for some emergency. It was another sixty-mile drive by the time I arrived at Kokee for the last workers' check-offs. My day's work was done. But I still had to return to the office in Lihue and post every worker's time in the master chart.

I came home exhausted. The family circled around me and plied me with questions. But dear Umma's concern was, "It isn't too hard, is it, Pedro-ya?"

My own chief concern was the distance of daily travel. I couldn't use the family car and deprive them of transportation. I had to do something about it right away. Fortunately, the next day was Saturday. Early in the morning I went to the Lihue Ford Company and looked over all the available used cars. There was one I liked—a 1930 Model-A Ford coupe with a rumble seat. I bargained hard and purchased it with no down payment and monthly payments of forty five dollars. I thought that was a stroke of luck. With my wages, it would be easy to meet the payments. On Monday I reported to work in my own car and dressed properly for my part: gabardine breeches with leather leggings over work boots, and a short-sleeved khaki shirt with two large pockets bulging with pens and pencils. I felt like a veteran timekeeper.

I played my role faithfully and discharged my duties efficiently. The big boss of the construction company was quite pleased with my performance. Moreover, I learned some valuable lessons in economics and politics. I discovered that the road-building work force came from two sources: First, the main supply of labor came from veteran road builders who traveled wherever there were road-building jobs. These were mature and sometimes aged men who had left their families behind to follow the jobs. And second, the rest of the road gang was made up of local youths—those fresh out of high school or those who had left school to work.

Another lesson had to do with economics. One day, after recording the time for all the men reporting to work, I stopped to chat with a foreman. The job was for widening the narrow country road that led into the town of Lihue. In puzzlement, I noticed the widening was only a foot on each side. "Say," I asked the foreman, "why don't they widen it a little more so that the traffic could move more safely?"

The foreman looked at me with a silly grin and said, "If we did that, we wouldn't have any job next year!"

After a month of conscientious labor, just when I felt I was fast becoming somewhat of an expert on the cost of labor in road construction, I was jolted out of my newly earned niche by a telephone call. It came from a totally unlikely source: a Hollywood movie producer. An independent company had come to Kauai to film a picture, and the director wanted to see me for a part. The appointment was made for Saturday, my day off. I didn't ask how they got my name.

The director, Mrs. Louis, as everybody addressed her, was a rather friendly woman approaching retirement age. I learned that she had directed some of Charlie Chaplin's early pictures. Searching for local talent, she was told about a Peter Hyun who had experience in the theatre. She said that it wasn't much of a part, but very important for the picture.

"What is the story like?" I asked.

"Oh, it's only a commercial script. Young American tourists, a man and a woman, meet on the island. They hit all the high spots of the island together, climaxing in a Hawaiian *luau*. They fall in love with the romantic island but not with each other. They meet a tragic end when the hero burns to death in a sugarcane fire." *Cane Fire* was the name of the movie. Mrs. Louis went on, "There is a Chinese butler in the service of our hero. The butler dispenses with more philosophical wisdom than necessary physical service. It's a part for comic relief. Would you be interested?"

"Yes, Mrs. Louis," I answered. "I always thought I would get in the movies someday, but I certainly didn't dream of doing it on the island where I was born." We both had a good laugh and sealed the deal with a handshake.

I don't remember if we even talked about the money. "See Harry," she said. That was Harry Gantz, her husband, who was the manager of the company.

On the set the next day I met the stars, Mona Maris and Robert (I don't remember his last name). She was supposedly a South American fireball, and he an actor with considerable stage experience. Rather than watch the acting, I was more interested in the motion picture techniques.

I observed the actors did not learn their lines before their appearance; they learned them on the set just before shooting the scene. Indeed, why bother with the lines, since there were only two or three lines at the most in each scene to be shot. The rehearsal also took place just before the shooting. The director designed the movements and dialogue of the scene, and the actors followed through. The camera man followed the action and would make some comments and suggestions to the director, such as: "Don't let Mona turn her back to the camera completely." "Have Robert come a little closer to Mona when he enters the room," and so on.

The rehearsals completed, it was time for "places!" and "action!" The director or the camera man is not satisfied, so they shoot the scene again. A simple scene lasting only a few minutes might be repeated three or four times. Sometimes a scene consisted of an actor entering the room and hollering, "Is anybody home?" This scene also could be shot over three or four times to get the picture the director wanted.

The whole production had nothing to do with theatre. The picturization of the performance depended not in the sustained emotional development of the actors, but upon the clippings and editing of the director and the film editor. Motion pictures, I concluded, were not theatre; they were mechanical quilts. Depending on the caliber of the director and the camera man, the quilt could turn out to be a hodgepodge or a beautiful, harmonious creation.

In any case, I learned and had my fun. I, the butler, appeared in lots of scenes—for "comic relief"—until the end. My climactic scene was to run through the furious *Cane Fire* and rescue my pet baby pig. My performance must have really pleased Mrs. Louis and the camera man—no retakes.

When all the shooting was done and Harry Gantz handed me my check—I don't remember how much—Mrs. Louis asked to see me. Shaking my hand with both of hers, she gave me a surprisingly warm greeting. "Peter, I want you to know," she said, "that you were the best actor in the whole picture." Then she added her parting words: "If ever you come to Hollywood, be sure to come and see me."

# 7

# RETURN
# TO THE
# THEATRE

$P$apa called me. "Pedro-ya! Here's a letter for you."

No wonder Papa was excited; it was from New York. And I couldn't believe it was from May Sarton. With trembling hands, I opened it and began to read:

"Greetings, salutations and lots of love, etc," it opened. She then plunged into the matter at hand. "Peter, I am working with my own company. We'll open our first play at the Austin Memorial Museum in Hartford, Connecticut in two weeks. I want you to stage-manage the show for me."

Out of nowhere the old flame shot up inside me. I called her on the phone. It was May who answered. "I'll be there a week before the opening," I told her.

I had to move quickly: pick up all the loose ends, settle all the bills, visit all the people on the island to say goodbye once again, and take off in a hurry. Once again, I boarded the Matson liner *Lurline* and headed for Los Angeles. There was no fanfare this time; no party of friends to send me off with leis. And once again I was sailing in the tourist cabin in the ship's hold.

In Los Angeles, no longer a strange city, I called Mrs. Louis. Pleasantly surprised, she gave me her address and directions to get there by taxi. To my great surprise I found her living in a very modest apartment. So, I discovered not everyone in the movies lived in mansions and palaces.

"*Cane Fire*," she said, "was not a hit but will not lose any money." She told me again how impressed she was with my acting talent. She said that they were casting *The Good Earth* with Luise Rainer and Paul Muni. They were looking for an Oriental to play the part of the son. Casually, she picked up the phone and dialed.

"Hello, Irving, this is Mrs. Louis. Fine, fine! I'm calling to tell you I have with me a fine Oriental actor who would be perfect for the older son in *The Good Earth.* Hold a second. Yes, he can come right over."

I was completely in the dark. Mrs. Louis hung up the phone and turned to me.

"Peter, that was Irving Thalberg of MGM. He's casting *The Good Earth,* and he's looking for someone to play the part of the son. Go to his studio right away—he'll be waiting for you." She sprang into action: called a cab, gave directions to MGM (Metro Goldwyn-Meyer), and rushed me off.

Thalberg didn't look like a Hollywood tycoon, but more like an ordinary businessman. He gave a perfunctory greeting and said, "I want you to go and see Max; he'll give you a screen test."

Following Thalberg's direction, I walked around the immense studio lot and found Max's office. When I knocked on the door, a man opening the door said, "Oh, yes. You must be Peter; come in."

He went to his desk and thumbed through some papers. He turned to me and said, "Well, Peter, I can take you on Thursday for your screen test."

"I am sorry. I can't stay here until Thursday. I am on my way to New York, and I have to be in Hartford, Connecticut, by Wednesday."

"But I can't take you before Thursday."

The temptation was great; to crash into the movies! I loved Pearl Buck's *The Good Earth* and had deep admiration for Paul Muni. But how could I disappoint May Sarton? Which road? The movies or May? No question; once more May won me over hands down. "Sorry, Mr. Max. I have to be on my way."

So I left Max's office. I left behind Mrs. Louis, Irving Thalberg, the screen test, and a possible career in the movies.

In New York, I took the train to Hartford, where I bumped into a young actor who used to be in the Civic Repertory Theatre's Apprentice Group. He took me to the boarding house where he was staying and talked the landlady into taking me in as a boarder. It was really a stroke of luck to have found a room so quickly. The modest price for the room included dinner. However, the dinner was served in a different home where everything was strictly kosher. It was very good for me; I learned so much about the life style of orthodox Jews.

They studied the teachings of the Talmud—the Holy Bible of the Jews. They not only studied, but lived by the teachings of the Talmud. Moreover, their faith was handed down to their children. Before the sun set on Friday, they would light candles throughout the house. Except for these candles they would not switch on any other light throughout the night. The code of kosher as applied to food was and is absolute. Pork or any of its by-products were never touched or eaten. The code against pork was derived from their experience of finding pigs' carcasses often diseased and unclean. They would not mix meat dishes with dairy dishes. To make certain, two sets of dishes were kept: one for the meat dishes, another for the dairy or milk dishes. I was the only non-Jew, but I observed all the ethics and codes they taught me with great respect.

The Austin Memorial Museum in Hartford was a privately endowed little museum with some collections of paintings and sculptures. The unusual feature of the museum was its little theatre with a two hundred-seat capacity. It had a beautiful stage completely packed with modern equipment. May was indeed fortunate to have its use for her group and their first production. Just as the Studio Players was my first venture into directing my own theatre group, this was a first for May. She, too, was putting to the test her idea of the theatre, which we had discussed over so many midnight candles.

At the rehearsal, May introduced me to the members of her company. With the exception of two or three men, including myself, the rest of the members were women—young, aspiring actresses with very little experience. From the beginning, I made up my mind to keep my hands and nose out of the directing. May accepted this and never asked for my ideas, criticisms, or suggestions.

For their first undertaking, May chose an ancient Greek comedy in three acts newly translated into English. I didn't ask where or how May got hold of the property, which had never been done on the American stage. I thought that the strangeness of the play was part of the fascination for May. The plot dealt with the ancient theme of mistaken identity. Its humor, unless brilliantly staged, could not hold the audience through three acts and two and one-half hours.

I also detected another weakness: There was no cohesion among the group. Aside from their respect for May, there was no collective spirit. Each one was a star in his or her own right and performed to prove it. But the greatest obstacle was the personal emotional involvements among the members of the group, particularly the rivalry for the attention and affection of their director, May Sarton. Such emotional entanglements inevitably would affect the creative process of the entire group.

And it happened; the performance did not reach beyond the individuals. There were some brilliant moments, but they were isolated and independent of the whole. The end result was a patchwork of bright colors and dark shadows. May's direction was very sensitive, but a bit arty. And the audience was not much help. They were the elite members of Hartford society—patrons of the arts. They were reserved and conservative in their response. Occasionally they broke out into soft, stifled, styled laughter in response to the broad comedy on stage. Several performances in Hartford failed to move either the local or the New York press.

I felt very sorry for May, who had poured all her energy into the group and production. I realized that I felt she was the most beautiful woman I had ever known in my life and that I had almost given up my life for my love of her. Also, it was good to feel that I had sufficiently recovered from that trauma, with my emotional and artistic balance restored.

Before the company dispersed, May told me that she had an appointment with LeGallienne in New York. The purpose was to discuss the future of May's company with her. May said that she had mentioned my work to LeGalliene, and had received permission to present a short scene from my work with the Studio Players. That was a complete surprise. I went to New York, and hastily assembled the cast of *Uncle Vanya* and conducted hurried rehearsals.

The meeting with LeGallienne took place in an empty loft in midtown New York. At the loft were May Sarton and her company and several members of the Studio Players. With bated breath, we waited for LeGallienne's appearance. Her entrance was as dramatic as ever; her wind-blown silvery hair, her bristling blue eyes, and her leaping, positive strides all marked the unmistakable LeGallienne entrance.

She took a seat at center stage and welcomed us all. Her greetings, as always, were warm and very special. She called on May Sarton to tell her of her plans. She knew of May's venture in Hartford, Connecticut. May was a picture of humility. Very softly she said that she would go on with her company and that they would spend the summer living and working together.

Eva LeGallienne seemed impressed and asked, "Where will you get the money?"

"It's not the money I'm worried about," May answered. "I have the money. But we have no direction. I do worry about our reaching the goal."

"What is your goal?"

"To develop a competent, professional company to do productions of worthwhile plays."

"You have my blessings, May," LeGallienne said. "It's not going to be easy."

After more prolonged discussion of May's project, LeGallienne turned to me. "Peter, I understand you had a season in Boston. Let me see what you've done."

That was the cue for me to put on the scene from my *Uncle Vanya*. I felt sorry for the cast having to perform with only one run-through in a barn-like loft with no scenery, no props, and before a company of actors and Eva LeGallienne—but for the actors, the memory of their recent performance in Cambridge and the enthusiastic reviews in the *Boston Press* were still quite fresh. Along with the little audience, I watched the performance with intense interest. I was amazed and pleased to see them at ease and projecting the essence of the play. I had no premonition that I was about to face the most painful experience of my life in the theatre. The bombshell! Miss LeGallienne took the floor, supposedly for a critique of the performance.

"What right did you have to do *Uncle Vanya*?"

"What do you know about Chekhov?"

"Who told you you could stage *Uncle Vanya*?"

Once she launched her merciless attack, she could not stop. She exploded as though I had invaded her personal property. The harangue continued without pause for nearly fifteen minutes. It wasn't a critique; it was a sentence, if not an execution. No hatchet job in the annals of the theatre could have been as crude and cruel. LeGallienne was beside herself with rage. She couldn't stop her stream of vindictives. She sounded like Ibsen's Masterbuilder crying out, "Youth is knocking at my door!" And when she repeated, "What right did you have to do *Uncle Vanya?*" I got up and walked out. I would never see her again.

A few days later, I saw May. She asked, "Peter, why didn't you say something?"

"What could I say to a madwoman? To a person venting her vengeance over her own frustrations?"

From that moment thereafter, May Sarton and I traveled separate roads; she into the literary world, and I stubbornly following my destiny in the theatre.

The senseless bomb tossed at me by LeGallienne failed to deter my continuing search for my place in American theatre. The outburst of her anger and frustration did, however, inflict a deep, painful wound. Only after the pain had festered for a few days did I raise a serious question in my mind: How much of that venom was poured on me because I was an Oriental? Would she have been as vicious if the scene from *Uncle Vanya* had been directed by Howard daSilva or Burgess Meredith? Seeking consolation, I turned to my friend, Howard daSilva.

"Oh, forget it, Peter," was Howard's verdict. "She was out of her mind," he added. He wanted to know what my plans were. I had none at the moment.

"There is a group in the village," Howard said. "They call themselves Workers' Lab Theatre. I understand they are quite radical. Why don't you look them up?"

I found the Workers' Lab Theatre on Twelfth Street, just west of Broadway. It was located in a walk-up third-floor loft. A little stage was built on one end, and an enclosure for an office on the other. I met Al Saxe, one of the two directors. I asked a lot of questions, and Al answered without hesitation, "Yes, we are radical, because we are for organized labor. We develop Agit-Prop (Agitation Propaganda) productions and place them at their service."

"Where do you get the material?"

"We have writers. They go to the scene of a labor struggle, do research, and write up the script."

"What then?"

"Then we give it to the actors and let them develop the drama. As the director, my job is to organize the improvisations into a dramatic form." Then it was his turn to ask me questions: "How did you happen to come here?" "What have you done in the theatre?" And much more, such as "What's your feeling about the CIO [Congress of Industrial Organization] labor movement?" "What do you know about the garment workers' strike?"

I realized that he was probing not so much into my theatre background as into my ideological makeup. Realizing what he was after, I told him of my revolutionary roots in Korea and China. When I was fourteen years old, I told him, with a price on my head, I distributed union leaflets on the streets of Shanghai. That was enough for Al Saxe.

Then, delving into my experience in the theatre, he was impressed with my work as a stage manager in Eva LeGallienne's Civic Repertory Theatre and my own theatre venture in Cambridge.

"Okay," he said, "we welcome you to join us. But let me tell you the conditions. We live in a collective where your room and board would be taken care of. And whenever we have the money, we distribute it among the members for incidental expenses." He paused, then asked, "How does that sound to you?"

"That sounds great!" I answered.

I moved in and spent the first week attending and observing some rehearsals. They were impressive; such energy, vitality; I could feel the sparks the actors let fly. They were working with a script written by their writer, Peter Martin. He had gathered his material at the ILGWU (International Ladies' Garment Workers' Union) Hall and at the picket line in front of Ohrbach's, the major target of the strike. Ohrbach's, a newly opened store for women's wear, was located in the center of teeming labor struggles just off Union Square on Fourteenth and Broadway. The shop was notoriously anti-union and extremely crude in its exploitation of its employees. One of the demands of the strike was for workers' rest periods.

The script had been given to the actors for study, and at the first session of the cast there was a freewheeling discussion of the script. They would offer criticism and ideas. Peter Martin would listen carefully and make changes on the spot—an unheard of collaboration between playwright and actors.

The next day the rehearsal began in earnest. Scene by scene, the action and the dialogue were tossed in for improvisations. Al Saxe took notes of particular dialogue and action and incorporated them for the finished scene. With tireless work, the entire production was completed in a week. They took it to various locals of ILGWU to perform at their union meetings. I helped to carry the costumes and props in a suitcase. We traveled on the subway and reached the union halls in the Bronx, Brooklyn, and even on Staten Island.

The response of the workers to the performance was explosive. They could easily identify their own images, their dilemma, and their struggle; except that they had never expressed them so succinctly and so dramatically. The Agit-Prop performances accomplished one more thing: They inspired the workers to stay with their strike to victory.

Well, we couldn't mount an American Shock Brigade for the workers and farmers of the Soviet Union, but we did succeed in mounting the Shock Brigade American style.

I was intrigued by the technique used for the Agit-Prop productions. Everything was stylized and accentuated, as in a modernistic painting. The dialogue was not conversational, but was made more effective by shouting or whispering. Sometimes the lines were delivered in duets or in a chorus. The movements, too, were stylized. In keeping with the characters, the style of walks and all the body movements identified the boss, the exploited garment worker, the stool pigeon, the police, and so on. Original music composed and played on the piano by Earl Robinson further enriched the total drama.

The most successful production of the Workers' Lab Theatre was *Newsboy,* performed in 1934. It was the culmination and crowning glory for all the pioneering, experimental work they did. Defying all the conventions of the theatre, the little band of actors and directors dared to forge a new theatre form, a new concept, new dynamics of the theatre. It was a historical breakthrough.

*Newsboy* was the story of the collapse of the stock market and the resulting dizzying tailspin of the rich and poor alike.

For the first time on the American stage, blackouts were used for dramatic effect. Going even further, the technique of pictorial montage onstage was brought to life. *Newsboy,* along with the original music of Earl Robinson, did not waste a second to move swiftly to portray the agony of the human dilemma. The entire new experience in the theatre took only fifteen minutes! *Newsboy* was performed all around New York to rousing acclaim wherever it was performed. The New York Federal Theatre's *Living Newspaper* productions used the technique of *Newsboy*. The use of montage in *Newsboy* soon found its way to Hollywood, and the moviemakers adapted the technique on film with great commercial success.

The Workers' Lab Theatre reached its peak and began scanning the horizon for new territory to conquer. There was only one answer: Do an original full-length play. The directors and the writers put their heads together and came up with the play *The Young Go First*. It was the story of the CCC (Civilian Conservation Corps) camp under the WPA (Works Project Administration) program. Intensive research was conducted, including a visit to a CCC camp located in the forest of upper New York.

The basic objective of the CCC was to corral the unemployed youth, get them off the city streets, and send them into remote mountains to do reforestation work. The idea was fine, and the country received some benefits. The problem with CCC rose from the attempted militarization of the young. Army officers were in charge of its administration, and they imposed military discipline, conducted military drills, and converted the civilian corps into a military unit. The youth revolted, which was countered with harsher discipline. The living human drama was crystallized into a dramatic play called *The Young Go First*.

With the 1935 production of this full-length play, the Workers' Lab Theatre changed its name to the Theatre of Action. Among the new members joining us were Norman Lloyd and Jeff Corey and Nick Ray. We found enough money to lease a theatre, not quite on Broadway—the Park Theatre in Columbus Circle, which I believe was on West Fifty-ninth Street. William Randolph Hearst had built this theatre to further the acting career of Marion Davis. The luxurious five hundred-seat theatre had an enormous, well-equipped stage. The distinctive feature, however, was the private suite in the back of the balcony. It was furnished with plush divans and chairs where Hearst and his cronies settled with cocktails in their hands to have a private viewing of Marion Davis onstage. I don't believe there were too many such occasions.

And now a Korean director was sitting in the stuffed chair and watching the young actors from the village rehearsing a play about the CCC, one of President Franklin Delano Roosevelt's economic recovery projects. Acting in a full-length play was quite a change from Agit-Prop acting. The scenes didn't reach their climax with a slogan or blackout. They had to be developed slowly and with subtlety. They demanded sustained concentration.

After a week's rehearsal, the actors were beginning to enjoy their new theatre experience. They were bundles of talents as well as bundles of energy and fire. *The Young Go First* turned into really exciting theatre. It opened to an enthusiastic reception. The faithful followers of the Theatre of Action filled the theatre for the first few nights.

We then learned a few painful lessons. First, you do not dare put on a play in uptown New York without a star; the theatregoers follow the stars. They are the so-called upper-middle class people not only from the five boroughs of New York, but from the daily million tourists from around the country and the world. We, too, had followers, but they were in the union halls and on the picket lines. Even if they wanted, they could not afford the trip uptown and the price of a theatre ticket.

We also learned that the theatre critics were the lords and masters whose reviews of a production determined the life or death of a play. It mattered little who wrote, who produced, who directed, who starred, and how much it cost. With a stroke of a pen, the critic pronounced his sentence: a hit, a so-so, or instant death. Under the circumstances, it was a miracle that *The Young Go First* ran for two weeks before closing. And that was the end of the Theatre of Action.

That's when Herbert Biberman came to New York, bringing with him a play he saw in the Soviet Union, *China Roars.* He produced it as a season opener for the Theatre Guild. I met him at his first rehearsal. I introduced myself, offered a quick resume, and asked for a job. No, all the parts were filled. How about a stage manager? No, he had all the stage managers he needed. What appalled me was that he wasn't a bit interested in my China background.

About the same time, a new theatre group called Group Theatre appeared in New York. Its leaders were Lee Strasberg, Cheryl Crawford, and Harold Clurman. They were all followers of the Moscow Art Theatre. Besides a group of highly talented young actors, they also had writers: Clifford Odets and Irwin Shaw. Their first show was *Waiting for Lefty,* written by Odets. It was produced in 1935 on the stage of the old Civic Repertory Theatre on Fourteenth Street.

The play is about taxi cab drivers and their decision to strike—

shades of the Workers' Lab Theatre and Agit-Prop; blackouts, slogans, and audience participation. Receiving wild acclamation, *Waiting for Lefty* launched the meteoric career of Clifford Odets. Among the founding members of the Group Theatre, there was one Elia Kazan, who played the central character. He was destined to play a role in my theatre career before his phenomenal success in the movies.

One day I obtained an interview with Lee Strasberg; I was interested in joining the Group Theatre. It was a very painful experience. He asked me what my interests in the theatre were. Directing, I told him. Whereupon he launched a probe into my theatre background, not by asking about my experiences but about my knowledge of Greek, Elizabethan, and Shakespearean theatre. He rattled off the names of all the books of those periods and asked if I had read any of them. I said of course not. He didn't ask me what I knew about the Chinese opera or the Japanese No theatre. He ended the interview with the typical, "I'll let you know." I didn't expect ever to hear from him again. I didn't.

With the closing of *The Young Go First,* and with the funds of the Theatre of Action completely depleted, the entire group, including musicians and writers, staged an exodus into the New York Federal Theatre. We were all accepted, and with the thirty dollars a week each one was paid, we were able to maintain our collective and keep our bodies and souls together. Philip Barber succeeded Hallie Flanagan as director, and I was assigned to the Children's Theatre as director. I was given a free hand to choose a play and direct it. I decided on Molière's *The Miser.*

I had never read Molière in the original French. My two years of high school French were hardly enough to approach Molière in his native tongue. I became acquainted with him at the Civic Repertory Theatre. I had stage managed LeGallienne's production of Molière's *Would-Be Gentleman.* The social satire verging on hilarious farce captured the soul of the theatre completely. That prompted me to read Molière's other works.

I didn't know if *The Miser* had ever been done in the United States, but it was a challenge, and the facilities of the Federal Theatre offered a great opportunity to attempt its production. My basic concept was to stage Molière in the light of present-day society, to test and reflect Molière's characters and dialogue in modern American society. I designed the set and had it built by the Federal Theatre stage builders. One innovation used in the design was a slide beside the stairway. The miser would use it to slide down and catch the thief before he got away. The costume department either rented or made all the seventeenth-century French costumes and fitted everyone in the cast.

The show opened in a little neighborhood community theatre before an audience composed mainly of employees of the Federal Theatre. They were super critical, and their reception ranged from surprise and high praise to jealous ridicule. We publicized it in the midtown East Side neighborhoods—free admission. After a week, we gave up the effort. In hindsight, it was a mistake to offer a seventeenth-century French dramatist to the cynical inhabitants of New York's East Side.

Following this lesson, my next undertaking was much closer to reality. I conceived the idea that the theatre should not be the property of the rich; it should belong to the people. But the people never came near the theatre; it was a world apart. Well, then, the theatre should be taken to the people. My inspiration led me to build a mobile theatre.

With my ideas and design, a stage was built on the bed of a large truck. We had the proscenium, the spotlights, and the backdrop from the Federal Theatre. In addition, several microphones were hung up and connected to large loudspeakers. We would drive the truck to a neighborhood park, set up the stage, and give our performance. The play I chose was *The Emperor's New Clothes,* a perfect choice for the working people of New York. The vanity of the emperor (the rich), the farce of a naked emperor strutting before his people, all struck the people's collective funny bone. Their spontaneous laughter and applause confirmed my belief that the theatre belongs to the people.

One day, out of sheer curiosity, I visited the Puppet Theatre, another branch of the Federal Theatre. Watching the work of the marionette show intrigued me: sculpting and shaping the figures, designing and dressing them, and finally stringing and manipulating their movements. I was particularly moved by the eccentric motions of the marionettes, which satirized human movements.

I decided to do a marionette production. For the material I chose Eason Munroe's *Ferdinand the Bull.* I presented the idea to Phil Barber, the director, and he approved it instantly. Simon and Schuster, the publishers, also approved. It was probably the most elaborate and ambitious marionette show ever conceived and staged. What made it possible were the resources of the U.S. Public Works Program Administration. I had a talented writer from the writers' project do the narration, a composer from the music project to produce an original score, and a choreographer from the dance project to direct the dancing. I watched and supervised the entire production.

The head of the Puppet Theatre, whose name I don't remember, was a soft-spoken, kindly office manager. He didn't interfere with *Ferdinand;* he gave me free reign to do everything I wanted. The puppeteers began by molding the heads of every character in clay. Plaster of Paris molds were then cast, and when ready, papiermâché forms were struck out of the molds. They were then properly painted and decorated. Delicate hands and feet were carved out of soft wood. When all of the figures were assembled and costumed, they all came to life. They were then strung up with fine, almost invisible strings, all of which were tied to the controlling crossbars. The makeup and costuming departments completed the final touches for the formal appearance of the marionettes.

The most ingenious characters were the picadores carrying lances on horseback; the adorable characters, the banderilleros, with long darts trailing colorful streamers; the matador, or bullfighter, handsome in gold trimmed breeches and tunic. The hero of the show, Ferdinand, was a noble animal with great aloof dignity. The opening performance was done in a large community center theatre. The classic overture for a bullfight came over the loudspeaker as the lights dimmed and the curtain parted. Onstage was another theatre, the marionette stage. Applause.

The trumpet pierced the air, announcing the parade. As the picadores on horseback strutted onstage, the backdrop began to move, creating the illusion of parading around the bullring. Great applause! Now the banderilleros followed, waving their decorated darts at the crowd. More applause.

Following a short pause, the matador came on. A roar from the crowd greeted him. Waving his black tricorne hat, he bowed to the crowd again and again. Finally, they opened the gate, allowing the bull to enter the ring; Ferdinand! Ignoring the applause, with magnificent dignity the bull circled the ring in measured steps. Then he settled under the shade of a tree and surveyed the scene.

The blast of trumpets heralded the start of the bullfight, and the crowd roared in anticipation. But Ferdinand would not stir. The picadores came on, and using their lances tried to rouse the lethargic bull. No success. Next the banderilleros did their dance before the bull. Ferdinand wasn't interested; he gave a mighty yawn instead. In fury, the banderilleros poked a few darts at Ferdinand's shoulders—he was more annoyed than aroused.

Another blast of the trumpets. The matador, in all of his glorious splendor, accompanied by deafening applause, seemed to float into the center of the ring. Waving his black hat, he bowed gracefully in all directions to the crowd. He then cautiously approached the bull. He held up the red cape with his sword and stepped up to face the bull. To all the ceremonial maneuvers, Ferdinand paid not the slightest attention. The matador came closer and flipped his cape to the left and to the right. No, Ferdinand didn't wish to fight. He shut his eyes to all the commotion and went to sleep. Outraged, the matador tore off his cape and tossed it at Ferdinand, who slept on as the curtain closed on the marionette stage, followed by the theatre-stage curtain. The audience broke into applause as wildly as if it were in the bullring itself.

*Ferdinand the Bull* became the favorite of the neighborhood community center circuit around New York. Phil Barber then announced the big news: *Ferdinand* would go to the New York World's Fair; it would be featured in the WPA exhibit at the fair. Three daily performances drew audiences from around the country and the world, and every performance was met with enthusiastic applause and comments in many languages.

All the puppeteers, technicians, and stagehands were as enthusiastic as the audiences. None of us—the writers, composers, choreographer, puppeteers, not to mention the director—received special financial compensation beyond our regular weekly wages. At the time, it didn't occur to us that we should have some share of *Ferdinand's* financial success. We were all employees of the Federal Theatre and were guaranteed weekly wages of thirty dollars regardless of what we did at any given time. With such living conditions assured, we devoted all our time and energy to creative work. This was one of the profound lessons of the WPA for all the actors, writers, artists, and technicians in all the projects of the performing arts.

The search for my next project brought me in contact with two young writers—Lou Lantz and Oscar Saul. Fresh out of New York City College (CCNY), they had written a play called *Revolt of the Beavers*. They gave me the script to see if I would be interested in producing it. I studied the script, and the following week we met to discuss the play. Of course they wanted to know if I liked it or not.

"Yes, I like it very much," I assured them. "I like the allegorical concept; it opens infinite possibilities. I know you are completely wrapped up in telling the story of human struggles through the animal life of the beavers. That's all original and imaginative." Then I launched a serious critique. "You are telling your story not in a narrative or in a book; you are telling it in a play. The entire story must have dramatic interest, a dramatic development that reaches a climax."

"Well," one of them asked, "don't we have that in our script?"

"No, you don't."

"What can we do?"

"You have to rewrite it, and I'll help you."

We met every day and spent hours reconstructing and rewriting the play. In a few weeks, a new *Revolt of the Beavers* was born.

With Phil Barber's approval, I arranged the time and place for casting. At the appointed hour, I entered the room. My stage manager had placed a little table and chair at one end, and the actors and actresses sat in a circle around the room. As I entered, a deadly silence fell over the room. I could sense the instant charge of electricity from everyone. I walked over and slowly sat at the table. I circled the group with my eyes, making sure to look at every face. I noticed Jules Dassin, who had played the tailor in my *The Emperor's New Clothes*. A product of the Jewish Art Theatre, Dassin was an intense, talented actor.

When I completed my visual survey, I dropped my eyes to the manuscript on the desk. I held my breath and kept silent for a long minute. I raised my head, and looking straight at the assembled actors I spoke my first words: "I know what you are all thinking."

A long pause.

"You are all thinking, 'What the hell is this Chinaman doing here?' Right?"

Stunned silence.

"Well, let me tell you what this Chinaman is doing here. I am here to find out if any of you know how to act. I am also going to show you what acting really is, to show you how you can discover the kind of acting you never knew you had in you. Now, before we go on, any of you who don't care to work under a Chinaman may leave the room now." I waited in silence; nobody left. "Well, now then, we can go to work."

I had the stage manager pass the scripts around and gave time for them to study it. Before the reading began I told them the basic concept of the play and asked them to read the lines, not as they would read a story, but as if they were projecting them on stage.

Their first and subsequent readings were all impressive; youth, ambition, and dedication charged through everyone. Inwardly, I wished I could cast them all in the play. After several days of trials, I found the final cast. For the leading roles I found two young actors, Sam Bonnell and Kathleen Hoyt; for two other prominent roles, Joseph Dixon and Jules Dassin. It was Dassin who was destined to become famous with his *Never on Sunday*. And to play other key parts, I enrolled a few of the young veterans of the Theatre of Action: Perry Bruskin, Ben Ross, Lucy Kaye, and others. The whole cast numbered over fifty and included two groups of dancers, whose appearances between scenes were much like the Greek chorus. I was fortunate to have Oscar Walzer compose the original orchestral music that accompanied the entire show. I was equally fortunate in having Sylvia Manning of Martha Graham's school to choreograph all the dances.

We plunged into rehearsals in earnest. The play had a simple story line. The beaver world is ruled by a chief with absolute power. The working beavers are driven by bully police beavers. All the tree barks produced by the beavers belong to the chief. The working beavers receive very little and suffer with hunger. A rebellious young beaver secretly organizes the colony of beavers into a union. They draft and present their demands to the chief: better working conditions, no police surveillance, and a fair share of the bark they produce.

The chief breaks into a belly laugh. "What a joke! Little beavers telling me what they want!"

"Let's strike!" the lead beaver retorts, and all the working beavers agree by acclamation.

The chief snorts and predicts the beavers will go back to work when they are hungry enough. But the striking beavers hold fast, and the supply of bark for the chief depletes. He orders his police beavers to force them to work. They fail, and the bark supply drops to a dangerously low level. The chief calls the leader beaver and negotiates. They agree on a settlement: no overtime work—eight hours a day only, no police surveillance at work, and half of all bark produced given to the working beavers.

A victory celebration by the beavers would bring down the final curtain.

The rehearsals went at a rapid pace. All my experience as a director was being put to the test and was paying rich dividends. I was particularly pleased with my concept of stylizing the production; the speech and the movements in the allegory could not be presented in realistic terms. But by stylizing, the ideas and emotions could be accentuated. However, it demanded a very fine synchronization of speech, sounds, and movements. I felt *Revolt of the Beavers* would be the ultimate synthesis of all my work in the theatre.

One day, Phil Barber came to watch our rehearsal. Before leaving he said, "Come and see me when you've finished." In his office, before I could sit down, Barber said, "Peter, as I watched the rehearsal of *Beaver*, I decided to put the show on Broadway."

Stunned, I asked, "What did you say, Mr. Barber?"

"You heard me right. We are going to put *Beaver* on Broadway." No more questions and no discussion.

I rushed out to share the news with the cast, but they were already gone. The next day, before the rehearsal, I made the announcement to the cast. "Phil Barber has told me," I said in measured tones, "that *Revolt of the Beavers* will go on Broadway."

Stunned, unbelieving silence for a moment, and then pandemonium. Yelling and screaming, jumping and dancing, the actors lost all control. I understood and allowed the merriment to go on. After all, Broadway meant the pot of gold at the end of the rainbow. It was every actor's dream. Eventually, the uproar subsided, and that's when the trouble began.

We ran through a rather lackadaisical rehearsal and ended it quite early; I sensed everyone was anxious to get away to break the news. The next day the rehearsal turned into a strangely indifferent recitation. I decided it was only the aftermath of the excitement about going on Broadway after all the years of work and dreams. But when the indifference persisted for several days, I was alarmed.

One day, I stopped the rehearsal and addressed the cast. "What's the matter?" I asked. "You have all stopped performing. Tell me what's troubling you all."

No reply—total silence.

The next day, I was called into the office by Phil Barber. When I entered the office, I found him nervously shuffling papers on his desk. Finally, he motioned for me to sit down. "I have some bad news for you, Peter," he said. "The cast of your *Beaver* has told me that they don't want to go on Broadway with you as the director. They asked me to find a name director."

I was in shock. I recovered only to murmur, "I'll be damned!"

Barber made a feeble attempt to console me. "Peter," he said, "it's a shame. *Beaver* is your show from start to finish. And now this disgraceful situation."

"I can't believe it!" I moaned.

Following a long moment of silence, Barber continued. "Peter," he said, "if you want, I'll cancel the whole production."

"No!" I jumped. "Don't do that, Mr. Barber. 'The show must go on.'"

"The sad thing is," Barber said apologetically, "that we have already leased a Broadway theatre, and we can't face an actors' strike at this stage."

"And have you also found a 'name director'?" I asked.

"Elia Kazan of the Group Theatre has agreed to take it over."

"Kazan?" I was amazed. "True, he's not a 'Chinaman,' but he's an actor—he has never directed anything as far as I know."

The next morning I met the cast at rehearsal. They were all standing around, fidgeting nervously.

"Please sit down," I said, as calmly as I could, "and don't be nervous. How can you go on Broadway with such fragile nerves?" I waited for them to settle in their seats, then I said, "Mr. Barber has told me all about your determination not to go on Broadway with a Chinaman as the director. He said he would cancel the show if I wished." I allowed that to sink in, then continued. " 'Absolutely not,' I told Mr. Barber. So you'll all be sure to have your chance to perform on Broadway." I picked up my script and stood up. My parting words were, "I am really ashamed of all of you."

The following days I sank into a deeper and deeper depression. The nearly ten years I had spent in the theatre floated through my mind, and throughout, the scenes I had blocked out reappeared in sharp focus—the racial prejudice, slurs, insults. I had battled them all and had refused to allow them to interfere with my work in the theatre. "The theatre," I repeated to myself over and over again, "should be above such human frailties." That's an ideal not to be found in reality.

The following days and nights—even in my dreams—I wrestled with the question, Should I or shouldn't I go on with the theatre? Ten years! That's a big chunk of one's life, especially out of one's youth. Yes, for almost ten years I had devoted all my time and energy to the creative world of the theatre. I studied and I labored, and I had moments of great joy and satisfaction.

But throughout all this time, I had also lived through pain and suffering springing from racial prejudice and discrimination. All my waking hours I had to be on guard, on the streets and in the theatre. Finding a place to live in New York City was a painful ordeal. In response to a "For Rent" sign, I would walk up and ring the doorbell. The man or woman opened the door and with a startled face gave me the distant and choking, "Y-e-s?"

"I would like to see the apartment for rent."

"Oh, that! It's already rented."

It was always the same answer. Finally, I had to resort to subterfuge. I would find a Caucasian friend to go and rent the apartment for me.

The racial prejudice and slurs I faced inside the theatre were even more painful. I could understand and forgive the insults of the stagehands—their ignoring my orders and their refusal to follow my cues. After all, I reasoned, they were an uneducated, ignorant lot. But the actors! They were artists, enlightened intellectuals. Well read, and versed in human affairs. And by the very nature of their work as actors, they had to be highly sensitive to human feelings. Some of them even composed music, wrote poems, and painted pictures.

Yet they were totally blind and insensitive to racial discrimination and prejudice. They laughed at racist jokes. They called people by their racist labels: dago, pollack, kike, Chinaman. I flinched every time I heard "Chinaman": To all Americans, it seemed, "Chinaman" and "laundryman" were synonymous. Time and again, in the polite company of gentle people, I would be asked if my family were in the laundry business. They couldn't possibly guess how searing and painful the name-calling was. How could they know they were insulting not just me, but all of my ancestors? The genealogy of the Hyun family proudly records thirty generations—nearly one thousand years—of generals, ministers, literati, and diplomats. "Chinaman!" hurled at me also insulted Korea's four-thousand-year history and culture. Throughout its history, would-be conquerors invaded Korea; they came from Mongolia, China, Russia, and Japan. They all failed. None of them could break the spirit of the Korean people for independence and freedom. Some invaders took longer than others, but in the end, all retreated. The Koreans preserved their national identity and freedom.

For years I fought the insults off; I pushed them into the dark recesses of my consciousness—so I thought! No, the hateful scenes did not disappear; the hurt always resurfaced at the most unguarded moments: on the streets, in the restaurants, and even in a public park. I had to hold my breath when going anywhere accompanied by an American woman. I had to be alert and be prepared to fend off the assaults of stares and glares.

However, these silent encounters on the streets were bearable compared to those in the theatre. Various versions of "Hey, Chinaman, what are you doing here?" would be flung at me backstage, in the dressing rooms, in the hallway. The success of the *Revolt of the Beavers,* which culminated in the "revolt of the actors" against me, a "Chinaman," was the final blow. I had to call myself a Chinaman and challenge the actors to accept me as the director, or leave. Why such prelude and backhanded apology to work in the theatre? It was grotesque and ludicrous! If I were to go on, I shuddered at the thought of spending the rest of my life fighting and struggling against the unseen phantom. I had to save myself from such ingrained evil; I had to refuse to be mired in the filth of racial prejudice. My mind was made up.

At the last rehearsal, I bid farewell to the cast and the theatre. I parted with a short message: "You are going on Broadway without me. I hope some day in the future, you will remember this day and feel the burden of shame. Now when the curtain goes up on *Revolt,* be sure to remember all the directions I have given you."

*Revolt of the Beavers* was opening on Broadway. Like an old horse running back to his barn at sundown, I went to the theatre to see it. I was surprised to find in the program that it was directed not by Elia

Kazan, but by Lewis Leverett and Peter Hyun. Evidently, Kazan had given up and handed the show over to Leverett, another member of Group Theatre. And good old Phil Barber must have insisted on adding my name to the program. The essence of my concept for *Revolt* was there: the stylized speech and movement. I marveled at how great the production was. There was only one weakness: It was not an inspired performance!

I left the theatre early, and that would be the last time I had anything to do with actors and the theatre.

Hyun family, Shanghai, ca. 1919. *Left to right:* Paul, Soon Ok, Joshua, Elizabeth holding Mary, Alice. *Rear:* Peter.

Family group traveling to Makaweli for local family service, ca. 1928. *Front row, left to right:* David, Mary, Joshua. *Back row, left to right:* Reverend Hyun, Maria holding grandson Wellington, Peter, Paul. Note no shoes in front row.

Korean Methodist Church in Honolulu.

Methodist church and parsonage on Kauai.

Kauai High School orchestra; Peter Hyun *second on left.*

Peter Hyun as "Saong" in *Cane Fire,* filmed on Kauai, Hawaii.

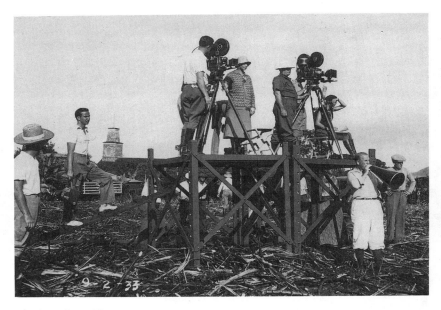

Filming *Cane Fire*.

Maria and Reverend
Hyun, ca. 1952.

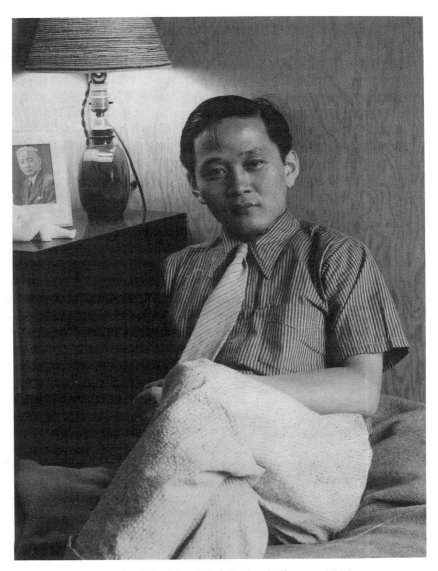

Director Peter Hyun of the New York Federal Theatre, 1936.

Peter Hyun *(center)* directs a production of *Ferdinand the Bull* by the Federal Theatre Marionette Workshop. Photo courtesy of the Library of Congress Federal Theatre Project Collection, George Mason University Library, Fairfax, Virginia.

Announcement of *Revolt of the Beavers*. Photo courtesy of the Library of Congress Federal Theatre Project Collection, George Mason University Library, Fairfax, Virginia.

Brothers Paul *(left)* and Peter Hyun *(right)* in New York, ca. 1934.

Technical Sergeant Peter Hyun with an unidentified companion at the Village Barn, Greenwich Village, New York City.

Major Peter Hyun aboard a Korea-bound troop ship, 1945.

Peter with his second wife, Luisa Stuart Hyun, 1992.

# 8

# NEW
# BEGINNING

The prodigal son had come home again and was embraced and welcomed by Papa and Umma, just like in biblical days. The years had etched new wrinkles on their faces, and their hair shimmered silvery white. Yet they were not bent; the old fire of rebellion still burned in their eyes and their hearts. After a lifetime of work in the church, Papa had finally retired and moved to Honolulu.

They asked no questions why I had returned. They knew I had quit the theatre and that what I needed was the protection and comfort of my home. They knew: Umma slipped away to the kitchen and began preparing the lunch. I knew it would be my favorite summer dish—ice-cold noodles with *kim chee* and fruit. Meanwhile, Papa began telling the news of our old Korean friends on Kauai. He said hardly any Koreans were left in the sugar plantations anymore. With their grown-up children, they had all moved to the city— Honolulu. A few of them were even engaged in business such as produce markets and furniture stores. Their sons and daughters, now secretaries, teachers, businessmen, and businesswomen, supported their old parents. Papa mentioned a few names I could remember: the Hong family of Puhi, the Parks of Hanapepe, the Chungs of Makaweli, and the Chois of Kekaha. Where were they now? All scattered on Oahu, especially in Honolulu.

In my own family there had also been startling changes. Brother David and baby Sister Mary were both attending the University of Hawaii. David was studying civil engineering and was wearing a captain's uniform in the ROTC. Mary was in social studies but more involved with a young man from California named Lindauer. In 1926, Sister Alice had returned to Chung, her husband, and four-year-old daughter in Korea. It turned out to be a mistake. Against impossible odds, she was granted a divorce and, leaving her daughter with Chung, returned to Honolulu in 1927. A few months later, she gave birth to her son. Father named him Wellington, not after the British general and statesman, but after Wellington Koo of China, whom Father admired for his political outlook and statesmanship. Wellington grew to be a bright and handsome boy, and when he was a year old, Sister Alice decided to go back to school. She left the infant in Umma's care and went to New York, where Sister Elizabeth still lived. She enrolled in New York University to study world literature and creative writing, supporting herself by working as a housemaid. She had returned to Hawaii in 1935 and was now, with Brother Paul—still the artist—producing block prints of Hawaiian flora and fauna on fabrics. It was the forerunner of Hawaiian prints for aloha shirts and swimsuits. Brother Joshua was the worker and the breadwinner of the family. He had followed his interest in carpentry from his high school days and had developed into a fine journeyman carpenter in construction. And as in his earlier years, he handed his weekly paycheck to Umma. She would then put a few dollars in Joshua's pocket for his spending money.

It seemed nothing short of magic to come home to find such adjustments among all members of the family. Who but my dear mother, Umma, could have achieved such masterful family management. She even managed to buy a house in the Kaimuki district and ensconced her not-so-young brood in it, except for big Sister Alice. Breaking away from Umma's world, Sister Alice dared to create her own. Without any money for a down payment, she bought a beautiful, sumptuous old house on Anapuni Street, in the heart of a quiet, middle-class neighborhood. I was afraid to ask how she engineered the miracle; I only knew she was the most resourceful, imaginative, and daring person. The house, with a suggestive Victorian appearance, had three huge bedrooms, an immense living room, and a spacious dining room. The kitchen, too, was generously large, and the circular table was the center of all social activities. Following the Hyun family tradition, all visitors were directed to the kitchen and treated to bits of delicacies with tea or coffee. There was also a *lanai*—a sunny, roomy porch that Sister converted to another sleeping room. Two Korean university students were boarded there and helped with the expenses.

My ever-enterprising sister soon sold the house at a big profit, enough to pay off the mortgage and buy a house on the hill above Manoa Valley. This one was designed and built by a German architect and was constructed entirely of lava rock. Its special feature was one hundred and two zigzagging steps that led from the road to the entrance of the house. Once inside, one was rewarded with a panoramic view of the valley and the sparkling waters of the Pacific. True to German taste, it was a massive structure. All the walls were a foot thick and all the windows and doors in heavy frame; there wasn't a squeak anywhere. Besides the two bedrooms, living room, dining room, kitchen, and bath on the main floor, there was a commodious guest room downstairs.

I moved in with Sister Alice and very quickly our home in Manoa Valley became a veritable refuge for sailors and soldiers stationed in Hawaii; they found their way to our home on their weekends off and on furloughs. They were from New England, New York, Chicago, and Indiana, not to mention the West Coast states of Washington, Oregon, and California. Their calling card usually was their union affiliation—AFL (American Federation of Labor), CIO —they knew somebody who knew somebody who knew me or Sister Alice. We welcomed them all and did everything to make them feel at home away from home; home-cooked meals, comfortable bed, and good company. Soon our home became the clearinghouse for all servicemen with a liberal bent.

Most of the time they were only overnight guests, but occasionally some of them came with a three-day pass, which signaled a celebration and a party. The one exception was a naval combat flyer named Irving. For one month he flew all over the Pacific on combat duty. When he returned alive, he was given one month of leave. That's when he found us. We let him settle in the guest room downstairs to unwind from the war. He did. He was not only a war hero, but a good union man to boot. We dined and feted him and paraded him before all our friends. But in the evening, he always sank into a melancholy mood, and it was always the same concern and worry— his girlfriend back in California. "Do you think she'll wait for me?" "Oh, what a beautiful girl!" "Maybe she'll find somebody else. . . ."

For a month, Sister Alice and I listened to his woes and plied him with food and comfort. His leave expired; he returned to his base.

That was not the end of Irving. After the war, Sister Alice and I settled in Los Angeles. We tracked and located Irving. He was happily married to his true love and was working as an organizer for the Electrical Workers Union. Sister and I were pleased with the happy ending of Irving's sufferings over his true love.

Another amenity of the stone house was a detached wooden cabin built on high stilts. It was spacious enough, and the entire wall facing north was encased in glass. Brother Paul was delighted with the daytime northern light, which was perfect for his artwork and for the fabric printing business. Sister Alice would buy rolls of linen at the India House. She would cut them into doilies and napkins and fray the edges. Brother Paul was busy designing shapes of the hibiscus, bird of paradise, and anthurium, among others, which he would then carve onto wood blocks. Finally, using delicate, waterproof colors, the designs were printed on the linen. It required the sensitive touch of Brother Paul to produce the most beautiful table settings.

I was the self-appointed salesman. I would pack the samples and hit the road. I started with the main department stores. The buyers were impressed but reluctant to try such a brand-new item. Refusing to take no for an answer, I would persuade them to take them on consignment on a fifty-fifty basis. With such arrangements, I was able to place them in all three major stores and deplete our stock entirely. Within a week, we received phone calls from all three stores with new orders. Paul now had to work late into the night to meet the demand, and Sister Alice had to search for other sources for the material.

I now called on some of the better-known gift shops in town. They, too, were hesitant at first, but when told that the department stores were selling them like hotcakes, decided to carry them as well. As the demand grew, we also altered the financial arrangements. No longer on consignment, but cash on delivery, and not fifty-fifty but sixty-forty, with the larger share to the manufacturer—us.

Sister Alice then conceived another idea: Why not print the flowers on sport shirts for both men and women? Again, Paul designed the pattern, carved them onto wood blocks, and had them printed on shirts—front and back and some on sleeves. I took the samples to our customers. The buyers were surprised and delighted.

"Why didn't we think of that?" they moaned in chorus. The shirts were an instant success. The stores provided the shirts and paid us for the printing. The net result was far more profitable than the doily and napkin line. Why didn't we contract a commercial textile firm to mass produce the aloha shirts and table sets? Why, we could have become instant millionaires! Ah, but that's not the way of life with the Hyuns. Our family tradition inspired all of us to be the initiators and erectors, but never hoarders and amassers. And I was searching for some undertaking of my own to contribute to the family welfare.

One day, I accidentally met a Korean gentleman farmer who raised carnations and sold the flowers to Hawaiian lei makers. I asked if I could go into farming.

"Why not?" was his answer. "I know where there's some acreage available. Go, lease it, and I'll help you get started."

The novel idea of becoming a farmer struck a responsive cord in me. I had always harbored a romantic image of farmers, and I knew both Umma and Papa loved to grow things. I drove out to Koko Head, a nearby suburb of Honolulu, and looked at a piece of land for lease—three acres, one two-bedroom bungalow, a wood-burning stove in the kitchen, and an outhouse. I signed the lease on the spot.

Umma and Papa were delighted to move out of the city and to have a plot of land to grow something. Learning to raise carnations was not easy. There was so much work separating the slips from healthy plants, planting, weeding and watering, waiting for them to mature and blossom. The stems of blooms were cut and bundled, one dozen blossoms in each bundle. At the crack of dawn, I would take the flowers to the market. I couldn't get more than ten cents a dozen. Rarely did I bring home more than three dollars. Even though they had expended so many hours of back-breaking labor, both Umma and Papa were delighted to see the money they had earned farming. There had to be a better reward for their labor.

Casually examining the produce market, I discovered most of the produce was brought over from the mainland. No wonder they were so expensive! The most expensive item, I discovered, was cucumbers—five, ten, and up to fifteen cents apiece. Well! Why couldn't I grow cucumbers? I went to the Department of Agriculture at the University of Hawaii and raised this question. The counselor was quite sympathetic and promised to make a study of the feasibility of my plan. But first he asked me to bring him a sample of soil dug up from beneath the surface. I complied, and a week later I reported to his office. He had assembled all the necessary information to raise cucumbers in Hawaii. However, this information raised more questions than answers.

First the soil: The volcanic soil of Hawaii lacked sulphur, lime, and alkali. Certain fertilizers were recommended to remedy the deficiency. After plowing the field, I would need to cover it with a thin layer of the fertilizer and, using a rake, mix it well with the soil, and water it daily for a week before planting.

The seeds: A certain brand of hybrid cucumber seeds from Japan, considered to be hardy and fertile, was suggested. They should be planted in circular patches of two and a half feet in diameter, three to four feet apart. They should be watered generously twice a day—early in the morning before sunrise and late afternoon after sunset. Within a week, the cucumber plants should break out of the ground.

"Watch it," the counselor warned, "because that's when your troubles will begin. In the night, the cutworms will emerge out of the ground and have a feast cutting up the young plants." It sounded ominous. "To save the crop, you must have a bag of brown sugar mixed with arsenic in a three to one ratio ready for intercepting the cutworms. As soon as the plants appear, sprinkle the sweet poison around every hole before retiring. In the morning you should see some dead cutworms." (It was amazing to see the carcasses of cutworms lying in a circle in every patch. When the plants grew their main stems, the worms ceased their attack.)

"In two to three weeks the vines will begin to spread, and that's the time for mildew."

"Mildew?" I was puzzled.

"Yes, mildew, the most deadly disease."

"How can I tell?" I asked.

"Oh, you will," the counselor assured me. "The disease attacks mature leaves, leaving patches of white. And when you discover them, you must set fire to the whole plant immediately. Don't touch or move the diseased plant. If not burned, the mildew can spread over the whole field in a matter of days and kill the entire crop." (The mildew happened exactly as predicted.)

"Within four weeks, the field will be covered with little yellow cucumber blossoms and they will invite another enemy—Spanish flies. These flies will lay their eggs in the center of the blossoms so that they remain in the fruit. As the fruit grows, the eggs will hatch and feed on the meat of the cucumber. When fully grown, and you pick the fruit, you will find only the shell; the inside of the fruit would be completely filled with tiny worms—maggots."

I didn't believe this particular warning until I did find some perfectly good-looking cucumbers that broke open to touch, exposing a revolting bunch of maggots. To prevent the flies from infesting the whole field, I was instructed to use a special chemical spray that, without harming the plant, killed the flies—eggs and all. Carrying a large can of the chemical strapped to my back, I pumped with one hand and sprayed with the other. Swarms of Spanish flies—with pretty green wings—descended on the field in the morning. I had to be there early to meet them with my spray. In the afternoon, the school of flies returned for another visit, and I had to meet and fight them with my sprayer. The fruit-bearing season over, the flies disappeared, and thanks to the university counselor's instructions and my faithful spraying, we found only a few maggot-infested cucumbers.

In six weeks, we began harvesting. The sight of Umma and Papa picking cucumbers in the field was beautiful and joyful. They were so carried away; they would fill their baskets in no time, dump them on a large canvas, and return to pick more. It was my job to grade the fruit according to size and shape—numbers 1, 2, and 3. number 1 fetched ten cents a pound at the wholesale market; number 2, seven cents a pound; and number 3, five cents a pound. We picked twice a week for three weeks, beginning with three hundred pounds, the first picking, to a thousand pounds at the height of the season. It brought a tidy sum of money—enough to meet all the needs of Umma and Papa.

The news of our successful cucumber farming spread to all the neighboring farmers, who all happened to be Koreans. They all switched their farms from carnations to cucumbers. I went around and told them to have their soil analyzed.

"Never heard of such a thing," they admonished me.

I warned them about the cutworms.

"Been farming all my life, but never heard of 'cutworms.'" They lost nearly half of their crop to cutworms.

Then came the mildew. I pleaded, "Ajutsi!—Uncle—please burn that patch with white spots right away!"

"Burn?" He put me in my place. "What do you know about farming? Burn perfectly good-looking plants?"

A few days later, I again visited their cucumber farms. A pitiful sight—the entire crop collapsed from mildew.

"Ajutsi," I said sorrowfully, "you should have burned the first mildew-infested plant."

"Nonsense," he said. "You know what happened the day before yesterday? A pregnant woman came to visit and walked all around the field!"

Another memorable family event at that time was the marriage of my baby sister, Mary. I wasn't even aware of any courting going on, nor did I have a glimpse of the young man doing the courting. He was among the many young men from California who came to Hawaii to engage in "national defense" projects in place of the draft for military service. Walter Lindauer, of German parentage, a patternmaker, came to Hawaii to work in the naval shipyards. I met him only days before the wedding. He seemed gentle and warm, but I was uncontrollably angry. Sister Mary had just begun her study at the University of Hawaii. The marriage would cut short her education, and Walter Lindauer was the cause of it.

I was rather surprised, however, that Umma and Papa readily consented, and the wedding ceremony took place in our living room on Anapuni Street, Papa conducting and attesting to their marriage vows. I didn't know where or how they were going to spend their honeymoon. I was only sad to see Sister Mary move out of the house to live with her husband in a house only a few blocks away. My fury and anger didn't subside. One evening, I even tried to pick a fight with my new brother-in-law. The unreasonable fury wouldn't leave me for a long, long time—until the day baby Sister Mary gave birth to her first child, a beautiful girl named Ruth. Papa promptly attached a Korean middle name, Myung Jin (Bright Star).

She was my first niece, whom I loved and treasured dearly. All my anger disappeared, and I was at a loss as to how I could beg for my brother-in-law's forgiveness. I merely remained silent on the subject and allowed time to heal the wound. Life certainly has its strange twists and turns. In time, Walter, whom we all called Lindy, the patternmaker, blossomed into a poet and a painter. His poems always searched for the deeper meanings of life, and his paintings of unusual technique—delicate and microscopic etchings in black and white—

were like the delicate weaving of a silkworm. Their ethereal images provoked the imagination and reached out and touched the universe. Neither his poems nor his paintings caught the eye of the commercial world, but Lindy refused to compromise; he kept his faith in himself and in his art.

Moreover, he and Mary reared, in addition to Ruth, two bright and handsome sons, Paul and Karl. I attended Paul's (the older son) wedding. Now an architectural draftsman, he married the beautiful daughter of an old California family. It was Hawaiian style: outdoors and full of flowers, leis, and music.

Karl, the younger son, was a talented pianist. Before his graduation from high school, he gave a recital. It was the brilliant performance of a teenager showing potential for a great musical career. Alas, it was not to be. He traded his music for a girl and got married.

As for me, I hadn't yet found an answer to my predicament. To be a farmer was a challenge, but the fun lasted just one cucumber season. The farmer's world was not for me. I had to find some occupation, a skilled labor, a trade, not to mention a self-identity.

While pondering this dilemma, I ran into a young fellow who casually mentioned, "Say, Peter; they need a rodboy where I work. You wanna take the job?"

Without knowing what and where the job was, I said, "Sure, why not!"

The following day, I became an instant "rodboy." The job was in Pearl Harbor, the biggest U.S. naval base in the Pacific. The job of a rodboy was just that—hold up a seven-foot rod marked with measurements at designated points for the surveyor to take a reading with his instrument. I felt foolish holding up the rod eight hours a day. But I liked getting up at the crack of dawn, packing a lunch pail, catching a ride to Pearl Harbor, punching a time card, and starting work at 8:00 A.M. I liked the feeling of being a worker.

Moreover, I became interested in finding out the purpose of the mysterious operation. After several weeks of work as a good, reliable rodboy, I became friendly with the "levelman." He was the man who took the readings through an instrument called the "level," secured on a tripod. Every day, I would ply him admiringly and respectfully with new questions. He would respond with pride and tell me he was drawing a topographical map. It was intriguing; I had never heard of such a map—a map of the horizontal contours of the land. The more admiration I showed, the more he was willing to exhibit and explain his knowledge.

As the ultimate reward for my faithful work, one day he offered me the level to look through and take a reading. Gratefully, I looked into the instrument and read the measurement; it was in feet and inches. He then looked through the instrument and checked my reading and declared it was correct. "Say, Peter, it's right on the gnat's ass!" I learned "gnat's ass" was his favorite description of accuracy.

The work of a rodboy was not always monotonous and boring—for instance, the day we had to crawl under a giant, empty water tank to take measurements. While lying on my back under the tank and taking measurements, the immense tank exploded with sounds like thunder. No one had told us there were welders inside the empty tank driving rivets. There was no way to escape. We had to lie there and take the punishment. When the riveting stopped, we would resume our work, only to be stopped again by the machine-gun fire inside the empty tank. Finally, when we crawled out, my ears were ringing and my head felt as if it had been emptied of its brains by the man-made thunder, leaving only an empty chamber filled with dull echoes of the painful explosion. I do believe that is how my hearing was damaged and that it caused the gradual loss of hearing.

I soon became his assistant. He would send someone else to hold the rod and let me stay with him and write down his readings. All the observed elevations were based on a point with an established elevation, called the "benchmark." After months of work I had earned enough of his confidence that he let me take his place whenever he felt like taking it easy. I not only took the readings and recorded them, but also drew the topographical graph from the notes. That was the whole function of a levelman.

Every day was an adventure; we never knew what sort of work we would be performing until we arrived for work at 8:00 A.M. and our levelman picked up the job assignment for the day. The assignment varied each day, but usually it was a simple, routine job like checking the foundations of barracks or laying out grades for a new road. But every now and then there were surprises.

The greatest surprise I had was checking the measurements of a giant airplane hanger—150 feet wide, 200 feet long, and 100 feet high. Checking the measurement of the building on the ground was easy enough. But we had to climb up the steel girders to the roof of the hanger and take measurements. To do that, the rear chainman— that was me—held the steel tape at one end; the head chainman walked across the hanger and took the measurement. After releasing the chain, I had to walk across and continue with the measuring. The "I" beam that spanned the hanger was barely six inches wide. I saw the steel workers standing straight up and walking across the beam, not minding that they were over a hundred feet up. As hard as I tried to convince myself it wasn't too difficult, I couldn't stand up on that narrow beam. I kneeled and slowly crawled on all fours.

"Don't look down!" my partner screamed, "or you'll freeze." I didn't understand what he meant.

"What's freeze?" I asked.

"If you freeze while crossing the beam," my partner explained patiently, "you will become immobilized; you will become frozen to the steel beam, unable to go forward or backward."

"What happens then?"

"Then we would have to bring a super fire truck ladder, climb up, pry you loose, and hand you down."

As frightened as I was, I refused to freeze.

In six months, I mastered all the tricks of a rodboy as well as all the science of a levelman—and then it happened. One morning, the levelman failed to show up for work. The boss called me into his office and asked, "Peter, do you think you can handle this job?" and handed me a roll of blueprints; it was a road-grading layout.

"Sure, Mr. Jones, I can do it."

"Well, take it."

That was how I was able to get my foot in the door of a new trade: surveying.

There remained one more hurdle, that of a "transitman." This was much more complicated work, using an instrument called a transit. The transitman not only had to align a perfectly straight line, but also had to lay out and check degrees of curvature. Just as a navigator would chart the course of the ship, the transitman would stake out the curve of a road for the road builder to follow. The work of the transitman seemed almost like magic. Aspiring to elevate myself to the higher position, I spent evenings restudying my high school geometry; and now as a levelman, I worked closely with the transitman.

And, of course, I had to show my respect for his superior rank.

Such recognition of rank was very important in all trades, I discovered; in carpentry, in electrical wiring, and plumbing, or with operators of all kinds of machinery. By according him complete respect, I earned the friendship of the transitman, who in turn accorded me opportunities to ply him with questions. He was only too eager to display his knowledge and skill. Soon, he allowed me to look through the transit and check the alignment. And without any strenuous effort I became, ipso facto, his assistant.

The first anniversary of my employment as a rodboy was approaching. I was proud to realize what a faithful and loyal worker I had been; I hadn't missed a day, hadn't been late to work, and hadn't made any serious mistakes. As though in recognition, Mr. Jones, the boss, one day called me into his office once again.

"Peter," he called in a serious tone, "we need another transitman." He paused, and I felt my heart beating faster. "Do you think you can handle the transit?"

I had to be very cautious with my answer. I replied with deliberate hesitation, "Well, Mr. Jones, you can try me."

"Yes," Mr. Jones announced, "I have already decided." Handing me a set of blueprints, he said, "These are the new offices we are building. Study it in the office this afternoon. Ask any questions you have, and let me know if you can handle the job."

That was the day that gave birth to a brand-new, full-fledged surveyor. I was especially pleased with the raise in pay, enabling me to make a larger contribution to Sister Alice's family budget. That was October 1941. Within two months my new job was to be rudely interrupted by the Japanese attack on Pearl Harbor.

December 7, 1941, was a Sunday, my day off, when I could sleep all morning. But a loud radio woke me. Irritated, I said, "Hey! Turn that damn radio off!"

"Peter, get up and listen!" someone yelled back.

"What's going on?" I slowly sat up on my bed.

"Pearl Harbor is being bombed!" I heard distant rumbles and the tatooing sounds of machine guns.

"Boy, they sure know how to make their military maneuvers realistic." I knew the U.S. fleet had just returned to Pearl Harbor after staging extensive maneuvers in the Pacific. I took it for granted that the broadcast was the climactic conclusion of those maneuvers.

Reluctantly, I got up, washed, and sat at the table for breakfast.

The radio kept blaring, broadcasting a blow-by-blow account of the bombing. Now they named the attacker—the Japanese! That was most puzzling. Why hadn't they identified the attacker during all the hours of broadcasting? Still disbelieving, I began to listen more carefully.

Several hours later, the bombing had ceased and the broadcast began describing the results: serious damage to two battleships, one cruiser, and two destroyers. Fortunately, the aircraft carriers had not followed the fleet to Pearl Harbor; they were still out in the open sea. The account also mentioned damage to a dry dock and some buildings. Any human casualties were unknown. The unbelievable report began to sink in, and serious questions surged in my mind: "Will they come back to finish the job? Will they land on the island for military occupation?"

Toward evening, the broadcast repeated warnings against the Japanese attack and possible landing. The advisory also ordered citizens to remain indoors and to report to police any suspicious acts or movements of people. The atmosphere around the house was becoming tense. Five of us were in the house: me, big Sister Alice, her son Wellie, younger Brother Paul and our boarder, a Korean college student named Thomas Choi. The heavy load on the telephone lines made it practically useless, but after repeated tries, we got through and reached the house in Kaimuki where Papa and Umma lived with Brothers Joshua and David and Sister Mary. We assured each other all was well. My father was furious. He got on the phone and shouted with anger, "I told the dumb commanding general at Fort Shafter the Japanese were planning to attack Hawaii, but he wouldn't listen!"

For the following two days, I was forced to remain at home and listen to the radio. All traffic into Pearl Harbor was halted—nobody could get in or out. A special notice was given to all civilian employees to stay away. Then on the evening of the second day, the naval authorities notified all employees to report to work the next day. A series of emergency laws had been promulgated by the military, including an Island-wide blackout from sundown to sunrise and a curfew forbidding any presence on the street after sundown.

Early the next morning when it was still dark, following military orders, we drove without any lights to Pearl Harbor. It was dawn when we got there. Even before arriving at the main gate, I saw shrapnel scattered on the road. They had no time to clean up the souvenirs left by the Japanese bombers. Another new procedure was the body search of everyone boarding the ferry that took us to Ford Island, where we worked.

On the ferry, chugging along across the broad harbor, I could see the havoc wreaked by the Sunday morning surprise attack. All the dry docks were a panorama of skeletons of twisted steel beams with ships toppled over, and the three-story buildings that housed the navy personnel were not there. When we reached the dock on Ford Island, I saw the real destruction. The heavyweights of the U.S. naval power, the battleships, were all sunk. Only their super-structures showed above water. The war bulletins over the radio had reported two battleships "damaged" in addition to one cruiser and a destroyer. I learned then that the war bulletins were not factual reports, but screened fabrications for the public.

The most horrible sight I saw was in the middle of the channel where the airplane tender had been anchored. The ship, with a complement of more than three hundred sailors, was completely sunk in the deep water. Knowing everyone on the ship had drowned, not even an attempt was made to save any life or to raise the ship. We used to throw a fishing line out into the channel before starting work, and when we quit, we would pull in the line and take the fish home. "No more fishing in the channel," we ruefully said to each other. "They are too fat feeding on sailors!"

With the bombing of Pearl Harbor, the life-styles of everyone living on the islands changed. All island security was placed under emergency martial law. Even a traffic ticket required an appearance before a military marshal. All ships handling passengers as well as cargo were commandeered by the military, curtailing shipments of food and beverages from the mainland on which the population of Hawaii depended. There was an immediate frenzy of food hoarding, rapidly depleting all grocery stock.

It seemed alcoholic beverages were even more precious than food. All existing supplies of liquor on the islands were frozen. Everyone of drinking age was required to carry an official permit to buy alcoholic beverages. The drinking population suddenly rose to almost 100 percent of all males and females twenty-one years of age or over. No one in our family drank very much, but we obtained four permits. When a new shipment of booze arrived in Honolulu from the mainland, the military government announced the date of sale. For a day or two, business on the island was at the liquor dispensing stores. Each one with a permit had the choice—provided they were in stock—of a case of beer, a bottle of whiskey, or two bottles of wine. With four permits, our family obtained two whiskey rations and one each of beer and wine. Our drinking friends had their standing orders to pick up the liquor at our home at cost.

Under the military, Hawaii also had a total blackout from sunset to sunrise—the only place in the United States and its territories to have such a blackout. As it turned out, it was not necessary. The Japanese force, except for a few sneak submarine attacks, never returned to Hawaii. The blackout not only wiped out all evening activities such as the movie theatres, restaurants, and saloons, but replaced them with drinking and gambling in the house with blackout curtains drawn. Undoubtedly every night there must have been innumerable and bizarre things happening to people all over Honolulu, including me.

On Saturday nights my friends and I would gather at a designated house prepared for an all night poker game. I would arrive before dark with my bedding and one case of beer I had just obtained from the liquor store. All together there were seven of us with seven cases of beer. After a few rounds of beer, we settled at a poker table, each buying twenty dollars worth of chips. Also, each player—except me—placed a stack of twenty dollars bills behind their chips. The game we played was "table stakes"—one could bet as much as he had on the table. Money was no object; everyone worked on defense projects, and got paid high wages, but with the blackout had nowhere to spend the money.

The boys were especially glad to have me come to the poker game, because I always lost. However, I saw to it that my loss would not exceed fifty dollars. The rest were playing for high stakes, and their winnings or losses mounted into the hundreds. What really set me down was not the loss of money, but the continuous flow of beer through the whole night. They were all good drinkers, and they seemed determined to deplete the entire seven cases of beer. It was awesome to see them emptying bottle after bottle with no visible effect. With a concerted effort I drank three bottles—the absolute limit—and I paid dearly for the sin.

At the crack of dawn, having lost all of my fifty dollars, I picked up my bedding and took leave of the gamblers. I got in the car feeling the unsettling effects of three bottles of beer. I managed to get out of the driveway and turn onto the street. For a split second, all my senses lapsed. While blinking desperately to regain control, I felt the ground rocking under me. In that instant the car plunged into a ditch. The noise and the jolt sobered me, but too late. I was able to get out of the car and survey the scene—I needed help. I returned to the house to see the boys winding down their last game of poker.

"I crashed my car into the ditch," I announced.

"What!" They gave a collective yell.

"Wait, Peter," one of them pleaded, "wait till we finish this last hand." I had to stand there and watch them settle all the accounts: cashing in chips, counting their winnings and losses.

"All right, Peter, let's go and see. . . ." The six boys filed out and followed me to the scene.

"Say, that's a beauty!"

"Lucky you didn't fall in all the way."

"I'll go get my car," one of them volunteered. "With the chain I have, we might pull the car out of the ditch."

They worked as though they had pulled cars out of ditches all their lives. The chain was secured on the bumper of my car and the driver spit out orders: "When I give you the signal, you guys give all you got and push the car."

I only stood there watching and hoping the rear bumper of my car wouldn't fall off.

"All right, you guys, get ready." The driver raced his engine a few times, then yelled, "NOW!" The engine roared and the guys gave a mighty heave, screaming, "Let's go!"

I couldn't believe my eyes. My car leaped over the ditch and bounced on the road. I never went back to the poker game and I never drank three bottles of beer again.

Having mastered the use of the level and the transit, I considered myself a full-fledged surveyor. With a year's work I graduated from rodboy to surveyor. More than anything else, I was grateful and proud to have found a new trade to earn a living since leaving the theatre two years before. Working for a defense contractor in Pearl Harbor, I not only learned a trade but also received some valuable lessons in economics. I discovered that all defense contracts were awarded on "cost-plus" basis. The government paid the contractor for all the costs of material and labor plus a given percentage of the cost as profit; the higher the cost, the bigger the profit. The contractor had no trouble padding and raising the cost. The sure method was waste—rampant waste of material and labor.

I witnessed such an operation while working on a new airfield on Ford Island. I did the surveying and laying out of the runway; its dimensions and grades. First a fleet of tractors excavated two feet down the entire planned airfield, nearly a mile long and two hundred feet wide. Then came the graders, who leveled the ground and determined the rise and fall as well as drainage of the field. The equipment and labor for the runway foundation alone must have cost a small fortune. Next, a fleet of dump trucks hauled in crushed rock from a quarry many miles away. First, no. 1 rock, or the coarse pieces. When the entire field was covered, steamrollers rolled over them and pressed them down.

Next came truckloads of no. 2 rocks—medium-sized crushed rocks. The relay of dump trucks continued until the entire field was covered. In came the steamrollers. They rolled over and over and pressed down the second layer of rocks. Then the dump trucks hauled in no. 3 rocks—finely crushed rocks. It took several days to cover the whole field with the last layer of rocks for its foundation, and a few more days to roll over them to tamp and press the rocks down. Then came the last stage of constructing the runway—covering the field with asphalt. The asphalt plant was also miles away from Pearl Harbor. A relay of dump trucks loaded with hot asphalt kept pouring it over the rocks, immediately followed by the steamroller. It took several days to finish paving the runway. I thought there should be some sort of celebration; there was none.

Several days later, one morning I was horrified to see tractors digging up the newly paved runway. It was like throwing mud on a newly painted masterpiece. What madness, I thought; who could have ordered such a sacrilege? Yes, it was the cost-plus contractors. Belatedly they tested the temperature of the asphalt and discovered it was some degrees below the required temperature. So they plowed it under and paved the field all over again. No, they didn't test the asphalt's temperature at the plant. They took its temperature after it reached the airfield and the paving was almost finished. So, they repeated the whole process of cleaning up the used asphalt, retamping and rolling the foundation, and resurfacing the runway with new asphalt of the correct temperature. In short, the contractors more than doubled the cost of building the runway.

I didn't try to figure what the final figure of the "cost-plus" contract was, and what it must have cost the U.S. government—the taxpayers. It was all the more frightening when you realized that the same "planned" inefficiency was being perpetrated all over the Pacific: on Kwajalein, Midway, Wake, and Guam, to mention only a few. The defrauding and cheating of the U.S. government for billions of dollars was a common practice long before the Pentagon procurement scandal of 1988.

There is one thing we can be sure of: Life moves on, and with it my destiny. I had to get out of the tragic confines of Pearl Harbor. I applied for a job with the U.S. Corps of Engineers—the responsible body for all military construction not under the control of the U.S. Navy. The job was for a surveyor. On the basis of my experience, I was hired as a chief-of-party in charge of a surveying team. Under me, I had a levelman (I was the transitman) and two rodboys, plus the use of a Chevrolet station wagon. The job was also accompanied by a good raise in pay.

It was a terribly responsible job, and I wondered if I hadn't overreached myself. There was no room for any mistakes. My job assignment varied from day to day: locating sites for new barracks, recreation halls, office buildings, and laying out all access roads. I really had to study the blueprints before going out in the field, where I double-checked the benchmarks for elevation and the "azimuth" for positioning the building correctly. With sheer daring and guts, I survived the first months of initiation as a chief-of-party. My year's experience on Ford Island paid valuable dividends. I could tell the rodboys how to execute their job properly and to critically review the charts of the levelman. Together, we earned the respect of the supervisors as dependable, first-rate surveyors.

My one-year tenure with the U.S. Corps of Engineers produced two notable events. First, the most dramatic undertaking: One day, I was casually handed the day's work. I looked at the blueprint and shuddered. I was to go out to Barber's Point and lay out a complex fifteen-inch gun emplacement. The island was dotted with these long-range artillery as its first line of defense. Each gun had to be placed so as to provide for 180-degree coverage of firepower for a given area. It was of vital importance that duplication as well as dead open space be avoided. The idea of the enemy fleet sneaking through a dead spot of the artillery due to an error I might make made my heart palpitate.

After locating the gun emplacement, I had to lay out the narrow-gauge railway for transporting the heavy shells from the ammunition dump to the underground gun emplacement. There were a few curves I had to chart for the railroad—I was never too sure of figuring out the curvature. But miraculously, I completed the survey, and the huge gun and all of its accoutrements were in place. Fortunately or unfortunately, I didn't have the privilege of witnessing the test firing of the big gun.

The second memorable event took place in the impenetrable jungle of lantana and *kiawe* bushes on the Waianae hills overlooking the Pacific. I had the job of cutting through the bushes and surveying for a road. I never asked what it was for. My two rodboys, wielding razor-sharp cane knives, did a noble job of opening a path for my line and the offset markers. On our second day, as we cut through the bush, we heard the frantic squeals of wild pigs. Sure enough, we reached a nest of baby pigs; the mother pig had fled. I felt terribly guilty; I picked up one of the baby pigs and brought it home.

I built a cozy sty with a supply of water. I also bought a baby bottle with extra nipples and a supply of Carnation evaporated milk. The wild baby pig, whom I named "Waazo," took to the bottle with surprising zest. I prevailed on my Sister Alice to feed the baby while I was away at work. But I always cuddled him (I wasn't sure of its sex) and fed him his evening meal. I would call him by his name, "Waazo, Waazo, Waazo," to familiarize him with his name and my voice before giving him his bottle. Soon he responded to my call like a puppy.

I could now take him out of his cage, call him, and feed him. He was more than ready for solid foods. He gobbled up everything put in his bowl—leftover foods from the table, meats, vegetables, and rice. He loved rice! When three months old, he began to show tusks protruding at the sides of his snout. He still answered my call, "Waazo! Waazo!" and followed me wherever I went. I would even take a walk on the street with Waazo following me like a poodle. He grew fast and fat and his tusks longer and more fierce. The neighbors began complaining; their children were frightened to go out on the street. "Keep your wild pig off the street," they said.

I had no choice. I had a friend with a farm who raised pigs. He was delighted to have Waazo in his pigsty. He said the wild pig would make an excellent breeder with his domestic pigs. I drove Waazo to the farm and bid him a fond farewell. I swear he looked lost and sad in the sty with the other pigs.

A few months later, I went to the farm to visit Waazo. I looked into the sty and couldn't find him. I walked up to the house and asked my friend, "Say, where is Waazo?"

"He's gone," he said.

"Gone? Where?"

"Well, we slaughtered and ate him."

My heart sank. How could you? My baby Waazo! Ate him? Ate him?

# 9

## GOING

## TO

## WAR

Meanwhile, the war raged on. Hitler's Nazi hordes broke through the vaunted Maginot Line, which was to repel all invasions of France from the north. Practically unopposed, the German army marched through the Rhineland and headed for Paris. On the Eastern Front, the German army overran the Soviet Ukraine and pointed south toward Stalingrad. Italy's Fascist Mussolini, too, was having a field day. To conquer northern Africa, he began attacking Ethiopia. And the third member of the Axis, Japan, following the sneak attack on Pearl Harbor, was picking off and occupying islands in the Pacific. They demolished U.S. defenses, occupied the Philippines, and penetrated deep into China. They proclaimed Pan-Asian sovereignty over all Asia.

Forced to declare war against Japan, America waged an internal war against all Japanese in the United States—citizens and noncitizens alike. All Japanese in California and the West Coast, as well as in other areas, were rounded up and shipped to hastily erected concentration camps, all of which were located in inaccessible, remote areas of the country. No such policy was ever directed toward the Germans in the United States nor toward the Italians. Only toward the Japanese. This was an unforgivable blunder of President Roosevelt and his military advisers, a shameful blemish on the history of America that will never be wiped off America's conscience.

It was 1944, and I could no longer remain a civilian, driving around in a station wagon, pushing a transit and earning a fat wage. I enlisted. But getting into the army was not so easy for me. First, they were doubtful about my age—thirty-eight. Then they saw the scar on my back, a reminder of spinal surgery in 1940 for a slipped lumbar disc. When I insisted I was physically fit, they asked if I would sign a disability waiver. Of course I did; I would sign anything. My enlistment was approved; I was going to war to kill or be killed. I bid farewell to Umma and Papa, my brothers and sisters, and all my friends. In a few days, wearing an ill-fitting uniform, I joined the young inductees and boarded a liberty ship sailing off to San Francisco. We were heading to army camps for basic training.

Normally the trip to San Francisco took three days, but our ship followed an irregular zigzag course to evade Japanese submarines, so the crossing took seven days. For seven days and nights, five hundred inductees and enlisted men were locked up in a ship with no radio, nothing to read, and nothing to do. So the ship instantly transformed into a floating gambling palace. Everyone carried all the money they had saved working on defense projects. They were all going to war and had no inclination to leave any money behind. With the probable minimum of two thousand dollars each one carried, there was a million dollars, all in cash, floating aboard our ship.

The gambling was conducted on the floor in the hold or on the deck above. With no arm of the law to interfere, we could gamble unafraid from early morning until late at night, breaking only for meals. There were a few games of crap, but predominantly it was poker. It seemed somehow the professional or near-professional gamblers infiltrated our group and conducted well-organized gambling. All the poker games were run by "housemen" who dealt the cards, called the bets, and took a small cut from each hand. There were games for the small-fries with one-dollar limits and three raises. For the adventurous, there were games with limits of five, ten and twenty dollars; and, of course, for the big fish, there was the "table stakes" game.

The perennial losses at poker in Honolulu still fresh in my memory, I meekly sat in at a one-dollar limit game. I was all nerves. Then a very strange thing happened; I couldn't lose! I would draw two pairs, three of a kind, and even a straight, flush, or full house. The luck held all day, and I won a sizable amount. Well, I had nothing to lose; I joined the game with higher stakes. At the five-dollar limit game, my luck held. I was raking it in. I grew so confident, I even bluffed and won. This kind of winning streak went on for several days, and my winnings were growing by leaps and bounds.

Why not ride my luck and join the big time? On the fourth or fifth day, while our ship pitched and rolled, I got a seat at the ten-dollar-limit game. I took the poor suckers for a ride. I just could not lose! I began to be cruel. At a seven-card stud game, with nothing showing, I would raise. The one with an ace showing would raise me back, and without hesitation I would raise again. And invariably, I would draw a triple and beat the other guy's two pairs. I couldn't believe I was really winning the kind of money bulging in my pocket.

I raised my sights and joined the twenty dollar game. Same thing; I still couldn't lose. It was as though a magic spell had been cast over me. I even thought perhaps it was a divine reward for my patriotic move to join the army and go to war. Whatever it was, I couldn't stop winning. Soon, a rumor spread among the soldiers that there was a "card shark" aboard—me!

On the last day on the gambling ship, I joined the table stakes game with no limits on raises. This was big-time gambling; a dog-eat-dog affair with no quarter given. Yet I was calm and confident—I only had to let lady luck take care of me. And she did. I won two out of three hands I played. Each pot was worth several hundred dollars. When the bell for the evening chow sounded, I picked up my winnings and walked away. And I did what I thought was a smart thing; I didn't go back for more. Next morning at sunrise, our ship passed under the Golden Gate Bridge and docked at the military pier at McNeil Island. Only after we landed and were deposited in barren barracks and I found a quiet corner did I dare take out all of the stuffed money and count it. It was more than five thousand dollars. I wished those poker players in Honolulu who took all my money could see the bundle I had won. I found a bank at the post and immediately purchased five thousand dollars in traveler's checks. The small fortune stood me in good stead throughout my basic training. Every Sunday I would take a few soldiers with me to town and treat them to a rich brunch. When they saw me signing a check for payment, they would ask, "Are you a millionaire's son?"

From McNeil Island, we were loaded in boxcars and took off. No one knew where we were going. After a couple of days and nights, we were told that we were headed for Fort Sill, Oklahoma. It sounded like a never-never land. I found Oklahoma a bleak, deserted land, especially with the winter wind kicking up dirty-brown dust.

But this was what I had asked for, and I was prepared for the worst. The basic training got underway. It didn't take long to learn what was really basic: discipline and regimentation. All our activities and movements were done by the numbers. We did nothing unless we heard an order, barked by the sergeant, the lieutenant, and sometimes by the captain. There was no such thing as daily routine; every movement and activity was performed by orders.

When the wake-up bell rang, no extra snoozing was allowed. We were expected to jump out of our bunks, get our teeth brushed, faces washed, rush back to our bunks, make our beds, and stand at attention for inspection. The sergeant marched down the aisle, checking that every bed appeared neat and properly made up. Invariably, he would stop at one or two beds judged not properly made and pull off the covers. The occupants would rush over and make the beds over again. Each violation was called "a geek" and punished with either latrine duty (cleaning the toilets) or kitchen duty (peeling potatoes and washing pots and pans).

The next bell was for breakfast. Rush over, get in line, hold out your mess kit, and let the kitchen helper fill it, usually with scrambled eggs and fried potatoes and bread. The Sunday special had a piece of bacon added, and if one hurried, he could run back for a second piece—but he had to be sure to finish all food in thirty minutes.

Now we had fifteen minutes to attend to our personal needs and report for drills in the field. The drills were also designed to discipline the soldiers and train them to instantly respond to commands. "Attention!" "At ease!" "Attention!" "At ease!" Over and over again. "Forward, march!" "Company halt!" "Forward, march!" "Company halt!" Over and over again. "To the rear . . . march!" "To the rear . . . march!" Over and over again. It seemed silly at times, but the result was that we could execute the steps in our sleep. That was exactly the purpose of basic training: to have everyone in the group perform in unison, whatever the command, without question, without hesitation. After the rough first two weeks, our company began to move smoothly, responding to all the commands, including some quite complicated ones.

We were then given training in artillery—Fort Sill was the artillery training center for the U.S. Army. Our assignment was to master the handling of 105-millimeter howitzer artillery pieces; after studying the mechanics of the gun, we began learning its operation. Here again, the important factor was discipline. A squad of six men was assigned to each gun. At the command, we took our positions. At the next command, two men picked up the shell and passed it to the gunners. They slid the shell into the breach and locked it. At the third command, the sighter spun and set the gun for the proper trajectory. The last command was for one member of the crew to pull the lanyard and fire the gun. The six men manning the gun rotated their positions so that every one could step into any position and perform. The target some miles away was unseen, so the firing depended solely on the mathematical computation of distance to the target. My brief career as a surveyor came in very handy. Each firing was observed, and it was reported to the gun crew how far they had missed; for example, clockwise, to eleven o'clock, and the distance over or under the target. The sighter would make a quick adjustment and fire again. Again the report of the miss. It was adjusted and fired again until the shell hit the mark and exploded.

Usually, the howitzers were used against enemy infantry positions, more as harassment than for destruction. But the bull's-eyes and near bull's-eyes could tear up an uncountable number of soldiers in the enemy trenches. No record was kept on a gun crew, so I had no idea how our crew fared in the hits and misses. But in my M-1 rifle firing, I got not only the score but the target as proof. My ROTC experience with the rifle served me well; I received a medal for "sharpshooter" and the two stripes of a corporal.

The military training became more and more realistic as our basic training advanced. We were given instructions on how to deal with malaria-carrying mosquitos and with women who carried gonorrhea and syphilis. As practical training, when leaving camp and going to town, we were required to carry a small prophylactic kit—we called it a pro-kit—with us. The kit contained two condoms, a piece of soap, and a tiny towel. But the most serious training dealt with nighttime operations. Among them was the use of a compass at night to find our way to our own outfits. In the dead of night, we would be driven out of the camp and dumped in some remote wilderness miles away. By using the compass, we were supposed to find our way back to the camp. Being the corporal, I was responsible for my squad. Reading the map and the compass by lighted matches, we groped our way, through the wilderness like a bunch of blind men. After hours of heavy breathing and fright, we saw the lights of our camp. There were some squads who got lost, and a search party had to be dispatched to look for them.

Another type of night training was in the simulated mine fields. A stretch of an empty field was seeded with military land mines; the only thing missing in them was dynamite. It was replaced with a pinch of gun powder that, when touched off, would make a deafening noise as though a hundred firecrackers were exploding simultaneously. Every squad would stretch out, crawl on hands and knees to cover every inch of the field, and search for the mines, presumably planted by the enemy. When a mine was detected, with the aid of a flashlight we would carefully disconnect the wire and defuse the mine. It was very slow and tedious work; but it was a life and death matter, and in spite of the cold night, we would all sweat. Every now and then we would hear the explosions go off: They were reminders for us of how many men would have been torn to pieces. Fortunately, my squad came through the field unscathed.

The most miserable operation was the night maneuver. Carrying our duffle bags, we marched through and around the woods. Without exception, the winter in Oklahoma was the coldest I had ever lived through. Six inches of snow did not help. When the marching ended around midnight, we were given the command to bivouac. We would open up our duffle bags, pull out and pitch the pup-tent, take out our sleeping bags, and spread them over the snow. To prepare myself for such an ordeal, I took a trip to Oklahoma City the week before. There, I got in a taxi and asked the driver to take me where I could buy some liquor.

The state of Oklahoma at the time was a "dry" state. Alcoholic beverages were outlawed. For that very reason, there was more liquor flowing in Oklahoma than in the neighboring "wet" states. One only had to know where the flow was. The taxi driver was the natural guide. The driver took me through a dark alley and stopped. I got out and climbed a dark stairway to the second floor. Someone looked through a peephole and opened the door. Inside, I was amazed to see shelves loaded with an elaborate display of bottles like any ordinary liquor store. I asked for a pint of scotch.

"What kind?" the man asked.

"Do you have Johnny Walker?"

"Red or black?"

"Give me the red label."

"Fifteen dollars."

Fifteen dollars for a pint of scotch in 1944, plus the cost of the taxi and bus ride to the city, made it a very expensive bottle. But it was worth all the trouble and money. Before hitting the sack in the snow, I opened the bottle and began guzzling—the only way to keep myself from freezing. After a while, I felt sufficiently numb and didn't feel a thing lying in the sleeping bag on the snow.

The six weeks of basic training was coming to an end. Everyone began fidgeting mentally. Where would they be assigned? The outfit they dreaded the most was the infantry. As I was mulling over my fate, the company commander, a captain, took me aside and asked, "How would you like to go to officer training school?"

I was speechless for a second, but I found my answer. "No, thank you, sir." Frankly, I didn't want to leave all my GI friends.

Equally surprised, the captain took a deep breath and asked, "Where would you like to go?"

"The military language school at Fort Snelling, sir."

With army travel papers, I took the long journey by train and bus from Fort Sill, Oklahoma, to Minneapolis, Minnesota. Fort Snelling in Minneapolis was a solid old establishment: three-story brick buildings lined in a row facing a well-landscaped court with a lawn and old fruit trees.

I reported to the office and presented my papers. The officer in charge asked which language I was interested in studying, Chinese or Japanese. "Japanese," I answered. Since my purpose in enlisting was to reach Korea, it seemed the Japanese language rather than Chinese promised a shorter road to Korea.

The dormitories in the brick buildings were completely filled, necessitating a number of temporary tents, each heated by a wood-burning, pot-bellied stove. It was April, a time for the warmth of spring. But the Oklahoma winter followed me, and it was freezing cold. In fact, it snowed toward the end of May, nipping all the blossoms off the fruit trees.

I began attending my Japanese class. I judged it was an intermediate course, consisting of conversation, reading, and writing. When I was growing up in Seoul, I was forced to study Japanese. Even though I had hated it, I still remembered some of the Japanese that was pounded into me from the age of eight until I was thirteen. At the sounds of Japanese spoken in class, some of the words and phrases would be roused from my memory and pop into life. I began remembering and speaking Japanese I hadn't used for over thirty years and had thought forgotten. Every day I discovered new words and expressions, and most interestingly, good pronunciation and intonation as well. Similarly, in writing, the visions of Japanese characters would appear in my head, and I would write them down on paper.

It was a crash course, five hours of class every day. The language study was oriented toward military application. When we graduated in four months, we were expected to interrogate Japanese prisoners of war and translate captured Japanese military documents. Every Saturday morning we practiced such field problems. An interesting sidelight was the assignment for me to lead the weekly orientation meetings. Moreover, I was given free reign to select whatever subject related to the war, present it, and have the group discuss it. It was quite an honor and an opportunity. We spent a lot of time discussing the relations of the Allied nations as well as their leaders. We discussed racial discrimination, especially within the U.S. Armed Forces. The discussions brought to light the level of the GIs' education, intellect, and interest; it was not too high.

Sundays, two to three hundred GIs would desert the confines of the camp and descend on the city of Minneapolis. The most important thing for everyone was to find a good restaurant and indulge in belly stuffing. An enterprising Japanese family appeared and opened a restaurant in the center of the city. Their Sunday business from dawn to dusk must have made up for the weekdays' slack. With a full stomach, the GIs' next interest was searching for girls. The USO (United Service Organization) was a fun place. There were pool, ping-pong, and card tables (no gambling), and dancing with the hostesses to the radio or phonograph music. Dating, if any, was strictly "on the side." The USO hostesses were all respectable young ladies volunteering to entertain the lonely GIs.

The more desperate ones would take to the streets, or the more affluent ones would visit the hotels and motels. Always curious, I would join a bunch and accompany them on their street hunting. It was not only distasteful, but barbaric to see the GIs accosting and treating the streetwalkers like pieces of merchandise. They showed no shame or qualms bargaining with the girls. I never saw anyone walking away with a girl, so I surmised that they got their kicks just bantering with them. I was amazed to see that most of the girls walking the streets were American Indians. I had never seen or met any Indian girl.

Fortunately, I found another kind of Sunday diversion, I visited various churches. I was received with warm welcomes, and some of the parishioners took me to their homes after the service. It was most interesting to find out where they and their parents had come from; I found a preponderance of Germanic and Slavic roots. It was even more interesting to learn the kind of work they did and how they managed their living. My surprising discovery was that they all had the same humor and fun, as well as worries and trepidations, of Korean families living in Honolulu.

Near the end of the third month at Fort Snelling, I was called in by the commanding officer. Of course, I was anxious to know what prompted the unusual order. When I entered the office, the commander politely asked me to sit down, whereupon he took out a roll of white paper and handed it to me. "Corporal Hyun, this is your diploma," he said.

"But, sir," I didn't know quite what to say. "But, sir," I repeated, "I have another month to finish the school."

"Yes, I know," he smiled, "but we decided to graduate you sooner. Let me explain. They brought a bunch of Japanese prisoners of war from the Pacific theatre. They have been placed in Camp McCoy, Wisconsin. They need an interpreter right away, and you have been recommended to take the job."

I was completely baffled. "Sir, I would like to have finished the school. But if they really need me, I must go."

"That's the spirit, Corporal Hyun." He handed me the diploma and shook my hand.

"Sir, how soon do I have to be there?"

"Tomorrow. All papers are ready for you to travel and to report at the headquarters of Camp McCoy. And you are promoted to tech sergeant. Good luck." He shook my hand again.

Once more, with army travel papers, I was headed for another unfamiliar place. From Minneapolis, there was no shortcut to Wisconsin. I had to go to Chicago first by train; then by bus into Wisconsin. We skirted the city of Milwaukee, then the river town of LaCrosse. From there, it was less than an hour's ride to Camp McCoy. It turned out to be a vast, sprawling army base. Having so much ground, so many barracks, and a remote location, it was perfectly suited for a POW (prisoner of war) camp. They already had Italian prisoners occupying one enclosure, and a compound holding German prisoners. I never found out where they had come from. Now the latest addition was a separate compound for the Japanese POWs.

I was taken there by a captain the very next morning after my arrival. The prisoners, about 150 of them, stood in formation in the open field, and I was introduced to them as a new person in charge. I addressed them in the polite form of Japanese, calling them "anta"—the honorable "you," instead of "omae"—unworthy "you." I received no applause, but I detected no hostility. The group was dismissed, and I made a tour of the camp to see what sort of facilities they had and what their living conditions were.

In the course of this initial inspection, I got the biggest shock of my life; the prisoners were not Japanese, they were Koreans! Oh, what an outburst of mutual appreciation we all had. The Korean prisoners could hardly believe that they had traveled so far from their homeland to find a Korean-American soldier to look after them. Almost the entire week was spent in getting acquainted. There were endless questions both from them and from me. By gathering bits of information from each one of them, I was able to draw a fairly clear picture of their odyssey.

Almost all of them came from agricultural villages of eastern and northern provinces of Korea; there was no South Korea and North Korea then—only one Korea. They were seized by the Japanese military and shipped to Japan, where they were transferred to a bigger ship and taken to the Pacific islands seized by the Japanese: New Guinea, Guam, Marshall Islands, and so on. The Koreans were used as slave labor for the construction of military bases. The group of prisoners brought to Camp McCoy were all from the Marshall Islands. The Japanese there, both military and civilian, including women holding their children, jumped off cliffs into the sea to escape being captured by the Americans. The Koreans refused to commit suicide, were taken prisoner, and were brought to Camp McCoy.

When they were convinced that I was really a Korean in American uniform, they pleaded for their first request: rice. They hadn't eaten any rice for a long time; I understood. I made an urgent request for rice to the quartermaster, and within days sacks of rice were delivered to our camp. I ordered special rations of Chinese cabbage, chili, garlic, and ginger. Together with some meat I had obtained for them, their cooks prepared a feast of Korean food. They all believed I had performed a miracle. Within a week they had meals of rice and their beloved *kim-chee.*

Their next request was to have their letters sent to their homes. I had to disappoint them by informing them that, because of the war, no mail could be delivered to Korea. I could only promise that I would personally carry their letters when I went to Korea. Eventually, I was able to fulfill this promise by mailing some of their letters in Seoul. The letters carried the first news to their families that their sons were alive and well. Some of the prisoners showed me poems and songs they had composed, all about their yearning for their homeland; it was very touching and moving.

The commander of the camp, a captain, seldom visited the compound and couldn't care less what I did with the prisoners. I set aside a plot of land in the field and had them cultivate a vegetable garden. Eagerly, they plowed and planted their favorite vegetables: Chinese cabbage, radish and green onion for *kim-chee,* as well as lettuce and tomato for fresh salad. With their enthusiastic care, the garden thrived. They also built a coop and raised chickens. The eggs and chicken were served only on special occasions, such as someone's birthday.

In answer to their persistent requests, I also organized a class in English. Different groups attended the class during the day to learn formal as well as conversational English. They enjoyed imitating the English pronunciations, which to them were comical. Most of all, they enjoyed learning how to address a girl and what to say.

They were all very athletically inclined and loved to play baseball and soccer. Capitalizing on their interest, I organized a track meet, announcing the prize for the winners—a sight-seeing trip to town. The feelings ran high, and they all began training for the event. I recruited a few GIs to help me run the track meet. Amidst a holiday atmosphere, the track meet opened on a Saturday, with a number of GIs and officers attending. The first event was the one hundred-yard dash. After a number of heats, running barefoot or in heavy boots, the winners ran against each other in the final. Next came the high jump. In their heavy prisoner's garb and bare feet, jumping and negotiating the crossbar was more comical than inspiring. The prisoners as well as the GIs and the officers doubled up with laughter. A few competitors surprised everyone by clearing over five feet.

We then had the funny races. The potato-sack race produced a few casualties; so did the three-legged race. The finale of the meet was the mile run—ten laps around the field. The Koreans were traditionally known for their stamina and speed in distance running. As the runners changed lead after lead, the whole camp erupted with shouts and applause. Coming from the Japanese slave labor camps after having lived on starvation rations for months, after crossing the Pacific to land in Camp McCoy, Wisconsin, and without any time for training, here they were, jumping and running, forgetting for one day their homesickness, and having a whale of a good time.

Following the highly successful track meet, I organized a writing contest: songs and poems, on any subject they chose. This project was abruptly interrupted when I received a fifteen-day furlough. I assigned a sergeant and two GIs to look after the prisoners and took off for New York.

First, a surprise visit with Sister Elizabeth and her three children. The oldest, a boy, was not at home. He had received a scholarship to a private boarding school in upper New York and seldom came home. The two girls, approaching their teen years, were both very smart and pretty. Sister Elizabeth was still the devoted mother and homemaker. Her husband was still traveling around, and she still lived a lonely life in the big city. After a week of theatre and the movies, once again I left my Sister and her children and took a train to Washington, D.C.

I found the headquarters of the Office of Strategic Service and inquired about the possibility of joining them. The OSS was engaged in a highly specialized form of military operation. Upon completion of training, units were flown behind enemy lines and dropped by parachutes. Quickly, they were to establish their operating base and maintain contact by radio. Their mission was twofold: to gather military information on the enemy and to relay it to U.S. intelligence agencies; next, to sabotage and disrupt enemy operations. I was eager to join the unit being trained to be sent to Korea.

This plan, too, was disrupted when I visited the State Department. I met a young undersecretary in charge of Korean affairs. His name was McCune. The name sounded very familiar. Of course, it was the name of a famous American missionary in Korea. So the young man at the desk must have been the son of the missionary. I remembered that when Father was the minister of Jung Dong Methodist Church in Seoul, I used to play with the children of American missionaries. Especially in the winter, we all rode our sleds down the hill next to the famous Korean middle school, Pai-Jai Hak Dang.

When I gave McCune my name, it, too, must have sounded familiar to him. His face lit up and he asked, "Are you the Reverend Soon Hyun's son?"

"Yes, I am." We happily reminisced a bit and exchanged each other's family news.

Finally he asked, "What are you doing in the army?"

"I'm stationed at Camp McCoy in Wisconsin. I look after the Korean prisoners of war there."

"Listen, go get your discharge and come back. We have more important work for you." He scribbled a note on his official stationery, signed it, and handed it to me, saying, "Take this to the commander of Camp McCoy and get your discharge."

I cut my furlough short and rushed back to Camp McCoy. When I handed the note from the State Department to the commanding officer, he looked up at me with that "who the hell are you?" expression. The next day, the news of atom bombs obliterating Hiroshima and Nagasaki stunned our camp, along with the rest of the world. I didn't understand it myself, but I tried to explain to the Koreans the power of an atom bomb, which could wipe out a whole city.

Japan's surrender soon followed, and the preparations to ship out the Korean POWs then began. I got my discharge from the army and was bound again for Washington, D.C. Bidding farewell to the Koreans was heartrending. In a very short time, we had forged a close bond among us. They all swore they wouldn't forget me, and I pledged the same to them.

Young McCune was glad to see me again. "Peter, you have your wish; we are going to send you to Korea."

It was my lifetime dream come true. "But how soon and what will I do in Korea?"

He briefly explained what my mission would be. He projected that our armed forces would be stationed in Korea for some time and they would need all the help that they could get to establish and maintain good relations with the Korean people. "Your father was one of the leaders of the Korean people and of the Korean independence movement," he said. "So, you must have known most of his contemporaries. You will be invaluable in contacting those leaders and persuading them to work with the American occupation forces."

"They may object to American occupation," I interrupted.

"Yes, quite possibly. But Korea has been devastated by the war. There isn't enough food, medicine, or anything. They are going to need us to bring life back to normal. The big problem is that they don't understand us and we don't understand them. That's why we need you. You understand both the American and Korean views. You can help to bring us together."

"That's a very big order," I said. "However, all my life I've wanted to help Korea. I'd be happy to go and do all I can. When do I leave?"

"As soon as all the paperwork is done. But first, you must change your uniform." He handed me an envelope addressed to an army tailor shop. "Go there now, and report here tomorrow morning."

It was late morning when I arrived at the army tailor shop, where I presented the envelope to the receptionist. He took it and disappeared. A moment later an imposing figure appeared and ushered me to another room. I was left there alone for what seemed a long time. Another man appeared with a cloth tape around his neck; no doubt, that was the tailor. Without a word he began taking measurements: the length of my arms and legs, the width of my chest, and even the circumference of my head. The tailor conducted these mysterious maneuvers without a word. Finally, he did say two words. Pointing to a chair, he said, "Please wait." And I didn't say a word. In answer, I sat down with a magazine and waited for I don't know how long. The tailor returned with what looked like an army uniform, but strangely it was olive green, not khaki. He told me to take off my uniform and put on the uniform he handed to me. It was an officer's uniform! The pants, the coat, and even the overseas cap fit perfectly. He asked me to sign a slip of paper and told me I could go. An instant transformation from sergeant to major! Gingerly, I stepped out of the shop and faced the world. A group of GIs passing by looked at me and executed smart salutes. I looked around to see whom they were saluting. It was me! How strange!

With a hearty handshake and affectionate pats on my back, McCune bid me farewell and wished me all success in Korea. Carrying all the War Department papers, including a brand-new ID for a field grade officer of the U.S. Army, I flew out to the West Coast. At last I was on my way to Korea.

# 10

# RETURN
# TO
# KOREA

My destination was Seoul, Korea, not as a member of an OSS-trained group to be dropped by parachute behind enemy lines, but in an army officer's uniform with valid travel papers.

The conditions for flying halfway around the world only a month after Japan's surrender in August 1945 were not without hazards and adventures. The first leg from Washington, D.C., brought me to Hamilton Air Base in northern California. There, I languished for several days waiting for a flight accommodation. One morning, I got an early call to board the plane leaving for Honolulu. Stuffing all my possessions in a duffle bag, I ran to the boarding gate on the double. I stood in a line that moved very slowly, and just as I reached the gate, the guard closed it, saying, "Sorry, that's all. Next flight, tomorrow."

Frustrated, I dragged myself and the bag back to the barracks. I cursed my luck for missing the plane by just one turn of the turnstile. Next morning, over the radio, I heard the horrifying news; the army transport C-54, leaving Hamilton Air Base, went down five hundred miles short of Honolulu. No account of casualties. I was so shook up; I couldn't decide whether it was a bad or a good omen for my projected trip to Seoul.

Regardless, the next day I got on the four-propeller C-54 bound for Hawaii. No, it didn't go down five hundred miles short of Hickam Field, Honolulu. There we only had to wait for refueling, then took off on our way to cross the Pacific. The pilot located a speck in the ocean and landed there safely. The mound of sand was called Kwajalein, where the ingenious U.S. Navy Seabees had installed a couple of quonset huts and fuel storage tanks for ships and planes. Loaded with a fresh supply of fuel, our C-54 took off again, now headed for the island of Saipan. From the air, the island looked more like a real land mass; deep green jungles and jagged peaks pointing at us.

The pilot landed on a well-paved runway and brought our plane to a stop by the side of a settlement of quonset huts. We were informed of an overnight layover. After a quick lunch in the GI mess, some of us got on a little truck and took off for a tour of the island. It was truly a tropical island, with impassable jungles and soaring peaks of mountains. Nestled in hillside jungles were some tiny dwellings here and there where the native Saipanese lived.

The truck came to a stop; it was the end of the road. The driver had warned us we would have to walk through a rough trail to reach the cliff. We all wanted to see the famous cliff from which the Japanese committed suicide en masse. The driver, leading with a machete, had to slash and chop through parts of the trail that were overgrown with giant ferns. Suddenly, we came to a wide open space where blinding sunlight greeted us. "This is the place," the driver announced. All of us walked to the edge of the cliff and looked down. A sheer drop of more than a thousand feet braced against an angry, bottomless ocean. And it really happened here only a few months before our arrival.

Saipan was the last stronghold of the Japanese Imperial Navy. When the U.S. Navy surrounded Saipan, the Japanese were cut off on the island; there was no escape. The commander warned them not to surrender, saying anyone captured by the Americans would be tortured to death. The only escape was suicide. So, the mass *harakiri* —except no dagger, no self-embowelment; they just jumped off the cliff.

There were no eyewitness reports of the horrifying event. We only know that all the Japanese soldiers, all the Japanese laborers, and their families assembled in the clearing and at a given command jumped to their deaths. I can imagine some reluctant youngsters who had to be pushed off from behind, and infants in their mothers' arms screaming piercingly. There was no report either whether the commander who ordered the mass suicide had followed the last of his people and jumped. The only survivors were a group of slave laborers brought over from Korea. They did not believe the Japanese commander; they were not convinced the Americans could be as cruel or crueler than the Japanese.

When the U.S. forces occupied Saipan, these slave laborers were rounded up and shipped to the POW center in Camp McCoy, Wisconsin. That was when I was sent to Camp McCoy to take care of a "bunch of Japanese war prisoners" from the Pacific theatre, and it was I who discovered them to be Koreans, not Japanese.

The next leg in my flight was an extra long one: Saipan to Manila, on the same old four-propeller C-54. It was a grueling and nerve-wracking overnight flight. At dawn, we flew straight into the rising sun—a happy and beautiful sight. We landed at Clark Field, a part of the U.S. naval base. It was already the middle of September, but when we walked down the plane we could feel the humid air rising off the ground. We checked into our flimsy wooden barracks to wait for the call to catch the flight for the next and last leg to Seoul.

The Philippines, Manila in particular, was the battleground of U.S. and Japanese forces: the siege and capture of Corregidor, the "Death March" of U.S. troops through the jungles of Luzon, the battle on the beaches of Leyte. It was General Douglas MacArthur who said, "I shall return" as he was being run out of Corregidor. Eventually, he did return, defeated the Japanese, and put its commander, General Yamashita, on trial as a war criminal. I attended one of the sessions of his trial. The Japanese general who was responsible for thousands of Americans who died in the "Death March" appeared in his uniform bedecked with rows of medals. He surveyed the audience and the prosecutors with a haughty and disdainful air, as though he were reviewing a complement of his troops. And he barked his answers to the prosecutor's questions like a military commander. He would never admit or recant the atrocities committed by the Japanese troops under his command. He was found guilty and was executed by hanging.

Accompanied by several others, I drove to town to survey the sites of battles against the Japanese, who decided to wage a street-by-street battle. And in order to save the lives of the GIs, General MacArthur ordered the troops to blast the Japanese with artillery fire. That artillery siege not only killed all the Japanese in sight, but completely demolished the city. There were no buildings still standing. The mammoth federal and post office buildings were just so much rubble. Near the dock I saw the Filipino longshoremen unloading a ship. The sun beat down mercilessly, and the temperature registered over one hundred degrees. I couldn't believe men could work in that heat without collapsing. There, across the bay, I saw a strange sight: a hundred-foot tall brick chimney standing proudly—no damage. How was it possible? I was more than curious and asked several Filipinos nearby.

"Oh, that," one man answered casually. "That's a brewery owned by General MacArthur." He claimed that when the Japanese retreated inside the brewery, MacArthur ordered his troops to hold their fire. Instead, he sent in foot soldiers to fight the Japanese. True, many American soldiers lost their lives there, but they saved the brewery.

There were other reasons for the GI's disaffection for General MacArthur. Among them was this wartime story. When the Japanese forces were nearly wiped out in the Philippines, to be safe, General MacArthur staged a landing of U.S. forces on the Leyte beaches far north of Manila. And when assured of absolute safety, he staged the historic "I shall return" scene for posterity. The camera crews were ready. They captured the scenes of the landing ships unloading U.S. troops, who then waded ashore. More landing ships unloaded General MacArthur's staff members. And finally, the general himself, holding a long cigarette holder, alighted. The cameras ground at a furious pace. The general actually stepped into the shallow water and waded ashore. The general had indeed returned. I asked many GIs about the staged landing; I didn't hear a single kind word from any GI.

It was like an oven inside the barracks. Lying stark naked, I was drenched in sweat. I would run over to the latrine, get under the shower, and turn it on. It took all of five minutes for me to cool off. Dripping wet, I would go to the bunk and lie down. Within minutes, it seemed, the cool shower water evaporated, and I began sweating again. I had to dash over to the shower and cool off again. Wouldn't you know, it was at such a moment the call came over the speaker: "Flight for Okinawa and Seoul ready. All aboard in ten minutes." I never moved so fast—dried off with a towel, put on my clothes, packed the duffle bag, and ran to the boarding gate, on the double. Then it happened again. Just as I reached the boarding gate, the guard bellowed, "That's all until tomorrow." And wouldn't you know, the morning news the next day reported the C-54 went down only a scant mile from the harbor of Naha, Okinawa. Now I asked again, was this a good or bad omen for my trip to Seoul?

The next day, we landed safely at Naha, then flew to Seoul and finally landed at Kimpo Airport. At last I got off the plane and stepped on the mother earth of Korea. A couple of GIs approached and asked for my ID. I pulled out my new ID and showed it to them. The soldiers snapped to attention and saluted, and I acknowledged with a peremptory salute. Carrying my gear, they led me to a jeep. This was the initiation into my new life as an officer. The fifteen-mile drive from Kimpo Airport to Seoul was filled with startling rediscoveries. After twenty-six years of absence, I could still recognize some of the landmarks of Seoul: the Central Railway Station, Severance Hospital, and the beautiful, ageless South Gate. But the people on the streets didn't look the same as I remembered. Instead of baggy pantaloons and long, white frocks, most of the men wore smart Western suits, and the swagger in their walks was also new. I searched in vain to see a man wearing the traditional tall, black hat, a common sight when I was growing up in Seoul. The briefcases some of them carried further symbolized a new era for Korean men.

The women, too, were not left far behind. No longer did they appear shy and meek in public, the customary image of Korean women. They did not yield the right of way to men on the sidewalks; they kept walking in straight lines. Except for the elderly, the women were also dressed in Western clothes, an unbelievable sight in the old days. Moreover, I saw a few women carrying briefcases, as though in defiance and claiming equal status with men.

The jeep halted in front of a high-rise building. The GIs unloaded my gear and announced, "Sir, this is your headquarters." They saluted and drove off.

The guard at the entrance, a corporal, rushed to pick up my gear and led me to the admissions desk. This couldn't be an army barracks, I thought to myself; this must be a hotel. Yes, indeed, I was being quartered in the famous Seoul Hotel, which was being used as U.S. Army officers' headquarters. I did have to share a room with another officer, a lowly lieutenant.

My first meal at the officers' mess was just as impressive. Even though we all sat on benches at long tables, we didn't have to stand in line carrying mess kits. The GIs served our food on plates. The embarrassing service was surpassed only by the quantity and the quality of food. All the time I spent in the army, I had no idea that the distinction between GIs and officers was so extreme.

The next morning, after yet another sumptuous breakfast, I started to explore the city and visit some of my favorite childhood haunts. I commandeered a jeep and started off. Sadly, I could not locate the house my family and I had lived in before leaving Korea, nor any of my uncle's mansions. They were all gone, replaced with modern buildings. I was disappointed and despondent. Then I found Papa's church—the Jung Dong First Methodist Church—still intact and standing proudly. Only the original aged hue of the bricks was lost, replaced by a new coat of bright red paint. The old minister's home, where the eight of us children had such a frolicking time growing up, was also gone.

Through persistent searching and questioning of strangers in the neighborhoods, I did succeed in locating Eun-Yim Umonee, my childhood nurse. She was living in a little apartment above a store far beyond the West Gate. She opened the door and stared, speechless. Little wonder; it had been twenty six years since we last saw each other.

"Don't you recognize me, Eun-Yim Umonee? I am Pedro-ya!"

"*Aigo! Aigo!*" she cried, and threw her arms around me. With tears streaming down her face, she pulled me into the room. She handed me a cushion to sit on the bare wooden floor. She couldn't stop her tears nor her rapid-fire questions. "Your Umma and Papa, how are they? Your sisters and brothers, are they all married? I knew your poor sister, Soon-Ok, died in Shanghai. Your beautiful sisters Mi-Ok [Alice] and Myung-Ok [Elizabeth], where are they now? And your three brothers, did they all go to college?"

And on and on; she couldn't exhaust all the questions that had been stored for twenty-six years. All the while she sat close by me, held my hand, and rubbed it in gentle rhythm as though I was still a child and she was rocking me.

This was the same woman who took care of me in my young years. Whenever I was in some distress and cried—oh, how I could cry!—she would lift me and give me her ample breasts, one to suckle and the other to hold. Next to my mother, she was the most beautiful woman in the world. She had aged, of course, but her beautiful face was still there. Finally, she released my hand, stood up, and went into the kitchen. It was a tiny kitchen equipped with a portable gas-burning stove. While she was chopping and puttering, I plied her with questions of my own.

"What happened to your husband?" I asked.

"Oh, he died years ago."

Even as a child, I thought of him as a drunkard and believed he would go to an early grave.

"Where is Eun-Yimee, your daughter?"

"She is teaching in a public school—she should be home soon."

"And her brother, Soo-Bok? What does he do?"

"Soo-Bok works in a factory, making something. He'll be home soon also."

My dear old nurse begged me to go to the living room. She followed and set a little lacquered table in front of me—it was the traditional dining table. Soon afterward, she carried a huge porcelain bowl and set it on the table—it was my favorite summer dish, *nang-myun,* or cold noodles. She then brought in several kinds of *kim-chee* and placed them next to the soup bowl. Such a delicious, impromptu luncheon reminded me of her talent for cooking. She would, on a moment's notice, stir up a lunch or dinner whenever friends came to visit my parents unexpectedly.

Just as I swallowed the last drop of soup, Eun-Yimee arrived home from school. I couldn't believe the sight of her; so tall and shapely. I couldn't believe this was the same girl who had spent her childhood with me. When we were six or seven years old, we both got under the same blanket, where I first discovered the tender shape of a female. And she, too, discovered the male body by feeling and exploring all over me. And here she was, demure and alluring, a beautiful schoolmarm. We were so shy with each other, we hardly carried on any conversation. A little later, her brother, Soo-Bok, returned from work and joined us. I remembered I used to call him behind his back, "the slow wit." Very quickly I found that the years had not accelerated his wit. I felt very sorry for him. Just the same, it was a happy reunion, and we were all elated; but it would be the last time I ever saw them.

Through Eun-Yim Umonee I found the whereabouts of my aunt, possibly my only close living relative in Korea. She was still living in the same neighborhood where most of the Hyun family used to live—away from the noise of the city. Auntie's house, with the wooden gate and heavy iron knockers, the immaculate courtyard with flower pots, and the raised, gleaming wooden parlor evoked memories of the house where my great-grandparents had lived. I took off my shoes, left them on an enormous stepping stone, and walked into the parlor. The parlor in a traditional Korean house occupies the center, with bedrooms on either side. The front of the parlor is left open. This is where visitors and guests are entertained. Auntie was already there.

I knelt and bowed, two hands clasped in front of my face, and bent down until my forehead touched the floor. Once an American asked what the significance of touching the ground or floor with one's forehead was. I explained it was a thousand-year-old tradition and is an expression of one's humility and is the highest respect paid to elders.

I first saw Auntie at her wedding, when she married my uncle; I was eight years old. In her bridal costume, with her eyes shut as required by tradition, exchanging tiny cups of wine with her husband, her face radiated sheer beauty. I had never seen such a beautiful face before. And today, when she must be near or over sixty, her face still held that beautiful gleam. She begged me to come and sit near her.

With repeated "*Aigo-cham!* Oh, heavens! *Aigo-cham!* Oh, heavens! You are really our Pedro-ya! I couldn't even dream I would see you again and have you sitting with me in my house." She couldn't continue; she heaved a deep sigh and repeated, "*Aigo-cham!* Oh, heavens! *Aigo-cham!* Oh, heavens!"

I, too, was speechless; I simply caressed her hand.

Then, as if the dam had broken open, Auntie poured out all the questions she had stored for twenty six years. She had always admired and respected Papa and Umma, and her concern for their health and well being was not just a casual inquiry. Amazingly, she remembered the names of all my brothers and sisters. While asking for their educational and marital status, she described each one of us succinctly from her memory. And true to Korean custom, she wondered if I were hungry. She was apologetic about her disinterest in household affairs and explained she didn't know what there was in the house to eat; she said I had to wait until her daughter, Hai-Sook, came home from work.

When Hai-Sook and her brother, Hyo-Sup, came home, they both greeted me with traditional bows. We were cousins, but I was much older, hence the bows for recognition and respect. With the exchange of only a few words, I was convinced they were deeply concerned with the political developments in Korea. Hyo-Sup, a young man in his early twenties, was a great soccer player and somewhat of a national hero. He was appalled by the ways of the American military government (AMG) and baffled by the division of Korea by the big powers into two Koreas. I felt ashamed while listening to his accounts of what the AMG had done to squelch all newborn activities of the people since liberation from the slavery of Japanese rule. Three days before my arrival in Seoul, my favorite uncle died of a simple cold that had developed into pneumonia. And his daughter, Hai-Sook, a doctor, couldn't find any medicine to save her father from dying. After the surrender, the Japanese had left Korea without any medical supplies.

"But do you know," Hyo-Sup exploded, "the AMG has a warehouse full of medical supplies. If given to the people, it would have saved not only my father, but hundreds of others also."

"I must go to his graveside and pay my respects," I said.

"But the Hyun ancestral home where my father is buried is nearly forty miles away," he said. "It's too far to walk."

"I'll see if I can get a U.S. Army vehicle so that everyone in the family could go."

A few days later, I had good news. I would have a U.S. Army personnel carrier with a corporal for a driver. I telephoned Hyo-Sup to have everyone ready to leave early the next morning.

When I arrived at Auntie's home, the army truck created quite a stir; a crowd had gathered, and what startled them the most was the sight of me in a U.S. Army officer's uniform. I could hear them speculating:

"Is he American or Korean?"

"Can't you see? He's an American officer."

"Yeah, but he looks like a Korean!"

I spoke to them politely. *"Nyee, na nun Hangukin im ni da."* ["Yes, I am Korean."]

This aroused even greater surprise.

"Did you hear that?"

"Did you hear that?"

"He spoke Korean!"

"He spoke Korean!"

Some people in the crowd were clapping and jumping.

And I was surprised to find in Auntie's house more than twenty people waiting to take the ride to Whang-Gol, my ancestral home; dear Auntie had marshalled all the relatives in Seoul to take the trip together. I had never seen them before. Auntie introduced them to me—my second and third cousins, nephews and nieces, and their parents; my uncles and aunts. After polite greetings, they climbed up on the truck and crowded its open deck. Of course, my dear cousin Hyo-Sup, his younger brother Myo-Sup, and Hai-Sook were there. Auntie and I sat in the front.

It was an exhilarating journey. Leaving the East Gate of Seoul behind, we were in the open country. For the first time since my arrival, I saw the expanse of open fields and the hills beyond screened by thick forests. The sight of the peaceful countryside evoked some of my childhood memories. Having spent all my childhood in the city of Seoul, I had yearned to see life in the country. Then a visiting aunt from my mother's family agreed to take me with her to her home in the country. I was elated to have a chance to ride on the train. The spectacle along the railroad passed so swiftly, I could hardly keep up with the varying scenes: patches of rice fields, clusters of thatched-roof houses, men, women, and animals working in the fields, and glimpses of children carrying heavy burdens on their backs and on their heads.

We got off the train at a tiny railroad station. My aunt told me we would have to walk to the village where her home was located. "It's a pretty long walk," she had warned me.

But before starting, she went to the market and shopped for provisions. I wondered and worried how my Aunt could carry all the supplies, when a workman with a *jee-gee*—the age-old wooden contraption with straw straps—appeared and loaded all the bundles on his *jee-gee*. Protruding from the load was the whole skull of a steer.

Pointing, I asked Auntie, "What's that for?"

"That's for my soup," she answered. "Enough to last through the winter."

These memories of my childhood flashed through my mind as we rumbled along in an American army truck. Auntie gave me the directions, and I translated them for the corporal. We got off the highway and rocked along a narrow country road that abruptly became very rocky. Now the ride was really rough, and I could hear the poor people in the open truck bed laughing and yelling.

"*Aigo-cham!*" ["Oh, heavens!"]

"*Aigo-cham!*" ["Oh, heavens!"]

Finally, we reached our destination, my ancestral home—an entire valley nestled between two mountain ranges. Everyone was happy to get off the truck. We were greeted by the *myo-gig*—caretaker of graves. He and his wife lived in the old house where my father once spent his childhood. The *myo-gig* led us to the hillside filled with mounds of graves of many generations past. We were all very solemn and trod over the ground reverently. The *myo-gig* then led us to the grave of my grandfather and spread a straw mat on which I could kneel and bow. The rest of the clan followed me two by two and paid their respects. Finally, we came to my uncle's grave. Thinking of his death only a few days before my arrival in Korea, and only for a lack of medicine, brought uncontrollable tears. I knelt, and with my forehead touching the ground, stayed in that position for as long as I could. Then I watched Auntie as she approached her husband's grave and performed the traditional woman's bow. Quite different from that of a man, using her hands and arms for balance, she slowly lowered her body until her whole body rested on the ground. She dropped her head and held it for a moment. Then she rose slowly and resumed a standing position. It was so graceful and beautiful.

When we returned to the house, we found the air filled with the tantalizing smell of *bul-go-gee*—literally, "fire beef"—the Korean version of barbecued beef. The *myo-gig's* wife evidently was cooking the whole time we were visiting the graves. And what a feast she spread on the table in the center of the parlor. Because of its limited space, only the elders could sit around the table, with bowls of steaming rice in their hands, helping themselves to *chap-chae* (mixed vegetables), *san-juk* (fried fillet of fish), the mouth-watering *bul-go-gee,* and the inevitable varieties of *kim-chee.* The youngsters were given plates loaded with food, which they carried to all the convenient spots in the court and gobbled.

Within an hour all the food disappeared, and the children disappeared in search of their own pleasure. Auntie, being the senior matriarch of the family, called for an impromptu family council. "We all welcome our Pedro-Si—honorable Pedro—who has traveled a very long distance to be with us today," she said.

Everyone present clapped their hands, and I bowed my head in appreciation.

"The most important business we have to settle today," Auntie continued, "is to agree on the heir of the Hyun family, who will take the title to this family estate and take care of it."

The estate occupied the entire Whang-Gol valley, comprised of tens of thousands of acres. Auntie then posed the question, "Who do you believe is the rightful heir?"

There was a visible stir among the elders present, but no one spoke. After a long wait of silence, Auntie spoke again. "As you all know, as the oldest son of Uncle Hyun Soon, Pedro-Si is the rightful heir. Do you all agree?"

"*Nee, nee*" [yes, yes], the elders replied.

"Very well." Auntie then proclaimed, "On behalf of all the Hyuns, I hereby designate our beloved Pedro-Si as the legal heir to our ancestral home."

I was stunned. I was speechless. I couldn't grasp the immensity of the honor, not to mention the responsibility. Instinctively I rose and, bowing to everyone, muttered "*Gomab-sumnida*—thank you. *Daidani gomab-sumnida*—Indeed, thank you very much." Then I began thinking out loud: "You know, I left Korea at age thirteen and for twenty-six years, I lived abroad. I went to school in China for four years, and have spent the rest of the years in America." I sighed deeply and continued in my meager Korean language. "Here in Korea, I am an ignorant person. I know nothing about property management, and less than nothing about farming."

There were murmurs of protest.

"Yes, I appreciate your confidence in me, but it would be unfair to you for me to accept this trusteeship."

"We'll all help! We'll all help!" Their earnest pleas were touching, and I felt a fleeting temptation to yield and accept the heirship.

But resisting it, I said, "Besides, I'll have to move and live here. It will mean leaving all my family, including my mother and father, and terminating all my work in America." Another deep sigh. "No, it's not possible, really. I hope you find someone next in line to manage the family estate. Again, I thank you very, very much!"

"Oh, then it will have to be Myung-Sup," someone spoke up. Myung-Sup was among the gathered; he was the son of a distant uncle and a concubine, which relegated him to a second-class status. Myung-Sup promptly accepted the position offered him.

Little did I realize that this turn of events would usher in tragic results for the Hyun family. Forty-two years later, in 1988, I returned to Korea with my son, Douglass. I was eager to have my son, born and raised in America, visit the land of his ancestors. I found Auntie, past ninety, still alive and well. From her I learned that we had lost our family estate. How? My cousin Myung-Sup, who replaced me as the heir, turned out to be a gambler. He sold our land piece by piece until only a parcel of fifteen acres remained. It was barely enough for the *myo-gig's* family of three to eke out a living by planting rice on the fifteen-acre field. We were thankful that my gambling cousin couldn't sell the hillside land with the graves of our ancestors. But the beautiful, enchanting valley is gone.

# 11

# THE AMERICAN MILITARY GOVERNMENT

The fate and destiny of the forty million people of South Korea were left in the hands of the American military, who ruled by orders and proclamations. The Korean people had no voice either in their promulgation or in the method of their execution. By virtue of the occupation of the country by the U.S. Seventh Army under the command of General John R. Hodge, the American military government assumed complete and indisputable power as the supreme governing body. This power extended not only over civil and political security, the distribution of food, medical supplies, and all necessities of life, but also over the press, the media, and all cultural activities.

As a liaison officer between the American and Korean representatives, I had the privilege of observing firsthand the operation of the AMG. Obviously, there were no advance plans nor any authoritative directives. Furthermore, from the commanding general down to the lowly private in the occupation force, no one had received any training nor were they qualified to assume the responsibility of ruling a foreign country, least of all a country whose language and culture were a complete mystery to them.

The gross disqualifications, however, were hidden behind a formidable protective screen—arrogance. Without exception, every member of the American occupation force I encountered assumed a superior attitude in their minds, over the unquestionably inferior Koreans. The Americans were well fed, well groomed, and well equipped with guns. Most of the Koreans, the poor devils, were starving or, due to a lack of medicine, sick or dead. And finally, they were helpless to protect themselves; they had no guns. The Japanese colonial rulers called the Koreans *baka!* (stupid!). American GIs promptly replaced it with "gooks," meaning the same. In tacit approval, General Hodge, in a public statement soon after his landing in Korea, declared, "Koreans are the same breed of cats as the Japanese." Little wonder the GIs coming out of the mess hall in the evening could be heard saying, "Hey! Let's go gook hunting!"

The Korean people had faced such national insults before. Throughout their four thousand-year history, would-be conquerors repeatedly invaded Korea from Mongolia, China, and Japan. They always came with overwhelming force, but, failing to subjugate the Koreans, in the end always retreated. Following Japan's surrender in World War II, the Korean people immediately organized themselves for self-rule. Under the leadership of Lyuh Woon Hyung, a fearless fighter for Korean independence under the Korean Provisional Government in Shanghai, the Korean People's Republic was established. Under its supervision, People's Committees were set up throughout the country. Their immediate tasks were, first, to disarm the remaining Japanese soldiers as well as the hated Japanese police. Next, the committees took over the distribution of food and medical supplies. The People's Committees went even further; they began confiscating lands belonging to absentee landlords and distributing them to the landless peasants.

One of the first acts of the AMG was to order the dissolution of the People's Committees. There were no explanations except the declaration that the Korean People's Republic and its People's Committees were Communist. I was appalled, but not surprised. I had seen a copy of the new "orientation" pamphlet distributed to the GIs in Korea. The theme of the pamphlet was that with the end of World War II, the real U.S. enemy was Communist Russia. The amazing revelation was that this bit of propaganda had been prepared under the Truman administration and published by the War Department even before World War II had ended. Pamphlets were shipped or flown overseas and placed in the hands of every GI for his "new orientation." At last the AMG was armed with a solid, basic policy and unswerving guideline: anticommunism.

One of the major projects of the Korean People's Republic was the revival and restoration of Korean culture, long suppressed by the Japanese. I visited the United Korean Cultural Reconstruction Society in Seoul. It was housed in a spacious three-story building formerly belonging to a Japanese business firm. The ground floor was occupied by the administration and planning offices. A modest room with a long table and chairs was reserved for meetings of the board of directors. The second floor was devoted to the literature, poetry, and music departments for research and creative development. The dance and theatre departments occupied the top floor.

I was there as an invited guest of the theatre department. I sat at a table with the chairperson, and a group of young men and women sat in a circle. I was totally unprepared when I was introduced as a theatre director from New York. My first remark was, "How did you know I worked in the theatre?"

"We know all about your work, Mr. Hyun," the chairperson answered. "We know you worked with Eva LeGallienne, with the Theatre of Action, and directed *The Revolt of the Beavers* for the New York Federal Theatre."

"But how? How did you gather all that information?"

"Well, even under the Japanese rule, we always tried to keep up with the theatre world, particularly the work of a director who happened to be a Korean."

"That is amazing; unbelievable!" Then I addressed the group. I lauded them for their research into the history of Korean theatre and for their adaptation to drama of the struggle of Korean people for freedom. As actors, directors, designers, and producers, they were in the forefront of not only the reconstruction of culture, but the reconstruction of Korea.

Following my address, there came a veritable deluge of questions.

"Where are Clifford Odets, Irwin Shaw, and Arthur Miller? What are they doing now?"

"Who owns the Broadway theatres?"

"What happened to the Theatre of Action?"

"What is the Group Theatre doing?"

I answered as best as I could, but to many questions I didn't have the answers. I felt overwhelmed by the vitality of the theatre group; it was vibrant. I thanked them for the opportunity to meet them and to learn a little bit of their work. As another surprise, someone stood up and made a motion to invite "Mr. Hyun" to be one of the directors of their new theatre. It was enthusiastically endorsed by the entire group.

Regrettably, I had to decline the honor. "I am now in the service of the AMG, from which I cannot resign. I have no recourse but to remain in my present position."

"Then, when you are discharged from service, will you come back and direct a play for us?" someone pleaded.

"First, I have to return to America, but I shall seriously consider your offer."

Less than a week after that inspiring meeting, by order of the AMG, the United Korean Cultural Reconstruction Society was outlawed and dissolved. The organization and its members were declared "either Communists or under Communist influence." Much of the valuable documents, literature, and equipment were seized and the doors to the building padlocked.

I also had the opportunity to participate in another kind of meeting—a meeting called by the policy-making body of the AMG. The problem was the arrival of a very large shipment of medical supplies; the surplus collected from the Pacific theatre of operations had been loaded on a ship and brought to Korea. The question was to decide on the method of its distribution, especially the critically needed penicillin. Much discussion centered around the idea of monetary returns for the medical supplies.

At an opportune moment, I presented the following proposal: Organize a special commission consisting of Korean religious and political leaders to take charge of the distribution of the medical supplies as a gift of the AMG. The authorities appeared impressed with my recommendation.

A few days later, the decision of the AMG was announced: The Korean Chamber of Commerce was appointed by the AMG to undertake the distribution of all medical supplies at "reasonable prices." This decision was in line with fostering so-called "free enterprise." The poor, most in need of medicine, were denied any benefits; and for greater profit, much of the supplies were channeled into the black market and smuggled to North Korea. Soon it was rumored that penicillin was available in North Korea and was much cheaper than in South Korea.

At the inception of the military occupation of Korea—by the Soviet Union in the north and the United States in the south—a joint commission was created to draw up a plan to establish a united, free Korea. The members of the commission were made up of representatives of the two occupying forces. They met daily, first to debate the proposal to mandate an Allied trusteeship over Korea. After nearly a year, due to mounting opposition by the Korean people, the idea of a trusteeship was abandoned. The debate then shifted to forming a consultative body of Koreans to formulate the plan for an independent government of Korea.

The debate lasted for another year on the question of who, among the Korean leaders, should be invited to sit on the consultative commission. Both the Soviets and the Americans maintained an uncompromising stand. The Soviets were adamant about excluding the extreme right-wing conservatives, and the Americans, while insisting on excluding the extreme left, was equally determined to bring in the conservatives—big businesses, rich landlords, and some religious leaders—in order to be assured of a Korean government aligned with the United States. The hope for a compromise on the formation of a united, free Korean government was futile. There were intermittent interruptions of the Joint Commission sessions, sometimes caused by a Soviet boycott, and other times by a U.S. walkout. The idea of the Soviet Union and the United States jointly forging a united and free Korea was doomed from the beginning. The final dissolution of the Joint Commission and the perpetuation of the 38th Parallel severing Korea in two were inevitable.

Toward the end of 1945, I received orders to be transferred to Chunchon, the capital city of Kangwon province, located about seventy miles northeast of Seoul. It is the nearest approach to the 38th Parallel, almost within shouting distance of the North Korean occupation forces. To satisfy my curiosity, I drove to the invisible dividing line, got out of the jeep, and slowly walked closer to the 38th Parallel. It was a strange sight in the north; there were no military installations, not even any barracks to house their soldiers. What I did see was a cluster of tiny, thatched-roof hovels of Korean farmers.

Soon, out of these hovels emerged groups of soldiers in North Korean army uniforms. In 1945, the deadly hostility between North and South Korea had not yet fully grown. Seeing me standing alone, the North Korean soldiers shouted friendly greetings and motioned for me to come over. Without any hesitation, I walked over to them. Recognizing my officer's uniform, they all saluted. I saluted in return and baffled them by speaking to them in Korean. I explained very quickly who I was and who my father was. They rushed over and shook my hand and led me into the hovel.

It was a farmer's house, either abandoned or requisitioned— low-ceilinged and windowless. Apparently the North Korean soldiers used the wood-burning stove in the kitchen to prepare all their meals. The American GIs would refuse to live in such squalid shelters. I was anxious to know where they came from. None of them were from any big city; they were all from small farming villages. Of course, they were even more anxious to find out where I had come from. I gave them a quick sketch of my wanderings, from Seoul to Shanghai, Nanking, Honolulu, to Indiana and New York. Their flood of questions about America was interrupted by the entrance of a soldier carrying a tray of cups and a teapot. In true Korean tradition, the leader of the group poured the tea; first cup for me, and the rest for the soldiers. We raised our cups high and drank to a united and independent Korea.

My job in Chunchon was to assist the military governor of the province—a lieutenant colonel, one rank above me—in carrying out the orders of the AMG, which were the surrender of all arms, dissolution of all Communist organizations, including trade unions, and return of all lands to their rightful owners.

All through my childhood I heard of the fabulous scenery of Kangwon province: the great "Diamond Mountain," the legendary Buddhist temples, and the beautiful seashore. I got a two-day leave, requisitioned a jeep with a corporal as driver, and started out on a sight-seeing trip. Soon after leaving Chunchon, we began climbing the mountains. The dirt road became narrower and winding. Some sections of the road had been washed away, and we had to drive cautiously. But the scenes above the cliff on our left, and the bottomless dense forest on our right, were breathtaking. The splashes of early autumn colors heightened the beauty even more dramatically.

With such an immense, colorful backdrop, there was also a human drama. Traveling in the opposite direction were groups of Korean men, women, and children, all carrying bundles—men on their backs, women on their heads, and children, on sticks over their shoulders. These were dispossessed farmers and their families in search of homes and food, all heading for the city of Chunchon and hopefully from there to Seoul. When the road got too narrow, we had to let them pass before we could drive on.

We slowly wound our way down the precipitous mountains, skirted around the Chaik-San National Park, past the seat of a famous Buddhist temple, Kuryongsa. We drove on as the setting sun cast a crimson net over the sea. It was almost dark when we reached the seaport city of Kangnung.

"We'll spend the night here," I said to the corporal. "How would you like to go to a Korean-style hotel?"

"Sir, that's a great idea. I always wanted to find out what it's like."

I directed him to leave the business section of the city and go to the outskirts. I read several signs saying "Lyuh-Kwan" (Inn) and stopped in front of an inn that appeared to be more spacious than the others. We parked and entered through the traditional front gate. The man greeting us was startled to see two of us in American uniform. I spoke to him in Korean, which surprised him even more.

He led us to the open parlor, where he took off his sandals and stepped up to the floor. We also took off our shoes and joined him. The host opened a sliding door paneled with rice paper. We entered the room, which was covered with oiled parchment. Impressive scrolls of calligraphy hung on one wall, and on the opposite side was a tall folding screen, the panels of which were decorated with inlaid pearls. At one end of the room, beside what seemed like a window, also paneled with rice paper, stood a wide chest of drawers. Our host slid the window open to a little garden full of voluptuous chrysanthemum blossoms. He then asked me when and how we would like to have our dinner served. I told him, and the host bowed politely and left us.

My corporal was curious to know what the tete-à-tete was all about. I told him that I had arranged to have our dinner not on two separate tables, but jointly on one table.

"But I don't see any table in the room, sir," my corporal observed.

"No, but there will be one when the dinner is ready," I assured him. "But before dinner, we are going to have a bath."

"Bath! Where?"

Just then, I heard our host announcing from outside that our bath was ready. We took off our clothes, leaving only our shirts and shorts on. At the door there were neatly placed two pairs of straw sandals. Our host was waiting for us. He guided us to the bath—a separate wooden structure. He handed us two enormous white towels, gave us some instructions, and left. Inside, over wooden slats, there was a huge circular wooden tub with steaming hot water. A water faucet and two small wooden buckets were placed near a wooden bench. I was first to get in, but very gingerly. Once we got acclimatized to the hot water, we submerged up to our necks, relaxed, and almost fell asleep in the tub. We shook ourselves out of the tub, and using the little buckets, doused ourselves with cold water from the faucet.

Back in our room, my corporal stretched on the floor, and I leaned against the wall. Both of us dozed off, we didn't know for how long, when we were awakened by the host announcing the dinner. We both got dressed and waited. Without any further ceremony, the door slid open, and a young woman bowed to us politely. She then carried in a miniature table loaded with bowls and dishes. She set the table down in the middle of the room and motioned us to come. She moved like a gentle breeze leaving the room, then in a moment returned with a miniature wooden tub. She lifted the lid, revealing steaming cooked rice. She filled a little brass bowl and handed it to me; and the same for the corporal. She then bowed, saying, "Not much taste, but please eat a whole lot" (traditional Korean humility).

I explained to the befuddled corporal what was on the table: short-ribs of beef soup, thin slices of charcoal broiled beef, steamed fillet of fish, and a collection of salads and *kim-chee*. Noticing the squirmish hesitation of the corporal, I picked up the chopsticks and sampled every dish, moaning, "Oh, that's good! Oh! This is delicious." What I didn't realize was that the corporal knew nothing about using chopsticks. I said, "Sorry, Corporal, they don't have forks in Korea; just use your spoon."

Eagerly, he plunged into tasting every dish. When he ate a bit of *kim-chee*, he froze for a moment; I knew the hot pepper got to him. But he ate every other dish ravenously, and his final compliment was, "This Korean food tastes pretty good!"

The young woman returned, and after moving the table away made up our beds. She opened the handsome chest and brought out two cotton padded mattresses and laid them on the floor. Next, she carried out two colorful silk comforters and placed them at the foot of each mattress. And last, she brought out two Korean-style pillows, which looked more like rolled-up bundles, and placed them at the head of each mattress.

To the dumbfounded corporal, I said gently, "It's all right, Corporal, to sleep on the floor; it's good for your back."

Early the next morning, after finishing our breakfast of rice gruel with more *kim-chee,* we drove to the seashore. The Eastern Sea, as Koreans call the Sea of Japan, with sparkles of morning sun, was magnificent. What intrigued me was the interesting formations of little rocky islands along the shore. All through my childhood I had heard about and seen pictures of the legendary Diamond Mountain. The rocky islands along the shore were the pieces cast off by the majestic Diamond Mountain not far from the coast. Though disappointed I could not visit the heartland of Diamond Mountain, I was thrilled to see the famed seashore of Kangwon province.

We turned our backs to the sea and headed for Chunchon. As we climbed the mountain range, we again ran into groups of refugees with heavy burdens trudging over the mountain to reach Seoul for a better life.

Back in Chunchon, I found Mr. Kim, the city's mayor. In my first visit at his home, I was impressed with his warmth and his bright, open mind. From him, I learned much about the town structure and politics. I began to visit him frequently, not only to learn more about the town, but also to make up for the lack of social life in the AMG. I was distressed to learn that there had been a strong trade union in the city, which the AMG ordered disbanded. Mr. Kim also gave me a veiled warning against a certain minister of a church; he wouldn't say exactly why.

One evening our conversation turned to his concern about the health of his wife. She had been suffering for some time with constant stomach pains. I offered to have our American medical officer examine her.

Of course, I acted as the interpreter while the medical officer of the AMG, a captain, examined her. It was the very first time for me to sit in at a medical examination of a woman. The diagnosis was quick and simple; the mayor's wife was suffering with a stomach tumor, and she should be operated on immediately. But where and how? The mayor told me there was a hospital in town that had been in disuse since the Japanese evacuation. Fortunately, Mr. Kim had access to the building. Three of us went to the hospital, a two-story brick building, to appraise its condition. Generally, the interior was fairly clean, needing no major cleanup. The operating room was located on the top floor. The captain was pleased to find the room immaculately clean and all the equipment, instruments, and supplies adequate. The only problem was the frigid temperature. The mayor assured us that the building could be heated to normal temperature. There was enough firewood in the basement, he explained, and he would immediately issue an order to fire up the heater. In two days it would be comfortably warm.

There was another requirement: nurses to assist the doctor during the surgery. The mayor had an answer for that also. He knew the nurses who used to work in the hospital. He would contact them and have them meet the doctor the next day. The problem was that they did not speak English and would need an interpreter. Needless to say, that would be my job. But first, before meeting the nurses, I had to learn all the Korean names for the surgical instruments. I spent the afternoon and the evening studying and memorizing the names. The captain held a dry run the next day, together with two Korean nurses who thought my Korean was adequate.

Two days later all was ready for the first surgery to be performed by an American doctor on a Korean woman patient, not to mention with a Korean-American interpreter to assist. The captain and I went to the hospital early in the morning. Then the two Korean nurses arrived. We all wore long white gowns and scrubbed our hands. One of the nurses brought long rubber gloves out of a sterilizer, a pair for the doctor and a pair each for the nurses. Soon the mayor ushered in his wife. The nurses took her to a dressing room and prepared her for the operation. She was brought back in a white gown and laid down on the operating table. The captain administered spinal anesthesia. After minutes of waiting, the surgery began.

I certainly was the most nervous person there. I had no idea that the human skin had so many layers. The captain deftly cut a long incision in the low part of the patient's stomach, spread the skin apart, and secured it with clips. He then made another incision in the second layer, spread the skin apart, and secured with more clips. I didn't squirm at the sight of blood because I was too busy interpreting the captain's orders for the instruments. Finally, the captain cut open the final layer of skin, exposing the inside of the patient's stomach. I held my breath when the captain dipped his hand into the gaping cavity. He swished his hand around, then inserted his other hand and dug in. With both hands the doctor lifted a solid mass out of the stomach; the tumor was in the shape of an inflated football. The nurse received the huge tumor in a pan and carried it out. I never found out what happened to the "football." Closing and suturing the wound was even more amazing than the cutting and opening. In the hands of the captain the surgical needle and the suture moved like an old shoemaker's needle. The stitches were so precise and uniform, it was almost artistic.

The mayor was so grateful and wished to offer the captain some money. I dissuaded him, saying, "He would be insulted." The operation was a great success, and a few weeks later they invited the captain and me to dinner. The very healthy wife cooked a delicious dinner with broiled pheasant as the main course.

At the AMG office not a day passed without emergencies, complaints, and petitions; the birth of a baby or a death; shortages of rice in the market and necessary repairs to a church roof. All the reports were received and duly recorded by the AMG.

One morning a delegation of several men requested an audience with me. They were brought to my office, where each presented his calling card. I glanced at the cards and found that they were a representative group consisting of businessmen, a landlord, and a religious leader. I was not a little surprised to see the name of the minister of the local church. It was the very man Mayor Kim had warned me against. I thanked them for their visit and asked if they had any special mission. One of them spoke up, apologizing for the intrusion.

"Teacher Hyun," he addressed me in the most polite and respectful term, "we thought we should express our gratitude for having you with us; and we all agreed we should welcome you at a dinner." He paused a moment to assess my reaction.

"Dinner? Where and when?" I asked.

"Tomorrow evening at seven at the Chunchon Restaurant," the spokesman answered, and added, "If it is convenient for you, Teacher Hyun?"

"Yes, quite. I'll be there. Thank you very much." They bowed repeatedly and backed out of the office.

The restaurant was known as the best and most expensive in town. I arrived there appropriately a little late; the leader of the delegation was waiting for me at the door. I took off my shoes and was ushered into a large room. I had never been in such a luxurious room in a Korean restaurant. A long table with a white tablecloth was set at one end of the room, and twenty or so people were already at the table when I entered. All got up and bowed, and I returned the bow to everyone. Together with the leader, I was led to the center of the table, and we sat on padded cushions. I was introduced to the party, and in return each guest was introduced to me. There was little doubt these men represented the upper crust of the Chunchon community.

The ending of the brief ceremony signaled the beginning of dinner. The table was already loaded with bowls of many kinds of salads and *kim-chee*. Four young women in native white costume carrying food led the procession. First they brought in huge tureens of soup and little wooden tubs of steaming rice. They served the soup in little brass bowls and the rice in pretty porcelain bowls. Everyone picked up their silver spoons and tasted the soup, complimenting loudly, "Oh, good! Ah, delicious!" There was a rhythmic clicking of the spoons and chopsticks, not to mention the appreciative exclamations of "Oh!" and "Ah!" as the dinner progressed. The celebrative mood was further heightened by the repeated filling of the tiny cups with *so-ju*—rice wine—by the pretty young ladies. They carried out the empty soup tureens and returned with trays loaded with platters of the meats—beef, pork, and venison—all delicately marinated and broiled on a charcoal fire. The aroma was tantalizing. The young women served the delicacies for each guest, prompting more ohs and ahs. And more *so-ju*, cup after cup. The ensuing toasts were inevitable.

"Our teacher, honorable Mr. Hyun!"

"To honorable teacher, Mr. Hyun!"

"To our esteemed honorable teacher, Mr. Hyun!"

The unbridled flattery bordering on adulation made me feel giddy and embarrassed. Fortunately, the toasts were terminated by the appearance of a man carrying an ancient Korean drum. Dressed in pantaloons and flowing tunic, he sat on a cushion and began to beat out a rhythm. The guests responded instantly with *"Jot-ta! Jot-ta!"* "Great! Great!"

When the drummer began singing an old Korean folk song, there appeared two young women in colorful costume. They bowed to the guests and began their dance. In my childhood, I had heard of the *ki-sang* entertaining the rich, but now I was actually experiencing it. The guests applauded and shouted, *"Jot-ta! Jot-ta!"* The singing and the dancing reached a crescendo, with the drumbeats and the movements sending the dancers to their final graceful bow.

Now, again, the three women in white were carrying in trays loaded with more food. They set them on the table and began serving: chicken and pheasant, steamed in delicate sauce, and fillet of fish fried in egg batter. These were first dipped in vinegar sauce before being dropped into one's mouth, then washed down with *so-ju*.

Once more, the *ki-sang* appeared with the drummer and danced —a more ribald and frenzied dance. Carried away, some of the guests joined the drummer in singing. I was at a loss; was I at a dinner party or an orgy?

No! Not again! The women in white were carrying in trays once more! What could it possibly be? Yes, there was more: *yak-bop* —honeyed "medicine rice"—nectar of persimmon, preserved chestnuts, and a cold and refreshing rice drink with floating pine nuts. With these delectable desserts and more *so-ju,* the mood of the party became more expansive. When the *ki-sang* and the drummer returned, a few of the guests jumped out on the floor with their own tipsy version of Korean dance.

It was nearly midnight when I trudged along the dark street on my way to my quarters. Two questions kept popping in my mind: What was the party all about? Why such an elaborate feast?

I didn't have to wait long for the answers. I got them the next day. Not too early in the morning, but early enough, the delegation reappeared in my office. The leader of the group was accompanied by four other men; I recognized only one, the minister of the local church.

The leader apologized for the "shameful merriment" the night before, then explained, "We don't very often have the opportunity to enjoy life. Everyone wishes to thank you for your presence."

Then another man spoke up and said, "We were very happy to have you with us because we are very anxious to have you work together with us."

I was unable to follow the drift, and blurted, "Surely, I am all for cooperation. But what kind of work can we do together?"

A third man spoke and came to the point. "In the Korean Tungsten Company," he said.

"Tungsten!" I nearly jumped out of my seat.

"Yes," the man calmly explained. "Mr. Hyun, the tungsten mine in Kangwon province is the largest in the world. The Japanese used to own and run it, and some of us worked for the company. In fact, Mr. Cho here," he said, pointing, "was an assistant manager."

"Well, that's all very interesting," I said, "but I know nothing about mining, least of all tungsten mining."

"Mr. Hyun," it was the minister speaking. "You don't have to worry about the operation of the mine. All our men are experienced workers and managers. They will operate the mine."

"Then what do I do?" I asked in puzzlement.

The leader answered with alacrity, "All you have to do is help us obtain the right to operate the mine from the American military government."

Suddenly, the whole approach of the delegation, beginning with the invitation to dinner, the elaborate feast, all became clear. They wanted to use me to obtain the AMG signature for the "transfer of enemy property" to the group, which would virtually give them ownership of the tungsten mine. Sensing my hesitation, the leader proposed what seemed to be the clincher.

Slowly, in measured tones, he said, "Teacher Hyun, we have already decided to make you the president of our company and to offer you 30 percent of the company stock."

Even in my stunned mind, I could comprehend the significance of the proposition; I would be an instant millionaire. Though quite difficult, I maintained my composure and replied. "Gentlemen, you will have to give me a little time. This would be a very serious undertaking."

The delegation rose from their seats, bowed politely, and assured me, "We can wait, Mr. Hyun. Please take the time you need. We are very anxious to have you working with us."

After their departure, I phoned Mayor Kim and told him I wanted to see him; not during the day, but at night after the city had gone to sleep. Making certain no one was following, I walked to the mayor's home and knocked on the door. The housekeeper didn't even ask who was knocking and opened the solid wooden gate. The mayor seemed to anticipate my mission and ushered me to his private room. I told him the whole episode of the horrendous dinner and the proposition that followed. I then gave him the names of the leaders, including the minister, and brief descriptions.

"I know, I know," the mayor said, smiling. "I knew they would be up to something like that." Then he dropped his voice and whispered, "You know who those men are? Notorious collaborators under the Japanese, who fed on the blood of their own people. As informers, they sent thousands of people to prison and death."

I was totally stunned. Putting our heads together, we exchanged ideas as to what could be done to deal with these culprits.

The next day I learned that the elaborate dinner had cost forty thousand won, equivalent to nearly three thousand U.S. dollars. I ordered the U.S. troop commander, a captain, to conduct a simultaneous search of six houses for any cache of arms. I reminded the captain, "You know all Korean citizens were ordered to surrender all arms and given a deadline that expired a month ago." I gave him the names and addresses of the six leaders of the group, including the minister.

At early dawn the next day, the captain staged a lightning raid and search of the six houses. They found rifles, shotguns, and a pistol in the minister's home. All six were arrested and locked up in jail. Frightened and angered, they told the captain to search the house belonging to the former trade union leader. There, the captain searched for and found a dagger and arrested the innocent Mr. Ahn. The unexpected development called for another meeting with Mayor Kim, who advised me of a plausible defense to save Mr. Ahn.

For the sake of "due process," a trial was held in the little courthouse in town. All six were found guilty and sentenced to a year in jail. Then the trial of the trade union leader took place. The captain who was prosecuting the case held out the evidence, a shiny dagger. Mr. Ahn testified and I interpreted.

"Why didn't you surrender this weapon?"

"Sir, because it is not a weapon."

"It certainly is; you could kill people with it, couldn't you?"

"No, sir. That dagger is not for killing people."

"No? Then what is it for?"

"It is our family heirloom."

"A dagger? Family heirloom? I don't understand."

"Your honor, please let me explain. As you see, the dagger is encased in a shield decorated with embroidery and silk tassles.

According to Korean tradition, a dagger is always tucked in the bride's trousseau. It is a symbol of protecting and preserving the honor of the bride."

"That is very interesting," said the judge, "but how can the bride preserve her honor with a dagger?"

Mr. Ahn patiently explained. "During the life of the bride, should she be dishonored in any way, she would use the dagger to end her life."

"That is amazing," the judge sighed; then declared, "Case dismissed!"

A few days later, I visited the jail where the six men were incarcerated. It was a windowless room of about fifteen by fifteen feet. The floor was covered with soiled parchment. In a corner there was a pile of cotton-padded mattresses and blankets; there was no way I could tell how dirty they were nor how long they had been in use. The prisoners' daily meals were pushed on trays through an opening under the door. Their toilet facility consisted of a square hole in the middle of the room, not more than eighteen inches wide. Into this hole the six men urinated and defecated day in and day out. I did not inquire how often the contents in the hole were removed, or by what means, if any, the terrible stench was controlled.

In spite of myself, acute feelings of pity swelled in me. But as I turned away from the horrible jail, I reminded myself that six of the group were still alive, not the thousands of victims who had perished by the direct or indirect actions of the collaborators, the six jailed men among them.

Not long after the disgusting incident, I received yet another invitation to dinner. This time the carriers of the invitation were two elderly women who certainly couldn't be former Japanese collaborators. Nevertheless, to avoid being involved in another get-rich-quick scheme, I asked a couple of questions: "Where will the dinner be held? Who will be present at the dinner?"

"Oh, it's just a family dinner at the home of Mr. and Mrs. Park." They added, "They are highly respected citizens in the community and very good friends of the mayor."

I was somewhat assured there wouldn't be any shenanigans, but to be doubly sure I asked, "Who else will be at the dinner?"

"Only one other guest—Dr. Lee. She is the only dentist in Chunchon."

A woman dentist; very interesting, I thought to myself. "Ladies, thank you very much for the invitation. I'll be there this coming Saturday evening at seven o'clock."

As they bowed and started for the door, one of the women turned her head and said, smiling, "Dr. Lee is very anxious to meet you."

I found the doctor, in her mid-thirties, quite attractive and very charming. I also noticed the two women who brought the dinner invitation hovering in the background and overseeing the dinner. At the time, however, I couldn't figure out just who they were. Mr. and Mrs. Park, my hosts, were very dignified and mellow. I was very appreciative of the homey atmosphere and, in contrast to the fancy banquet, the very delicious family dinner. I was pleased to observe that Dr. Lee seemed to show genuine enthusiasm for the dinner.

Mr. Park, a quiet old man, addressed me. "Mr. Hyun, I knew your father, the Reverend Hyun Soon."

I was surprised and pleased to listen to what Mr. Park had to say.

"Yes, I saw him and heard him preach."

"When was that, Mr. Park?"

"Must have been at least thirty-five years ago. He came here to Chunchon and conducted a Methodist revival service."

"I have heard from my father that Reverend Hyun was a very powerful speaker," Dr. Lee remarked unexpectedly.

"Yes, he was a man of faith, and his sermon moved everyone. And when he asked the people to come forward and be baptized, hundreds of men and women walked up and knelt before him. Instantly, they were all converted and became Christians."

"Well, Mr. Hyun," Dr. Lee spoke again, "like your father, you are also doing good work helping the Korean people."

Before I could respond to Dr. Lee's remark, out of nowhere the two women appeared and sat behind us, and one of them completely changed our conversation by asking no one in particular, "How old do you think Mr. Hyun is?"

Hearing no response, the woman continued. "Why, Mr. Hyun is almost forty years old, and he still isn't married."

Everyone broke into laughter, only to prompt the other woman to say, "Well, look at Dr. Lee. She is thirty-five, and she's never been married."

In embarrassment, Dr. Lee slapped the woman's knee and reprimanded her, "Dear Auntie [a polite form of addressing an older woman], who asked you to tell everybody my age!" Another burst of laughter.

"But it's no crime." It was Mrs. Park who commented soberly. "They are both waiting for the right man and woman to show up."

Now I felt embarrassed, and to stop the drift of conversation, I said, "I've been too busy to think about getting married." Then I added, "And I'm sure Dr. Lee must have been just as busy with her school and establishing her professional practice."

"Let's talk about something else." Dr. Lee dismissed the whole subject.

The next day I did what turned out to be a foolish thing: I telephoned Dr. Lee and asked if I might come and see her dental office. Honestly, I was merely curious to find out what a Korean dental clinic looked like.

"Of course, you are more than welcome at any time."

"I'll drop in after five, after finishing my work."

The dental clinic was a one-room affair in what would normally be the servant's room in Dr. Lee's home. Once inside I found the room as meticulously clinical as it could be. Modern dental chair, glass cabinet for medical equipment and supplies, and a sterilizer. The only thing lacking was an X-ray machine. I asked Dr. Lee how she was able to work without an X-ray facility.

"Oh," she said, "I send the patient to the X-ray lab in town."

I complimented her for her very fine dental clinic and told her it was comparable to any clinic in California.

She thanked me and quickly changed the subject. "You must be very lonesome, so far away from your home."

I parried as quickly. "Oh, Dr. Lee, I am so busy—I have no time to be lonesome."

She didn't or wouldn't believe me. She said, "Surely you must have some time away from your work, Mr. Hyun. What do you do or can you do all by yourself?"

I felt like I was being corralled. Speechless for a moment, I stared at her. She struck me as quite a beautiful woman, and I felt a burst of desire to embrace and kiss her. The moment passed, and I found myself telling her, "Oh, there are other officers. We talk and play cards, but most of the time I lie in my bunk and read."

Very wistfully, she said in almost a whisper, "I am very sorry for you, Mr. Hyun."

I still had another surprise the next morning. In my office, I happened to look out the window and saw the same two women walking up. What? Another dinner invitation? They came in, sat down, and took a deep breath as though they had been running. I was also breathless, waiting to hear their new mission.

"We heard," one of them said in a modulated tone of voice, "you paid a visit to Dr. Lee yesterday."

What could I say but yes.

"Dr. Lee is a rare and wonderful woman. Don't you think so?"

Again, what else could I say but yes.

"Mr. Hyun," the other woman took up the intriguing conversation, "you are old enough to get married and have a family."

No comment—I just fidgeted.

Dauntless, the woman went on. "You two would make a wonderful couple and become parents of beautiful children."

Only then, suddenly, it dawned on me that these two were not ordinary women; they were the traditional Korean matchmakers. In my childhood in Seoul, I had heard of the indispensable and clever work of the matchmaker, who was always a woman. Carrying a large bundle on her head, she would travel through rich neighborhoods and walk into any home she chose; the bundle on her head gave her that unquestionable right. Once in the house, after due salutations and greetings, she would place the bundle on the living room floor and spread it open. The lady of the house, together with all the household women, would sit around the bundle and examine the contents: threads of all colors, needles of various sizes, patterns for embroidery, and many tempting items that the women would pick up and enviously examine.

That's when the real mission of the tradeswoman—the matchmaker—was presented to the mistress of the house. "Dear Auntie [every lady of the house became her "Auntie"], your noble son is already fourteen years old."

"Yes, I know," the lady would acknowledge. "And he is becoming quite restless."

"Of course. We should find a bride for him."

"Do you have anyone in mind?" the lady would casually ask.

Before answering, the matchmaker would have to accommodate other women who wanted to know the prices for their selected items and conclude the transactions. She would quickly finish her business and wait for them to leave. At last alone with the mistress, she would reveal a very precious secret. "Auntie, I have two beautiful young ladies who are ready for marriage; one is fourteen years old, and the other fifteen."

"What's their family background?"

"The father of the fourteen year old, named Cho, is a teacher who trains boys for government examinations."

"That sounds interesting," the lady would respond.

"Wait, Auntie, until you hear about the fifteen year old. Her father, named Lee, is a palace physician, and she is very strong, ready to take care of all the work in the house."

"Have you told them about our son?"

"Not yet, Auntie, but if you wish, I would do so immediately."

"Well," the lady would muse, "as you very well know, our master has served as governor in three different counties."

The matchmaker would then be ready to prophesy a successful union very soon.

And I was now in the clutches of not one, but two, matchmakers. In my lifetime, I've had a few narrow escapes from "traps," but this encounter with Korean matchmakers made me completely helpless. Just to rid myself of these formidable emissaries, I said, "Ladies, I shall discuss the matter with Dr. Lee." And to hurry them away, I added, "Thank you very much."

How could I deal with this dilemma? The only answer: Run! Escape! Run!

Soon after their departure, I submitted a request for immediate transfer to Seoul. I made up a story and told it to my boss, the colonel. "My aunt in Seoul is dying. I must go and look after her and all her affairs."

At the crack of dawn the next day, armed with the official transfer, a corporal in a jeep drove me out of Chunchon, and within hours I checked into the officers' quarters in Seoul. Only then did I breathe easily and relax. I kept thinking, that was a close call; yes, a very close call!

A few weeks later, when I returned to the officers' quarters one afternoon, I got a message there was someone waiting to see me. Quite curious, I walked into the reception room, and there she was: Dr. Lee, the dentist from Chunchon! So, I hadn't escaped from her after all! I noticed at a glance she was very attractive. Her jet-black hair was rolled up in a knot and held together by a silver pin. She was dressed in trim Western dress, and her face shone as she looked up and rose from the chair.

I didn't know quite how to greet her. "What are you doing here, Dr. Lee?" I blurted.

"I came to Seoul to pick up some medical supplies." She sounded relaxed and at ease.

Not I. I was nervous as a cat, and, frankly, a little frightened. I said, "Let's go into another room where we can have some privacy." I ushered her into a little room and shut the door.

"Mr. Hyun," she said softly, "why did you leave Chunchon so suddenly?"

"Dr. Lee, let me be frank. Those two women, the matchmakers, frightened me."

"Why?"

"Because they were pushing me into marrying you."

"Mr. Hyun," she said almost in a whisper, "is that so frightening?"

"No, not really. But Dr. Lee, I am not ready to get married; I have too much work to do before settling down."

"Then, why didn't you come and tell me? I would have understood."

"I was a coward, I guess."

Dr. Lee stood up and bid adieu by saying, "I wish you good fortune in all your undertaking. And please remember me with kind thoughts." Before I could find words, she went out the door and disappeared.

My job was to discuss the policies and activities of the AMG with Korean religious and political leaders and to bring any criticisms, ideas, and suggestions back to the AMG administration. The idea behind this approach was sound and worthy, but in practice impractical, even deceptive. After all, the AMG was a military government ruled by military officers and by military proclamations. Invariably, the Korean leaders I met with would laugh when I asked for their ideas and suggestions.

"We are not fooled," they would say. "Our ideas and suggestions are useless. The AMG does what it wants to, regardless." It was cynical, but true.

One day, as I was driving around the city, I happened to look in the rearview mirror and saw another jeep some distance behind me.

Could it be—somebody was following me? To test my suspicion, I accelerated and turned into a narrow alley. Sure enough, the second jeep was still there. I stopped; so did the follower. Incredible! I was a member of G-2, Army intelligence, and I was being tailed by somebody else from the G-2. A spy spying on the spy! But I lost interest in keeping my eye and my mind on the "tail" and went on with my work.

Among the prominent political leaders I met with were Kim Koo, the last president of the Korean Provisional Government, and Lyuh Woon Hyung, the leader of the Korean People's Republic, which he organized immediately following the Japanese surrender ending World War II.

I knew both of them well in Shanghai during the tumultuous years when my father traveled to the four corners of the earth trying to raise enough money to sustain the Provisional Government. Kim Koo remained to the bitter end and kept alive the name of the Free Korean Provisional Government. Lyuh Woon Hyung was my special hero. He spent all of his spare time with young people. He was an enthusiastic booster of our Korean Youth Revolutionary Society and our baseball and soccer teams. Whenever we played against the Chinese or American teams, Mr. Lyuh was sure to be there, clapping, jumping, and yelling with encouragement. That picture remained with me all my life.

Both of these patriots—Kim Koo and Lyuh Woon Hyung—met the same fate. They both spent their lives in the struggle for Korean independence and had earned the respect and trust of the people. During 1946—1948, when the creation of a separate South Korean government became imminent, the struggle for political power centered around these two, plus the expatriate from the United States, Syngman Rhee, who held the inside track as America's favorite son. As the election for the presidency of South Korea neared, Lyuh and then Kim were both assassinated.

I also visited Park Huen-Young, the secretary of the Korean Communist Party. He, too, was one of my heroes in Shanghai. When the Provisional Government was struggling for survival, Park contacted the infant Chinese Communist Party and received financial aid, circa 1921—1922.

He organized a school and taught young Koreans, including me, about agrarian and industrial economy, about the working class and class struggle. It was all new to me. I had no idea of the signifi-cance of what I was learning. Nevertheless, Teacher Park's fervor was moving, and we spent days and nights studying. When I emigrated to Hawaii in 1924, I learned that Teacher Park had slipped into Korea and organized the farmers and the factory workers into unions and waged brave struggles against the Japanese. A price was placed on his head, and frequently the Japanese reported Park's capture, but Park always resurfaced and directed the struggle. The Japanese couldn't track Park down because he was protected by the people who revered him as their national hero.

The jeep that tailed me all over Seoul for weeks finally began to bear some ominous results. I was summoned to headquarters daily and subjected to intense questioning.

"Where did you go yesterday?"

"Whom did you visit?"

"What did you discuss?" And so on and so on. It was growing annoying and tiresome. So, one day, eluding my tail, I managed to go to the Korean Communist Party office through the back door. For-tunately, Teacher Park was there, and I had a chance to discuss my problem with him. I told him about the very unpleasant happenings, and about the very discouraging work I had to carry on.

Teacher Park wasn't disturbed. He said, "After all, the American military government is here for only one purpose; to establish a U.S. base and to convert Korea into an American colony."

After much discussion, I said, "Teacher Park, I want to resign my job and come to work with you."

He thought only a moment, then said, "Peter, I know where your heart is. But we have enough people in Korea; there are none in the U.S. who would plead and work for our cause. Go back to America and work for our independence and freedom from there." Of course, I took his advice.

When I bid him farewell in his dingy little office in Seoul, little did I realize that I would never see him again. To escape the inten-sifying attacks on all left-wing organizations, not to mention the Communist Party, by the AMG, Park fled to North Korea. There he joined the North Korean government and became its minister of for-eign affairs.

Early in the morning one day, I was roused by a lieutenant and two GIs. "Sir," the lieutenant addressed me, "you are under arrest."

I couldn't have heard right. I asked, "What did you say?"

"You are under arrest, sir."

I still didn't believe what I thought I heard. "Did you say, Lieutenant, I am under arrest?"

"That's right, sir."

"Tell me, Lieutenant, what's the charge?"

"I don't know, sir."

"Then tell me who ordered the arrest."

The lieutenant pulled out a piece of paper, unfolded it and thrust it at me, saying, "Here's the order, sir, duly signed by the chief of G-2 [Army intelligence]."

I took the paper and read it. The arrest order was for real. "Well, Lieutenant, where do we go?"

"I am to put you on the ship sailing for the States this afternoon. But the ship won't cast off until late in the afternoon. We'll go to the Makpo army camp nearby and wait a few hours there."

It was about an hour's drive to Makpo. We entered the huge military camp that was used as the staging center for incoming and outgoing U.S. soldiers. We passed rows and rows of barracks and stopped in front of a tent. The GI carried my duffle bag and the lieutenant motioned me to enter. The tent was barren except for a cot and a chair. I was offered the cot and the officer took the chair. I lay down, shut my eyes, and traced the recent events, trying to determine what triggered the arrest. The reports of the driver of the jeep that tailed me for days might have had some grounds, but I was almost certain my two visits to the Korean Communist Party headquarters were the clincher.

I opened my eyes and turned my head to look at the officer guarding me. I almost jumped out of the cot. A .45 automatic—an ugly weapon—was resting on the lieutenant's lap, undoubtedly loaded. Under any pretext, he could shoot and kill me. Maybe he already had such an order. Strangely, I was not frightened. What worried me was the little "black book" in my pocket. It contained the names and addresses of all the Korean religious and political leaders whom I had visited. If the black book fell into the hands of the G-2, everyone would be implicated. I had to get rid of it somehow, but any suspicious move and I could be shot on the spot.

Without moving a muscle, I called, "Lieutenant . . ."

"Yes, sir?"

"I have to go to the latrine."

"All right, sir; let's go."

The officer motioned me to lead, and he followed behind with the .45 jutting ominously from inside his coat pocket. Walking very slowly, two blocks away, I found the latrine. I was afraid the officer might follow me in, so I stopped at the entrance and said, "I'll be only a couple of minutes."

"All right, sir. I'll be here," he said.

Inside, I quickly pulled down my pants and squatted over one of the holes. Fortunately, there was no one else. I took the black book out of my pocket, tore up the pages and threw them down the hole. Fully relieved, I zipped up my pants and came out.

Back at the tent, I lay down on the cot and resumed my silent thoughts: Go ahead and shoot me. I've nothing to worry about now. And I actually fell asleep. I was awakened by the lieutenant saying, "Sir, it's time to go."

We were headed for Inchon Harbor, where I would be placed aboard a ship departing for the States. Inchon, the second largest port in South Korea, was known for its world's highest tide—more than thirty feet. Ships could come and dock during high tide, quickly discharge their cargo, and then had to sail out of the port before the tide receded, leaving nothing but mud along all the docks. This was the reason for the careful timing of my arrival at the harbor. It was high tide.

The lieutenant and I boarded a military launch, which carried us to a ship anchored miles away in deep water. Mission accomplished, the lieutenant saluted, and as the launch returned to port, he shouted "Good luck, sir!"

It was a liberty ship carrying a company of quartermaster corps back to the States. I got a bunk in the hold, where I stretched out and contemplated the strange twist of fate: A Korean American with a rank of major being expelled from Korea—the land of his ancestors—by the American military government. I was rather uneasy, suspecting that everyone aboard knew about my expulsion. Nevertheless, I ventured out and began pacing back and forth on the deck. There was no finger pointing; nobody paid any attention to me. I surmised the only one briefed about me was the captain.

Our ship had a layover in Yokohama. Capitalizing on the opportunity, I went ashore, got on the train to Tokyo, and located my dear

Sister Alice. It was a tearful reunion. I learned that she was also the victim of the same fate as mine. In a WAC uniform, she was arrested by the G-2 and deported out of Korea to Japan. Under house arrest in WAC headquarters, she was waiting for a ship going to Los Angeles.

I learned my ship was headed for Portland, Oregon. Resigning myself, I decided to relax and enjoy my enforced vacation. I took my three meals, got my exercise walking the deck, and spent the rest of the time reading.

One morning, while walking, I witnessed what appeared to be a very puzzling sight: a line of GIs passing some freight out of the hold and dumping it into the ocean. I moved closer to see what they were dumping. I couldn't believe my eyes; they were throwing overboard typewriters, adding machines, file cases, office furniture, and all kinds of valuable things. This was the day before we were to dock in Portland. Completely baffled, I asked some of the officers about the dumping. No, they didn't know anything about that. Then I corralled some GIs and asked nonchalantly, "What's all the dumping about?" And from them, I got the answer. With all that cargo, they would have to spend days in port checking and rechecking the inventory and filing reports.

"We are clean now," one GI said. "We won't have to hang around Portland for days; we can go right home."

From Oregon, I flew straight to Washington, D.C.—thanks to the army travel papers. For me, the capitol was a no-man's-land. I didn't know anything about NW and SW, not to mention NE and SE. But I could always use the telephone directory, through which I located several organizations such as the ACLU (American Civil Liberties Union), who might be interested in the case of my expulsion from Korea. I was advised to seek the help of Hugh DeLacey, the representative from Seattle, Washington. I had never dreamed that some day I would enter the offices of the U.S. federal government. As I was approaching the imposing structure, an odd feeling enveloped me: I was entering the American "Forbidden City."

Mr. DeLacey put me at ease; he wasn't at all like a politician, a man of smooth and glib tongue. He was genuinely surprised to see me and anxious to find out about my mission. Feeling perfectly at home, I told him the whole story of my odyssey: my family history; my appointment as a liaison officer for the AMG; my contacts with all the Korean political leaders, including the Communist secretary;

my arrest without charge or hearing; the incarceration with the threat of death; and my unceremonious expulsion from Korea.

Mr. DeLacey heard me out and muttered to himself, "Incredible! Unbelievable!" He said, "I shall submit a letter of protest to the Secretary of War, Patterson [it was the Department of War before it was changed to the Department of Defense], and demand an investigation and an apology."

Hearing the response from a member of the House of Representatives was satisfying enough for me. Of course, we never heard from Patterson, the Secretary of War. With such a twist of fate, my career in the American military government in Korea abruptly came to an end.

# 12

## MARRIAGE— BUSINESS— FATHERHOOD

Thrust into civilian life overnight, the necessary adjustments caused some problems. The most annoying was having to pay cash for every little necessity. A suit to replace my uniform, and among other items, I bought a couple pairs of socks. In contrast to the GI issue, they were colorful and good-looking. It felt novel but good to get into civilian clothes again, and the bright socks. At the end of the day when I took off my shoes, I saw no socks; they had simply disintegrated and disappeared. Someone explained this phenomenon to me; you see, there was a shortage of cotton during the war, so the DuPont textile mills produced ersatz thread to weave, among other products, men's socks, which just melted and disappeared under body heat.

I began my reentry into civilian life with a visit to my dear Sister Elizabeth living in the heart of New York's Chinatown. It was a moldy, old apartment with two bedrooms. Fortunately only her two daughters, Doris, ten, and Eleanor, eight, were living with her and her husband. Her son, Chang-Nai, was off at a boarding school, Viewpoint School, in the Adirondacks.

A visit to the school offered a pleasant interlude. A country estate had been converted into a boarding school. A vast circle of woods surrounded the school compound and the lake. Chang-Nai had happily adjusted to the boarding school and had been elected president of the student body and was doing well in all his classes. After a few days, the owner of the school, called Sunny by everyone, asked me if I would consider staying and teaching the children. I agreed to extend my stay for one month.

In the faculty, there was a young woman named Dorothy whom Sunny regarded as her adopted daughter. Her duties were to be the general assistant to all the teachers and the housekeepers as well. Another faculty member was a young man named Jack, who taught physical education and freshman English. Each day, when the classes and the study hour were over, and the kids tucked into beds, the three of us would get together. We would retreat to the empty bungalow at the top of the hill and have our midnight snack. Mysteriously, Jack would always produce a piece of thick steak—we never asked how he got it—and would prepare it according to his recipe. It never failed to be juicy and delicious. And just as mysteriously, he would produce several bottles of beer to wash down our steak. This nightly ritual went on for a while.

One weekend, Dorothy offered to drive me to New York City in her car. She dropped me off at Grand Central Station, and I went straight to Sister Elizabeth's. I gave her a glowing report of Viewpoint School and of the extraordinary lady, Sunny. Sister Elizabeth cooked a special Korean dinner for me, and we talked until the wee hours. From her I got news of Sister Alice. She had received an honorable discharge from the army and settled in Los Angeles with her son, Wellington, now a high school student. Brother David joined her and was attending the University of Southern California, studying architecture. Sister Alice, always resourceful, was in the midst of arranging for the emigration of the rest of the family from Honolulu to California.

The next day Dorothy and I met at the appointed hour and headed back to Viewpoint. She stopped once or twice and parked off the road, and we talked. She told me about her interesting visit with her friend and I told her of mine. We arrived at Viewpoint in time to have our midnight repast with Jack.

The very next day, I got an invitation to see Sunny in her "inner sanctum." As a beginning, she asked me how I enjoyed my trip to New York City.

"Fine," I said.

Then she changed the tone of her voice and said, "Peter, let me ask you a serious question."

With no idea of what was coming, I said, "Sure, Sunny."

"Peter," she said, "how would you like to marry my Dorothy?"

I was stunned, speechless.

"Peter, Dorothy loves you very much." Sunny broke the deadly silence. "You like her, too, don't you?"

"Yes, yes," I stuttered, "of course, I like her very much." I recovered enough of my senses to add, "But this is a very serious matter—I have to think it over. . . ."

"Of course," Sunny agreed. "Think it over and let me know."

I ran to my room and hurriedly packed my suitcase, called a cab, and got on a late bus to New York City. With no time to lose, I caught the first plane to Los Angeles to visit Sister Alice.

Once again, Sister Alice and I had a tearful reunion. Eagerly, we exchanged notes on what had happened after leaving each other in Tokyo. She was put on a ship sailing for Honolulu while I was sent to Portland, Oregon. She laughed when I told her about my protest with the Secretary of War, Patterson.

"You've never heard from him, have you?" was her mocking comment.

About this time, a general exodus to California of the Hyun family took place. It started with baby Sister Mary and her husband, Walter, and daughter, Ruth, emigrating to Mill Valley, California. This was followed by the major relocation of Sister Elizabeth and her children. What probably prompted the move was her husband, Kim's, resumption of his nomadic life—his closing his business and surrendering to the call of life on the road. Sister Elizabeth packed her two daughters and moved west to Los Angeles. She bought a liquor store and became its slave twelve hours a day. She would be happy later, nevertheless, to send her daughters to the University of California, Los Angeles, where both would do remarkably well. Her son Chang-Nai was left in the care of Sunny, practitioner of Christian Science and head of Viewpoint School. Before his graduation, Chang-Nai received a full scholarship to Yale University, which he would attend in the fall. Brother Paul was still on the high seas with the merchant marine, plying the Asian ports. That left Umma and Papa with Brother Joshua still stranded in Honolulu. Sister Alice was determined to rescue and bring them to California. Before we could fulfill that dream, we first had to find a way to make a living and support our parents.

We learned from Sister Elizabeth that the liquor store business made a pretty good living. With borrowed money—five thousand dollars (I didn't ask Sister Alice where the money came from)—Alice and I bought a liquor store on Bunker Hill at the northwest corner of First Street and Grand Avenue. Naturally, we named it the First Grand Liquor Store. Who could have guessed that some years later the store would become the main entrance to the Los Angeles Music Center. Bunker Hill, at the time, was the worst tenement district in all of Los Angeles, including the notorious East Los Angeles. More than forty thousand people lived within four blocks on Bunker Hill.

After sundown, it was a no-man's-land. How did two innocent Koreans survive there? It was all done by Sister Alice. On holidays, especially Thanksgiving, Christmas, and New Years' day, we packaged gifts for every kid in the neighborhood. Our store became the neighborhood institution. Bunker Hill had more than its share of holdups and robberies. Every little store expected to be the victim of a half dozen holdups each year. In four years of operation, the First Grand Liquor Store never suffered a single holdup. How did we account for that miracle? Our neighbors on the Hill—they protected us. Whenever a young stranger with a companion or two entered our store, a group of neighbors would appear and hang around the store until the strangers left.

"Do you know who those guys were?" they would ask us when the strangers had gone.

"No, who are they?"

"Gangsters! Holdup artists!"

I also conceived and introduced an innovation in the liquor store: a mini market. I learned to purchase meats and produce at the wholesale markets. I bought only the best cuts of meat, the best-known brands of processed meats and cheese. At the crack of dawn each morning, I went to the produce market and bought crates of lettuce, tomatoes, and bell peppers—all high quality. I installed two refrigerated display cases and mounted a very attractive display. It's not true that poor working people buy only the cheapest. They appreciate quality foodstuff as much as anyone else. Afterward, I also stocked some popular grocery items such as soups, corned beef hash, sardines, anchovies, and so on. Then the most unusual display of what was then called "Oriental food": soy sauce, sesame oil, along with catsup, mayonnaise and vinegar. Our mini market was an instant success; only a lack of space prevented its expansion.

Within six months, we amassed a fortune—one thousand dollars. Using it as a down payment and applying for my GI loan, we bought a house on the outskirts of Silver Lake. It was a magnificent Spanish stucco circa 1900. Located at the top of a hill on Micheltorena Street, the main floor contained two large bedrooms, a spacious kitchen, and a long dining room that led down to a high-ceilinged living room with a fireplace. The price of eighteen thousand dollars also included all the furnishings, draperies, and kitchen equipment, all of which were in very good taste. As a bonus, attached to the house were two one-bedroom apartments; one next to the main floor with a separate entrance, and the other in a semi-basement, also with a separate entrance. The rentals from the two units could pay more than half of the monthly mortgage payment. The most rewarding feature of the property was the vacant hillside lot that would serve as a garden where both Umma and Papa could grow all the flowers and vegetables they wished. We immediately wired the plane fare for three and asked Umma, Papa, and Brother Joshua to leave Honolulu immediately.

The family exodus completed, we settled down to a new way of life in Los Angeles—Sister Alice and I running the liquor store, Brother David pursuing his study of architecture at USC, Sister Alice's son Wellington finishing his last year at Marshall High School with high honors, Umma and Papa laboring on the hillside to start a beautiful garden, and Brother Joshua converting the two-car garage into a workshop to carry on his trade as a cabinetmaker.

The family life ran much too smoothly for comfort. I always thrived on wrestling with problems and struggling against challenges. Naturally, I found one. The desire and temptation I had buried deep inside me suddenly surfaced with a volcanic fire: I wanted to get married. Considering all the circumstances—a comfortable living, a house, not to mention my age (thirty-nine)—the time was ripe to get married and raise a family. I launched a concentrated hunt for a wife.

By 1946, there was already a sizable Korean community in Los Angeles, my hunting grounds. I began to attend the Korean Methodist Church, whose young minister, the Reverend Key Chang, was eventually to become my brother-in-law. There was a lively group of young Korean girls, all pretty and interesting. Branded as a legitimate footloose bachelor, the son of the famous Reverend Soon Hyun, I was courted by all the mothers of the young girls. After service, every Sunday, I would receive more than one invitation to lunch.

Accepting their invitations offered me an opportunity not only to meet the girls close up, but also to observe their home atmosphere.

I had always harbored a weakness for a nurse's uniform; the white gown and cap were beautiful and romantic. I learned that one of the daughters of Marie Lee, the daughter of a deacon in my father's church in Honolulu, was a registered nurse. I remembered Marie Lee had given birth to three daughters, the last two, twins. They had moved to Los Angeles some years before, but it seemed incredible that one of the twins had grown up and become a registered nurse. The other twin, Lila, was now the wife of the young minister, the Reverend Key Chang.

It wasn't too difficult to get all the information I needed to pay the young nurse a surprise visit. One Sunday afternoon, I drove to Los Angeles General Hospital and parked in front of the nurses' home. I reported to the housemother and said I wished to see a nurse named Anna Lee. She looked through her index cards and said, "She's not off duty yet, but she will be shortly if you wish to wait."

"Yes, I don't mind waiting."

Before I could settle down in the waiting room, Anna appeared and stood at the door, staring at me. Oh, she was the pretty picture I had imagined.

I stepped over and said, "I knew you when you were a little girl in Honolulu."

"Yes, I've heard of you, Peter," she said. "They told me a lot about you."

"I hope nothing bad."

"Yes, some bad, but mostly good."

So, she has a sense of humor, too, I thought.

She excused herself to change her clothes and returned in minutes in a pretty pink dress. "Where shall we go?" she asked.

"You must be hungry," I said. "Let's go eat something. Do you like Chinese food?"

"I adore it!" She sounded like a little girl, which I liked.

At the Chinese restaurant, I was also pleased to find her with hardly any inhibitions; she ate with full enjoyment, and with genuine pleasure she said, "Oh, this is really delicious!"

We finished the dinner with a pot of hot tea and almond and fortune cookies on the side. I don't remember what fortunes the cookies told us, but I noticed her dunking the pieces of cookies in the hot tea, so I followed and dunked mine. That's how I learned to dunk my fortune cookies into hot tea.

Coming out of the restaurant, it was still too early to take Anna back to the hospital dormitory. So I asked her if we could go for a spin.

"Sure," she answered readily. "Why not?"

The only so-called "lovers' lane" I knew of was above Griffith Park. We drove around the hill for a while, neither of us saying anything, and wound up behind the observatory. I found a viewpoint off the road, eased into it, and parked. Looking down on the lighted city below, we exchanged some banal remarks regarding the beautiful view. In between, the pauses of silence became longer and longer. Finally, I gathered enough courage to spit out, "Anna, may I kiss you?"

To my surprise and relief, she answered, "Sure, why not?"

I slowly kissed her very gently, like a gentleman should. Again to my surprise, she responded with her lips embracing my mouth. Excited, I pulled her close to me, held her face in my hands, and sucked her lips in my mouth for a prolonged moment.

"Oh, Anna," I gasped, "I have never kissed anyone like that in my life."

"Neither have I," she sighed.

We must have spent an hour enjoying and feeling at home with each other. Then my old self took hold of me and I said, "Anna, it's getting late, I'd better take you home."

The Sunday afternoon visits to the nurses' home became a ritual. We tried different restaurants for dinner, but always wound up behind the Griffith Park observatory. Eventually, when we lost all self-control and passionately embraced each other, it all seemed natural; I had no inhibitions, no shame. Our repeated physical unions convinced us both that we should get married and raise a family.

That's when the trouble started. Getting wind of our affair, Anna's mother, Marie, raised holy hell with her. "What's this I hear about you and Peter?"

"Well, we like each other very much," said Anna, trying to calm her mother. Anna then added, "We are going to get married."

"No! You must not see Peter any more!"

"Why not?"

"He's too old for you!"

When nothing could deter her daughter, her mother's final verdict was, "Well, Peter is a Communist!"

Even that didn't scare off Anna. Her father, Jason Lee, joined Marie and tried to break up our relationship. Jason really had very little to say in any of his family's matters. He lived with a young mistress in Chicago, and made an awful lot of money running an exclusive gambling house. The source of his gold mine was the American Legion Hall in Chicago where, with complete police protection, he ran a little Las Vegas. His regular daily cut from every table of black jack, dice, and poker ran into the thousands. He put some of his fortune to good use. He bought a house for Marie on Gramercy Place, which became known as the Korean Palace. And when his oldest daughter, Winifred, married Dr. Yin Kim, a dentist, he had a medical building built for him on Jefferson Boulevard. Now, on one of his rare visits home, he sided with Marie and strenuously objected to our marriage.

Anna and I considered the situation and agreed our only recourse was to elope to Las Vegas. Of course, I had kept Sister Alice fully informed of the progress of my relationship with Anna. She was not too enthusiastic about the match, but she expressed no objections. When informed of our plans for elopement, she said, "Good for you! Go! Go right away!" My nephew Wellington, Sister Alice's son, helped by driving us out to the Burbank airport. Left alone with a suitcase, we had a half-hour wait for the Las Vegas flight. We were both excited, and confused as well; we weren't sure whether to be happy or sad. Then suddenly, we were stunned to see someone walking toward us; it was the Reverend Key Chang, the husband of Anna's sister, Lila.

Stopping before us, he said awkwardly, "Hi, there."

"How did you find us here?"

"Peter, your sister told me."

"Well, what's the message?"

"Anna and Peter," his voice changed to a serious tone, "don't go away. Your mother wants you to come back. She wants to give you a real wedding."

"But she was so deadly opposed to our marriage."

"Well, she has changed her mind. Please come back. I'll take you home."

We had a long wait for the wedding. It seemed Marie decided

to go all out and make it the biggest wedding the Korean community had ever seen. She always took pride in putting on a show; show of wealth and prestige, proper form, and appearance. Invitations were printed in archaic type and mailed; gowns for the bride, the bridesmaids, and the flower girl had to be designed and fitted; tuxedos for the groom, his best man, and attendants; not to mention the decorations for the church and the altar, hiring the organist and ushers, and hundreds of other details all very important to Marie. I believe the church chosen was the First Methodist Church on Adams Boulevard.

Even before the church door opened, the wedding party was there for preparations; men in one room and women in the opposite room. Men didn't have much to do; discard our street clothes and put on the tuxedos and the patent leather shoes provided for us. There were altogether eight of us: the groom (me), the best man (Anna's brother), and six attendants. A makeup man came and dusted our faces with perfumed powder and brushed our hair in place. It was quite another scene in the women's room. It was strictly taboo for any man, especially the groom, to venture into the room. But I could imagine and guess: The fussing and fitting of gowns for the bridesmaids must be an endless tucking, pinning, and tying. The painful work must have been doubled and tripled when it came to dressing the bride and the little flower girl. I could only feel sorry for the torture Anna must have been going through.

It seemed like hours had passed when I looked at my watch; fifteen minutes to eleven! Fifteen minutes before the wedding bells were to ring. Soon, the ushers came to the door and told us to be ready for the wedding march. We had practiced this ceremony several times before, but my mind was blank. With the organ rumbling "Here Comes the Bride," I began the long journey down the aisle to the altar. I was impressed that the huge church was nearly filled. Marie's invitations had done the job. Besides the entire congregation of the Korean Methodist Church, there was also a sprinkle of my father's followers and their families. Nearing the altar I noticed the bride's family occupied the first three front rows on the left, and on the right the Hyun family, only a half of one row—Papa and Umma, my two sisters, Alice and Elizabeth, my two nieces, Doris and Eleanor, and Wellie, my nephew.

The picture of the beautifully gowned bridesmaids and the tuxedo-clad groom's attendants in the midst of huge bouquets of flowers was so impressive. Marie, the moving spirit of all the arrangements, must have been filled with pleasure and pride, which was exactly why she didn't want us to elope. The formal procedure of binding us as man and wife in marriage was also interesting. My brother-in-law to be, the Reverend Key Chang, for the benefit of the elderly Koreans, conducted the ceremony in both Korean and English. Both of us faithfully answered "yes" to all the challenging questions, exchanged our wedding rings, and duly performed the wedding kisses.

When we turned to march back down the aisle, instead of the customary wedding march, we heard someone singing the "Hawaiian Wedding Song"; it was Dr. Yin Kim, the dentist, the husband of Anna's older sister Winifred. I thought it was refreshing for a change, and Yin's voice was quite soothing.

I had already prepared a house to be our home. In the Silver Lake area, at 1640 Dillon Street, I took over the mortgage from Anna's brother Jason, whose marriage was breaking up. It was a delightful hillside stucco with two bedrooms, a living room open to the view of the city, a large linoleum-covered den, dining room and kitchen, and a fairly large backyard. We hastily unloaded all the wedding gifts, shed our costumes, and drove away for our honeymoon—Palm Springs bound.

We checked in at the Desert Inn and immediately christened our wedding bed. We spent three days, but not all of them in bed. In between making love, we wined and dined to reinforce ourselves. Yes, I had learned to drink a little wine. We danced and we visited the shops. And we even found time to go to a movie. I still remember the picture we saw, *Green Mansions*. It was the happiest three days of my life. They always said "all good things must come to an end." How right they were, whoever "they" were. We were on our way to return to the cruel realities of life.

For a wedding present, I stopped at a kennel by the roadside and bought a thoroughbred puppy—an English spaniel—for my wife. She loved the little animal and cuddled him in her arms all the way to Los Angeles.

For a few months we lived floating on air: that is, in love. Everything around the house was beautiful and glorious. The jacaranda tree in the front lawn, the morning glory vines over the backyard fence, and even the tall stone wall separating our house from our neighbor's; they were all beautiful. And inside, a beautiful kitchen, where I laid new plastic tiles. The four-burner gas range, the Whirlpool washer and dryer, and even the spare bathroom in the kitchen corner seemed so special and perfect. I lined the walls in the den with bookshelves and began filling them with my collections. The inviting rectangular table and chairs in the dining room, the two bedrooms, one facing the garden in back and the other with a balcony looking over the sprawling city—all were perfect.

Soon our home became the social center for family and friends. Birthdays and holidays were always celebrated at our home. On the occasion of the seventieth anniversary of Umma and Papa's wedding, we staged an authentic Korean wedding ceremony. My parent's friends made up complete traditional wedding costumes for the bride and the groom, Papa and Umma. They also prepared a wedding table with stemmed porcelain dishes loaded with all kinds of delicacies.

Surrounded by all our family and friends, the "bride" and "groom," both over eighty years of age and dressed in colorful costumes, were ushered in and placed on straw mats facing each other. They were now ready to bow to each other as a symbol of mutual acceptance as husband and wife.

Suddenly, Umma broke up the ceremony by shouting at Papa, "Listen; the first time we got married, I bowed to you first. This time, you bow to me first!"

Papa, laughing, obliged. Kneeling and bringing up his hands together to his brow, he bent over and bowed until his brow touched the floor.

"Hey, that's pretty good for an eighty-year-old groom," Umma said. She then rose, ever so demure and coy. She bent her knees and brought her hands down to separate the hems of her full skirt. In perfect control, she brought down her whole body to the floor and, half closing her eyes, lowered her head and bowed. The assemblage broke into applause. The wedding feast followed, with everyone digging into the mounds of delicacies on the wedding table.

Of all such happy events in the family, the happiest moment for me was when one morning Anna whispered to me, "Darling, I am pregnant."

Our first baby was born on February 9, 1949. Oh, what a beautiful bundle! With Anna's consent, of course, I promptly named her

Paula, after the great actress, Pola Negri. The first and the only time I saw her on the screen was in Shanghai, China, when I was fifteen. The picture of her beautiful face, her stately movements with such dignity, never left me. Like all fathers, I might be slightly prejudiced, but our Paula was really an extraordinary baby. Within weeks she began to recognize people and objects, and the first smile she gave me would have melted anyone's heart. I didn't realize I could be so absorbed and fascinated. Every day there were new discoveries, new revelations. And when she began responding not only with a smile and waving of her tiny hands, but also with dramatic gurgling sounds, I could hardly contain myself.

But my happiest moments with my baby were when, at the end of the day, I put her on my lap and I would sing to her the Korean lullaby:

*Dear Moon*
*Dear Moon*
*My dear bright moon,*
*Our great poet*
*Lee Tai Bak slept there.*
*In the heart of the bright moon*
*There stands an Eternal-Life tree.*
*Chop it down with a silver hatchet,*
*Trim it with a golden hatchet*
*Build a lovely house,*
*Bring my father and my mother*
*And live there happily forever and ever.*

Either the Korean lullaby or my soothing voice, or both, always helped her sleep soundly through the night.

Soon, she was walking and talking. By the time she was three years old, it seemed she never stopped talking during all her waking hours. Whenever we had visitors or a party, Paula preferred to join the adult company and enjoyed pitching in her two cents' worth. At one particular gathering, I felt rather embarrassed at Paula's performance and reprimanded her by saying, "Paula, why must you always have the last word?"

"And a good one, too, Dad," Paula shot back.

Our second bundle of beauty arrived on January 29, 1951.

Again with Anna's consent, I promptly named her Lena, after the great artist, Lena Horne. Not only was the artistry of Horne's performance unmatched, she did not hide her stand for equality, freedom, and justice for all people. When I met her some years later, I told her, "Miss Horne, I have been one of your admirers for many years. I admire not only your extraordinary gift to reach into people's hearts, but I also admire you for your uncompromising belief in freedom and justice for all people." Then I added, "In fact, I have a daughter whom I have named Lena, after you." She was thrilled and said, "I am honored, Mr. 'Hune.'" She gave me a photograph of herself, saying, "Please give this to your Lena and tell her that her namesake wishes her a wonderful life like mine."

With deep gratitude, I thanked her and left. I have always treasured that moment with Lena Horne.

My own Lena was yet another wonderment. Born of the same parents, yet how different she was from her sister! Not round and full like Paula, Lena was lean and delicate. Even as an infant, instead of flailing and bouncing, Lena was gentle and reticent. As the days passed I became mildly alarmed. No, I needn't have worried over Lena. I discovered she was endowed with hidden sensitivities. Her awareness of her surroundings—people and objects—was not exuberant, but sweet and gentle. Through her growth, she kept the pattern of her own responses, always reserved, very subtle.

With two beautiful daughters, I felt a yearning for a son. But how could I predetermine the sex of an offspring? Then, quite accidentally, I came across an article in a medical journal that dealt with the very subject I was mulling over: "How to Determine the Sex of Your Child." It was a report by two doctors in Sweden who had studied, researched, and compiled statistics of births in their hospital by their patients, with particular interest in finding what determined the sex of offspring.

Their report first confirmed that a woman conceives only during the period of ovulation, which follows her monthly menstruation. This period of ovulation lasts for three days. The child conceived at the early part of ovulation would be female, and the child conceived at the latter part of ovulation would be male. I marveled how with such a little margin of time to reproduce life, the human population exploded into billions! How powerful and inexhaustible human desires must be!

This was most interesting to me, and I discussed the phenomenon with my wife. First we agreed we would like to have a son. We then agreed to follow the medical thesis for a son. It was a year after Lena was born when we launched our experiment. Anna had to let me know when her menstruation began and when it ended. Then it was up to me to count the days and refrain from all intimacy. On the third day of ovulation I ejected my whole soul into my wife.

Lo and behold, Anna became pregnant again. By then, we had forgotten all about our little experiment. In due course, it was time to give birth. I waited until the birth pangs accelerated to every ten minutes, and as always, both Anna and I became excited. I led her to the car and drove to the hospital in a hurry. I paced the floor impatiently; then the nurse came and informed me, "Your wife won't be delivering tonight. You may go home and come back in the morning."

It was a long night, and I slept very little. I got up at daybreak, and to kill time drank a cup of coffee and munched on a bowl of cornflakes. I couldn't delay it any longer. I got in the car and drove furiously, dashed into the hospital, and entered Anna's room. I stopped at the threshold and looked at Anna. She was drained and pale, but greeted me with the happiest of smiles. "Darling, we have a son!"

I couldn't believe my ears. "Really, darling?"

"Yes, really. Go look at him."

At the nursery, I stood looking through a plate glass window. A nurse on the other side picked up a newborn and waved it at me. She turned the baby around. She patted the baby all over to let me know the baby was perfect. I just stood there and marvelled; the baby was really my son. The calendar on the wall showed October 15, 1952.

When Anna brought the baby home, I was eager to find a name for our son. I proposed Douglass, after Frederick Douglass. Anna thought it was wonderful. To me, Frederick Douglass symbolized not only the emancipation of an oppressed people, but the struggle for the final freedom and justice for the oppressed. I was confident our little Douglass would grow up and not disappoint his namesake.

With three beautiful children, it slowly dawned on me that one couldn't live on love alone; one must also have bread. But modern day "bread" came in a very expensive package. Bread to pay the house mortgage, taxes, and insurance. Then more bread to pay for food, clothing, and doctors. And bread left over for some enjoyment of life; an occasional party, some weekend excursions, and some contributions to worthwhile causes. Well, I had to face the world and search for a quick answer.

First, I enrolled in an evening school for a course in business. At the same time, I sought out people in various types of businesses and listened to their advice. Among them I ran into a man from New York who established an independent insurance agency. He suggested that instead of going to school, I could study the state insurance manual, take the test, and get a solicitor's license. I could then come and work in his agency, and while earning commissions, he would teach me all about the insurance business. He was convinced that my reputation in the Korean community alone should provide a good start in the business. He said next to food, clothing and housing, insurance was an indispensable item.

Though reluctant, Anna agreed with my stepping into the business world. I transferred the liquor store to my brother Joshua and started my career in the insurance business. I always enjoyed selling ideas and was quite successful doing it. Now I sold all lines of general insurance—fire, auto, liability. In a year, I had many clients, which provided a fairly good living. I also learned a valuable lesson. As a solicitor, all the business I obtained had to be placed in the books of a broker. That broker was the friend who had hired me. The business was then sent to the various companies who issued the policies and paid the commission, which usually ran 20 to 25 percent of the premium. The painful part was that the commission was split fifty-fifty between the agency and me. In short, what I did earn during the year was only half of the commission earned. Immediately, I took steps to obtain a license as an agent. Within two months, with the agent's license, I opened my own agency:

*Peter Hyun and Associates*
*Insurance Analyzing and Counseling*

That was on the letterhead and on my business card. I rented a room on Vermont near Santa Monica Boulevard. My first business call was at a little neighborhood market near where I lived. First making sure the man in the store was the owner, I presented my card.

"What's your business?" he asked.

"Analyzing your insurance program and counseling."

"Analyzing? What's that?"

"I study all your insurance policies to find out exactly what your coverages are and what the exclusions are; whether your coverages are for 100 percent or less. And most important, I determine if the premium you pay is the best rate available. You should have all such pertinent information before anything happens, not after."

"My agent never told me about such things. What do you charge for your service?"

"Nothing," I said.

"How do you make your living then?"

"Well, if I find your insurance program is good, your agent deserves to keep your business. But if it contains loopholes which would damage your interest, I, not your agent, deserve to have your business."

"What do I have to do?" the owner asked.

"Let me have all your policies; I'll give you a receipt for them. In a few days, I'll return and give you a complete report."

Of course the report, with charts, showed the policies contained numerous clauses and provisions that protected the insurance company more than the insured. Why do the agents sell such policies? Because they are working for the company. I decided to work for the people; it's more interesting and more rewarding.

An example is the case of a lawyer whose house I insured with a well-known company. For a very little more in premium, I inserted a replacement cost coverage in case of fire. A fire did break out and caused extensive damage. The adjuster set the value of the house less years of depreciation and percent of the house damaged by the fire. The owner was offered two thousand dollars as a settlement. When the lawyer called and told me this, I advised him not to accept it, but to insist on rebuilding the damaged area and have the insurance company pay him the replacement cost. The house was rebuilt. The accrued bills totaled more than eight thousand dollars, which the insurance company paid.

Another case involved a client whose very old automobile was totaled in an accident. The adjuster offered one hundred fifty dollars for the junk. I instructed the client not to accept, but to tell the adjuster that it had a great deal of sentimental value, and that he would like to have it repaired. The adjuster thought my client was mad; an old relic of a car—they couldn't even find the necessary parts. That's too bad, but the insurance policy clearly stated the car would be "restored to its original condition" after any damage.

"All right," the adjuster said, and offered three hundred dollars.

"No, sir, I don't want the money. I want it 'restored to its original condition.'" The adjuster was getting desperate. His settlement offer rose to five hundred dollars, then to eight hundred dollars. No, my client didn't want the money.

"All right. We'll give you one thousand dollars," the adjuster shouted. "That's final. You can take it or leave it."

"I'll take it," my client said. "Let me have the money." The adjuster handed him the check, saying, "Will you get rid of this wreck now?"

"Oh, no," my client replied, "it's all yours!"

Such stories quickly spread, and I was rewarded with referrals, which kept me quite busy. As a solicitor, my year's earnings were barely six thousand dollars. As an independent agent they climbed to nearly ten thousand dollars.

Now I added another avenue of finding new clients—by telephone. I attended a seminar on telephone technique in sales. It was amazing how, using this technique, I could pick up the phone, dial a number out of the directory and get an appointment with a stranger to analyze his insurance program. My phone calls were aimed at the higher-income class—doctors, lawyers, and business institutions. More than half of my interviews had successful results. When the casualty insurance program was concluded, I opened the subject of life insurance as an income protection plan. This was the logical wrap-up of all the insurance. At one meeting with a president of a savings and loan company, I wrote a life insurance policy for two hundred fifty thousand dollars.

The second year, my annual earnings climbed to seventeen thousand dollars. This was pretty big money in the early 1950s. Big enough, in fact, for us to buy an architect-designed house with a pool. Our mode of life changed suddenly. We dined out more often, and more frequently entertained relatives and friends. Our food and liquor bills doubled and tripled. So did our bills on gas, light, and telephone. We were living a rather affluent life, and that's when the troubles started. But let's not put the cart before the horse; let me come back to that later.

Fatherhood, especially being the father of three very handsome and bright children, I discovered, was the most taxing but enjoyable responsibility. I had to learn to recognize their needs and wishes. Their communications were unorthodox, but once I knew their silent languages, I found them quite precise and clear. They spoke through their expressive faces, intricate body movements, and primitive animal sounds. I got considerable help from the books by the famous pediatrician, Dr. Spock.

Digesting all the information, I evolved my own set of guidelines.

1. Never treat the children as inferiors. From infancy to their early years, I always spoke to them as equals. "Baby talk" was strictly forbidden in our household. When relatives and visitors indulged in baby talk to express their adoration, I asked them to speak to the children as their equals. The result was that the children learned to speak properly without going through the age of mumbo jumbo.

2. When they had a problem, I didn't offer them solutions; I led them to think for themselves and to develop their own reasoning power.

All three went through the same elementary, junior high, and high schools. They had their share of fun while attaining high scholastic standings. What I feel most fortunate about was that they did not fall victim to drugs, which were beginning to invade all levels of schools. Many of their contemporaries ended up in the arms of the law, and quite a few met tragic endings.

On graduation from high school, Paula applied for and received a full scholarship from Sarah Lawrence College in New York. From the day of her college graduation, she has worked in the field of music mass media and today is a vice president at Music Corporation of America (MCA) in charge of publicity and public relations. Besides directing her work with a large staff, she conducts a seminar to teach and train newcomers.

Lena, on a scholarship to UCLA, graduated with honors in art history. She received her master's degree at the University of California, Santa Barbara, and was then chosen to be among ten art students nationwide to receive a scholarship offered by the Whitney Museum of New York. It was an intensive course of study in the organization and operation of a museum of art. Since completing this very special study, she has been working as a curator in private art galleries in New York.

And Douglass, the biggest extrovert of the family, after finishing high school in Laguna Beach, studied photography at the California Institute of Art in Valencia. With complete photographic equipment provided by the school, he developed his own technique. He plunged into the highly competitive field of commercial photography and earned quite a reputation as a photographer of great originality. Today, he specializes in portraitures of well-known personalities, especially in the Hollywood movie industry.

With the consummate success of these three children, I feel proud and honored. Perhaps I did discharge my fatherhood responsibilities adequately.

# 13

## POLITICS— KOREAN WAR— DIVORCE

Once again, man cannot live on love alone, or bread alone, or even alone with love and bread. He still needs some meaningful participation in the struggles of mankind— that is, politics. Since June 25, 1950, the Korean War had been raging, and Korean people were dying by the thousands every day. Early on, I wanted to do something to help stop this senseless war. I joined the editorial staff of the *Korean Independence News,* a Korean-English weekly newspaper. Diamond Kim was the editor publisher, John Chun the Linotype operator and typesetter, and I was the editor of the English section. With little financial support, the three of us managed to bring out the newspaper and send it everywhere Koreans lived: to all the major cities in the United States, to Hawaii, and of course to Korea. Our editorial policy was clear: stop the war in Korea, oust Syngman Rhee, and tell all powers outside Korea— hands off.

We exposed Rhee's sordid background, which included extracting money from the Korean sugar plantation workers in Hawaii, who earned one dollar a day for eight hours of back-breaking labor, and issuing Korean national bonds to be redeemed when an independent Korean government was established under his leadership. We also exposed the motives and plans of the United States and the Soviet Union to establish their bases in Korea. We advocated an immediate cease-fire to allow the Korean people to determine their own destiny.

The supporters of Syngman Rhee in Los Angeles were outraged, and, with threats of physical harm, staged a drive to shut down our press. They branded the *Korean Independence News* and its staff as "Reds." This was taken up by the U.S. press and provided fuel for the rising McCarthyism. One evening, Drew Pearson of the "Washington Merry-go-round" devoted his entire weekly radio broadcast to "The Korean Communist Cell in Los Angeles." Naming names, he branded the staff of the *Korean Independence News* as totally Communist. That was not all; I began receiving late telephone calls from people screaming obscenities and ordering me to go back where I came from. I was forced to leave the phone off the hook before going to bed. I also began receiving postcards and letters with the message, "You dirty Red, go back where you came from."

To top it all off, one morning I heard the doorbell, and when I went to the door I found two young men who asked if I was Peter Hyun. One of them flashed his FBI badge and said, "We've come to ask you to cooperate with us." It meant, "Will you turn stool pigeon for us?"

I answered, "You are knocking at the wrong door," and slammed it shut.

They never came back. It was quite frightening to discover the police-state methods being used in America to intimidate citizens, and even more frightening to encounter so many bigots and racists who claimed to be Americans.

Then as a testimonial to the American way of life, I received an invitation to attend the founding convention of the American Peace Crusade in Chicago in 1951. Anna and I decided to attend, relying on an old friend to care for our children. We also offered to take three passengers with us driving to Chicago in our 1949 Studebaker four-door sedan—one a young Jewish woman student at Los Angeles City College, the other two African-American veterans of World War II. It didn't occur to me that we would face any problems because of our interracial group traveling together. We did.

The first day, after driving all morning, we stopped at a little diner somewhere in Arizona. We all sat at the counter, ready to order. The man in a dirty apron came to me and said, "We'll serve you, but not those two," his head pointing at our two black friends.

Stunned, I asked, "Why not?"

Without any hesitation, he said, "We don't serve niggers here."

Incensed, we walked out. After driving the rest of the day without any food, we stopped at a motel for the night. To avoid any further problems, I let the two African-American men out first, telling them we would wait to see if they got a room. When they did not come out, the rest of us also checked in. Next morning, we ate our breakfast separately.

We were now driving through New Mexico and stopped at a Standard station for gas and an oil change. Again we separated for lunch. We returned to the service station, paid the bill, and started off. We hadn't gone very far when the car suddenly stalled. It would not start. I hitched a ride, stopped at the nearest garage, and told them about my stalled car. They sent a tow truck and brought the car with its passengers. "Your engine is frozen," was the diagnosis.

"How come?" I asked.

"Well," the mechanic said, "there was no oil." Only then it dawned on me: The Standard station where we had stopped for the oil change just drained the oil and did not put in new oil. Accident? Impossible; another dastardly act of bigotry.

The mechanic loosened the frozen cylinders, poured quarts of oil in, and started the engine. "Well, it will run, but you have to watch the oil," he warned us.

Feeding the car a quart of oil every hundred miles, we drove into a little town in Kansas. It was rather late at night, and we were starved. We found a brightly lit restaurant and entered. There was a circular table by the window, and the five of us settled down. It was a large restaurant filled with a merry crowd. We sat there for fully ten minutes without any attention. I got up and went to the rear and asked to see the manager. I said to him, "We've been sitting at the table for ten minutes, and we would like some service."

"If you will move to this table," the manager said, pointing at a table in the rear corner, "we'll serve you."

"We like it fine where we are."

"Sorry," he said.

I went back and stood on the table. I waved at the crowd and shouted, "Listen; listen everybody! Are you all Americans here? Then listen! The manager refuses to serve us. You know why? Because we are with two friends who belong to the Negro race. Do you know who these two people are? They served in the U.S. Navy. You remember Guadalcanal, where American forces were cut off without food or ammunition? All of the Americans were facing death. Except for the quartermaster volunteer ship which broke through the Japanese blockade, they would all have died. Do you know who those volunteers were? Negroes—these two men among them. And you Americans, can you sit there and eat while they refuse to serve these black American heroes?"

Complete silence.

"Listen, you," the manager came over, "you stop that and get down, or I'll call the police."

To avoid a night in jail, I stepped down, and, leaving the crowd of silent Americans, we marched out.

Still feeding the car a quart of oil every hundred miles, we finally arrived in Chicago. And being present at the founding convention of the American Peace Crusade made it all worthwhile. Nearly a thousand delegates from every part of the country filled an immense auditorium.

When Dr. W. E. B. Du Bois appeared on the stage, the delegates rose to their feet with a thunderous ovation. We were under the spell of a great man—a renowned historian and scholar. He had participated in the formation of the World Council of Peace in Stockholm, Sweden, in 1949. In the same year in March, together with his associates, including Linus Pauling, Nobel Laureate in science, and John Rogge, former assistant U.S. attorney general, Dr. Du Bois organized the Cultural and Scientific conference for World Peace. The Cold War was heating up, and the conference proclaimed: Stop the war between the United States and the Soviet Union, and ban atomic weapons. This great man stood before us and presided over the founding convention for the American Peace Crusade.

After a daylong session under his leadership, the convention unanimously adopted three major platforms: Stop the war in Korea; Stop the threat of war between the United States and the Soviet Union; Ban atomic weapons. The delegates also unanimously pledged to return home and build an American Peace Crusade movement in their area. This auspicious beginning, despite all the obstacles raised by the hawks, grew into a ground swell and exerted a major impact in derailing the Cold War, electing Eisenhower for president on his pledge to bring peace in Korea, and creating interest in a U.S.–U.S.S.R. treaty to stop testing atomic weapons.

The five of us returned home to Los Angeles filled with inspiration and determination. With ourselves as the nucleus, we organized a peace conference. Invitations were sent to churches, cultural organizations, and different ethnic groups. The conference delegates heard our report on the Chicago convention and its resolutions. Then the question was raised: What can we do here in Los Angeles? After much discussion and exchange of ideas, a committee was elected and authorized to formulate the form and program of a Los Angeles peace movement. That's how the Southern California Peace Crusade was born, and I was elected its director.

Our work for the next three years, until the armistice in Korea was signed in 1953, was focused in the areas of mass education, public rallies, and the organization of peace centers. In a little office with an old mimeograph machine, and with volunteer labor, we printed thousands of peace bulletins as often as we could afford, and distributed them all over Los Angeles. A petition drive was addressed to President Truman, urging him to bring peace to Korea and save the lives of young Americans and Koreans. Los Angeles was in the grips of Olympic fever, scheduled to take place in Helsinki, Finland. With the slogan "Olympics for Peace," we mounted a petition drive. Among the religious leaders sponsoring this drive was a very enthusiastic Catholic bishop. With signature collection tables set up at major shopping centers, we collected nearly a million signatures. They were sent to Truman, but we never found out if he saw them.

Another highlight of our campaign was a peace motorcade. Over a hundred automobiles displaying peace slogans paraded through city streets showering peace leaflets, and ended at the segregated and depressed town of Watts. The results of such a demonstration were immeasurable; who could tell how many thousands of Americans were exposed to the idea of peace for the first time in their lives, and how many of them were moved to write letters to their congressmen and senators.

We also reached out to neighboring cities and towns to organize similar peace crusades. My main task in this field was to speak at schools, churches, and community centers. We succeeded in establishing centers in several towns, including Pasadena.

One day, a middle-aged woman came to my office in Los Angeles, gave me her name—Anita Schneider—and said that she was from San Diego. She was anxious to have a peace crusade center in San Diego. Could I help her? Of course. We held our first meeting with a half dozen people in her home. Thereafter, she was to be the leader of the group with whatever help I could give her. At the end

of one of the subsequent meetings, one of the people present, a professor at the University of Calfornia, San Diego, drew me aside and
whispered, "You be careful with that woman, Anita; her husband is a
chief petty officer in the U.S. Navy."

When we consider that such activities and drives were taking
place all over the country—from Maine to Florida, from Texas to
Washington—their impact on American intellectuals and workers
alike was resounding. The American peace crusaders of the 1950s
were the pioneers of the people's uprising for peace in Vietnam in
the 1960s.

One day, I received my medal of honor in the form of a subpoena from the House Committee on Un-American Activities. We
always called it the House Un-American Committee. But this was
no joke; it was very serious—I needed legal advice. I met with Al
Wiren, the famous civil rights attorney for the American Civil Liberties Union. I informed him of the subpoena I received and asked
for his advice.

"Well, what's your idea?" he asked. "What would you like
to do?"

"I would stand up before the committee and tell them just what
I think."

"And when they ask, 'Are you now or have you ever been a
member of the Communist Party?'"

"I would tell them that's none of their business. Political beliefs
and political affiliation are my own personal business."

"That's all very well and good," Mr. Wiren said, "but you can't
do that. You see, Peter, once you start answering in any way, you
have to continue answering. They will ask you where you were on
such and such a day, what kind of meeting was it that you attended,
and so on, until they ask you to identify some of the people you met,
and the discussions you had with them. And if you decide not to
answer any more, you will be cited for contempt of Congress and
sent to prison."

He continued: "Now, listen carefully, Peter. As to the question
regarding membership in the Communist Party, if you honestly
answer 'yes,' you will be charged and indicted under the Smith Act
and prosecuted for advocating the overthrow of the U.S. government
by force and violence. Upon conviction, you will receive a pretty
heavy sentence. But suppose you honestly answer 'no'; then they will

bring witnesses to testify they saw you at Communist meetings. Others will even testify that they knew you as a Communist. They can then charge you with perjury and send you to prison."

"So, I am damned if I say yes, and I am damned if I say no."

"That's exactly right," Mr. Wiren said. "And that's precisely why we have the Fifth Amendment to our Constitution, which protects us against self-incrimination. So, you see, Peter, you either do answer all questions asked and go to prison, or do not answer any question, and claim the protection of the Fifth Amendment."

For the first time in my life, I really got an insight into the importance and the meaning of the Fifth Amendment.

On the appointed day, I arrived rather early at Los Angeles City Hall, where the hearing or the process of defamation was to take place. On the stage an imposing long table and chairs were set, and on the table were a half dozen microphones ready to transport every word spoken by the committee members to the audience. It was a meticulously prepared stage setting. The members of the committee marched in and took their seats around the table, and the chairman declared the hearing in session. Following the appearances of two others who had been subpoenaed, I heard my name called. I rose and took the witness chair.

The chairman asked, "Are you Peter Hyun?" (He mispronounced my last name throughout the proceeding).

"Yes," I answered.

"What is your occupation, Mr. Hyun?"

"I refuse to answer on the grounds of the Fifth Amendment."

There followed a stream of questions dealing with my livelihood, my religious affiliation, and all sorts of seemingly trivial questions by various members of the committee; all of which I refused to answer. All these meaningless questions masked the real question the committee was interested in, and the chairman finally popped it:

"Are you now or have you ever been a member of the Communist Party?"

I offered him my routine answer: "I refuse to answer on the grounds of the protection of the Fifth Amendment against self-incrimination."

Finally the chairman announced, "Witness dismissed. Next witness."

"Oh, my God!" I gasped. It was Anita Schneider, the peace

crusade leader from San Diego. She answered all the routine questions confirming her identity.

Then, assuming a more serious voice, the Chairman asked, "Do you know a Mr. Peter Hyun?"

"Yes, Sir." Anita sounded well prepared. "Sir, I worked with him in the Southern California Peace Crusade, and I worked with him when he set up a peace crusade organization in San Diego."

"Isn't the so-called peace crusade a Red-front outfit?"

"Yes, sir, it sure is." Anita sounded almost rapturous.

"As director of the peace crusade, what did Mr. Hyun do?"

"He went around the country, waving the red flag, and tried to arouse the American people to believe we were a war-mongering country."

"To your knowledge, what else did he do?"

"Sir, Peter Hyun (pronounced correctly) is the number one agent of the Chinese Communist dictator, Mao Tse-tung, in the United States."

An audible murmur swept through the courtroom. The chairman took it all in stride. He didn't ask how she knew it and what evidence she had. The next morning, this bit of startling testimony made headline news in the *Los Angeles Times*.

The following Monday morning, I attended the sales meeting of the American National Insurance Company, of which I was a district manager. Arriving rather late, dead silence filled the room as I entered. I took a seat and followed the proceedings. Dick Thorne, the general manager of the company, quickly called the meeting to a close, and the attending sales agents dispersed. Dick Thorne asked me to come to his office. It was eerie—no one spoke a word to me as they left the room. I thought it quite strange as I walked into Dick Thorne's office.

"Please sit down, Peter." Dick sounded quite cordial. Leaning back with his hands at the back of his head, he spoke as if to no one in particular. "Before you joined us, the boys had a very serious discussion."

"What about?" I asked.

"About you, Peter. They were alarmed by what they read in the morning paper. They were in a quandary as to what they should do if it is true that you were a Communist agent."

"That's really interesting, because I was in a quandary myself.

The woman's testimony about my being the number one agent for Communist China was as much of a surprise for me as it might have been for you."

Inevitably, the sixty four-dollar question. Dick lowered his voice and asked, "Well, are you a member of the Communist Party?"

I, too, lowered my voice. "Well, Dick, before I answer you, I have to tell you what my lawyer, Al Wiren, a famous civil rights attorney, told me. When I confide to you whether or not I am a Communist, you will become my political ally by association."

Dick's mouth dropped open and he remained silent.

"If I tell you yes, you will have to testify that you knew I was a Communist in any future hearing. And if I tell you 'no, I am not a Communist,' you will have to testify as a sworn witness that you knew I was not a Communist." After a moment of silence, I asked, "Well, Dick, do you want me to give you the answer to your question?"

Dick heaved a big sigh and said, "Oh, Peter, forget it."

While such cat-and-mouse games were being played all over the United States, American young men were shedding their blood in the rice fields of Korea without knowing why. Bevin Alexander wrote a book on the subject called *Korea—The First War We Lost*. The real struggle, of course, was between the two superpowers—the United States and the U.S.S.R.

The Korean War, which began in June 1950, finally ended in July 1953, three years and one month after it started. Peace negotiations had dragged on from 1951 to 1953. The total casualties suffered during the period of peace negotiations were more than the total casualties incurred before the peace talks began. There were no winners, no losers; only the victims. There were no gains for either side. The final demarcation line, the military and political controls by North and South Korea, were exactly as they had been before the war.

The total battle casualties of the war amounted to more than two million killed and maimed, as well as untold millions of civilian casualties. Moreover, villages, towns, and cities, not to mention bridges, means of transportation, and factories, were all shattered in both the North and the South. The cost and the task of recovering and rebuilding the whole country was staggering; and there was no United Nations resolution to assist the reconstruction of Korea.

Along with the hundreds of thousands of families who lost their loved ones, the Hyun family, too, paid a heavy price in the Korean War: We lost our dearest Sister Alice and her only son, Wellington. As the oldest of the eight children in our family, Sister Alice was our counselor, guardian, and mentor. She was also our second mother; she mended our clothes and fed us when we were hungry.

Her most important role, however, was as our teacher. She taught us to be proud of the history of the Korean people and to offer our talent and energy in the struggle for our freedom. Whenever I was critical or scornful of another Korean, she would admonish me and teach me to love my people and try to help them. The highest duty in life, she kept reminding us, was to be patriotic and serve our own people.

At the time the Korean War broke out, Wellie was a second-year premed student at U.C.L.A. He was deeply concerned about his A-1 military draft status. He could be called up for army duty any day. He hated not so much the military training, but the idea of going to Korea and killing Korean people was absolutely impossible for him to accept. One day in July 1950 both Sister Alice and Wellie disappeared. With the possible exception of Umma and Papa, no one knew what happened to them. A few months later we received a letter from Wellie; it was from Prague, Czechoslovakia. Sister Alice wasn't with him.

He had enrolled in the medical school of the University of Prague, struggling with the language, his studies, and the means of earning his living. He conquered all three problems, and in three years he graduated and completed a postgraduate study in surgery, practicing in a well-known resort outside of Prague. He married a Czech girl, Anna Soltys, and became the father of a daughter named Tabitha.

Wellie went to the embassy of the Democratic People's Republic of Korea (North Korea) and volunteered his services. His offer was neither accepted nor rejected. Instead, he received a notice from the Czech government ordering him to leave the country within a month or he would be deported. All inquiries into the reasons for the deportation order were ignored, and Wellie guessed the only possible instigator of the drastic action was the North Korean embassy, which regarded all persons of U.S. background as spies. Wellie was helplessly trapped and learned that he would soon be deported to, of all places, Africa. He committed suicide.

We discovered that, after leaving Wellie in Czechoslovakia, Sister Alice had continued on to Moscow, then to Beijing, and from there to Pyongyang in North Korea. Park Huen-Young, formerly the general secretary of the Communist Party of Korea, and now the minister of foreign affairs in North Korea, was happy to see Sister Alice and hired her as his personal secretary. Their friendship dated back to the 1920s in Shanghai, when they silently shared mutual admiration. Once again, Sister Alice found her place to work for Korea and her people. At the time, I was editing the *Korean Independence News* in Los Angeles, where we had access to the North Korean newspaper.

Soon after the Korean armistice was signed on July 27, 1953, Kim Il-Sung, leader of North Korea, staged a ruthless purge. His target was Park Huen-Young, his minister of foreign affairs. This was not altogether unexpected. Park, who was a national hero and loved by the Korean people—North and South—was a threat to Kim's dictatorship. Park's national stature and his popularity overshadowed Kim's fabricated revolutionary background. Kim Il-Sung ordered the arrest of Park Huen-Young and thirty-nine of his associates, including Sister Alice. They were all found guilty of "collaborating with the United States" and summarily executed. She had spent all her life fighting for Korea, only to be executed by another Korean.

While the war in Korea was claiming thousands of lives every day, in my household a private little war was brewing. At the beginning, neither my wife nor I recognized the developing problem. Overnight, our home became the social center of our relatives and friends. Along with them, the number of newcomers swelled the circle of visitors, especially on weekends. The frolics around the pool cooled the hot summer days, and these frolics continued through the winter because the pool was kept heated. Invariably, the guests were served beer, wine, and cocktails, and soft drinks for the children. After sunset, the visitors lingered on, and Anna would load the dining table with all sorts of delicious concoctions of meats, salads, and sweets. And more drinks.

For a number of years all of us, especially our children, enjoyed the perpetual carnival atmosphere at home; we were having one long and hilarious party after another. Because I was the family treasurer as well as its manager by virtue of being the breadwinner, I was the first one to notice a surprising phenomenon. It was very interesting and also very painful. Our family budget rose in direct proportion to the rise in our living standard. Not only did our utility bills double and treble, but the bills for groceries, liquor, and "entertainment" far surpassed our previous family budget. It was alarming, and I mentioned this to Anna.

That was when the first serious rift began between us. Anna challenged me when I raised the issue. "What do you want to do?"

"Well, darling, I don't know," was my answer, "but we must do something to control the runaway budget."

From that point, Anna and I drifted apart. By the time the children were in their teens, she began spending more and more time with more and more friends away from home. Not long after this, Anna dropped a bombshell: "Peter, I want a divorce."

"What did you say?"

"I want a divorce."

I tried to marshal all my senses and sanity and not lose my mind. I found myself floundering like a drowning man. "When . . . when . . . how. . . . ," I mumbled.

I left the house in a daze. I couldn't bear to return home, so I spent a sleepless night in a neighborhood motel. When I came home the next day, Anna wasn't even curious about my night out. It seemed she couldn't care less about what was happening to me. The children were at school and we could talk freely.

"Anna, do you still want the divorce?"

"Yes, I do."

"Why don't we just separate and find out if you are really sure."

"I am sure now," Anna said, quite casually.

"Have you gone to a lawyer about this?"

"Yes, I have."

After that, there wasn't much left to discuss. "Do the children know about this?"

"Yes, I have told them we are divorcing."

"All right, Anna, I'll pack my things and move out."

I needed only two suitcases in which to stuff my clothes, toiletries, and important personal items, including the accounts payable folder containing all the bills from department stores. I checked in at the same motel, and for the first time in my life found myself sitting in a neighborhood saloon.

In a few days I found a one-bedroom apartment completely furnished except the kitchen. I went shopping and brought home a few essential items for housekeeping: pots and pans, plates and cups, a percolator, silverware, and for some unknown reason, a stainless steel strainer—which is still in my kitchen! Well, I was in business, cooking my own breakfast and dinner. Occasionally, I even had dinner guests when I cooked a fancy Korean meal. The greatest pleasure, however, was fixing my children's favorite dishes on weekends.

Shortly before the divorce became final, Anna raised the possibility of a reconciliation. Despite her desire to reverse the process, I observed that it was too late and that we were never really compatible. That was my last conversation with Anna.

Against the advice of my attorney, I did not claim one-half or any part of our community property. On the day of the final hearing, I appeared before the judge.

After asking me if I had been properly notified of the request for divorce, he asked, "For whatever reason, do you wish to contest this divorce?"

"No, your honor. No contest whatsoever."

Without any further ceremony, the judge declared our divorce legal and final. I was awakening from a horrible nightmare; the invisible heavy burden lifted. Seventeen years of marriage dissolved in a stroke with the banging of a gavel. My life in the New World and my determination to become Americanized had completed a full circle: new language, new customs, new education, new culture, new profession, new home, new family, and, finally, divorce.

But divorce would not be the final episode. Life began again with Luisa Stuart, who provided light, love, and laughter to my life for twenty-five years. My writing owes much to her wisdom and encouragement.

The fourth generation of the Korean-American Hyuns is represented by my two grandsons, Soon, age six, and Grant, age two. When I look at my grandsons talking, laughing, and playing, I see them as Americans carrying on the Hyun family heritage.

I am so proud of them, and I have a deep faith that they will grow into creative and productive adults who will make their share of contributions toward the betterment of human society.

# AFTERWORD

In the age-old Korean tradition, the family name, the family property, and all honor and responsibility are entrusted to the oldest son. And I had the misfortune to be the firstborn son. Not only my parents and grandparents, but all the members of the clan regarded me as the heir to the family tradition and lavished on me limitless indulgence. I was allowed to sit at the table of the elders and partake of the special food prepared for them. I always received the first new suit of clothes and sandals. Only after that, new clothes for my younger brothers. On special holidays such as my uncle's birthday, I would be taken to the festivities by Papa and Umma; younger ones—they stayed at home.

These traditional discriminations were openly displayed not only on special occasions, but even more openly in daily activities at home. There was distinction between the manner of speaking to the oldest son and to the rest of the children. Papa always took me with him when he went to the public baths where hot water was abundant. The rest of the family first had to heat the water in a kerosene can over an open fire and bathe in a tub. For my younger brothers, it was most tantalizing and aggravating at mealtimes. They had to sit and wait and watch the big helping of choice bits of food passed to me. Then they received their bowls, but not with too many choice bits. How such a Korean way of life must have hurt my brothers.

The status of my sisters was even one step lower than my brothers. Except for my oldest sister Alice, who was a little mother to all of us, the three other sisters had little recognition. Sister Soon-Ok, one year younger than I, was given more attention by virtue of the fact that she was an invalid; she had been bedridden from age ten until her death in Shanghai at sixteen.

Enjoying to the full all the privileges of a number one son, I was totally unaware of the anger and jealousy bordering on hatred felt by all my sisters and brothers. These stored animosities did not surface until our adult lives nearly a half century later. I was mortified and horrified to realize the hurts and pains my family role must have heaped on them when we were all young. The full impact of this did not fully crystallize until after Papa and Umma had both died. In vain attempts to redeem myself and to earn their forgiveness, I tried in many ways to belittle my place in the family and encourage my younger brothers to assume the leadership. But, alas, it was too late. Neither would their frozen hearts thaw nor their memories of pain ever quite disappear.

Having spent my childhood in a semifeudal society, and having transplanted myself into an industrialized democratic society, I was conscious and aware of the advantages and drawbacks of both. Living in America, I witnessed and cringed at the sight of some youngster cursing and attacking an older person. At the same time, the traditional confines and restrictions placed on Korean children restricted their ability to develop their talents. While I enjoyed as a young boy the privileges of being the number-one son, I can see how confining the traditional way was to my brothers and sisters.

The making of a Korean American is essentially a story of a cultural marriage. Such a marriage is consummated only after a prolonged period of engagement—ten years, twenty, or even longer.

At seventeen, a son of the ancient Korean culture, I was propelled into the New World called America. It was unreal: The streets, the buildings, the people and the language they spoke, all seemed like a scene in a dream. After living in Korea and China, once again I had to change my life drastically in this New World, or perish.

The immensity of the challenge dawned on me when I began to study the English language; it was a nightmare! I had studied and lived with three Asian languages—Korean, Japanese, and Chinese. I had also dabbled in Russian. But English, I discovered, was the most unreasoning language. The more I studied, the more complicated it became. Learning the grammar and memorizing the rules were of little help, for there were always exceptions to every rule. I was a prisoner of my own choosing. It was clear that I would never be free until I had conquered this devilish language.

Fortunately, I was born with the Korean stubborn streak: I refused to give up. For ten years, I struggled in agony, and suddenly one day, English was no longer a foreign language. The final testimonial of the long engagement between the Korean and the American cultures appeared in my sleep. In my dream, I was speaking not Korean as usual, but English. I awoke with a great sigh of relief and a feeling of overwhelming elation.

However, the trials and tribulations of the engagement did not cease. Learning and accepting the language of the American people was one thing; but accepting and being accepted as one of them was quite something else. The thousands of years of man's struggle for survival must have implanted instinctive suspicion, hostility, and hate of others. And the walls among people persist today.

"Hey! Chinaman!"

"Hey! Charlie!"

"Hey! Chink!"

These names were hurled at me at odd moments and at odd places—by a workman digging ditches, by a vendor selling apples on the street, by college students, artists, and professionals. How can such deep chasms in human minds be bridged? Will they ever be bridged? The tragedy is that these chasms dwell in the minds of all people; some carefully hidden, some disguised in polite smiles, and some bluntly exposed.

It took many more years for me to understand that the hostility and the hate came from two sources: ignorance and fear—the ignorance of another culture, and the fear of being exposed to it. The most effective weapon was laughter. People of different cultures laughing at and with each other could more quickly dispel their hostility.

"You think the Koreans speak funny English? You should hear the American missionaries speaking Korean!"

Laughter!

"Oh, yeah? You think Orientals with slanted eyes are funny looking? Ask a Korean farmer to tell you how the American missionaries look: Watery eyes, yellow hair, long nose!"

Laughter!

The sharing of laughter more than any books or lectures could draw us together and open the door for communication. Only communication can eventually wipe out prejudice, enlighten the ignorant, and neutralize hostility. True, it has taken more than thirty years for me to reach a state of mutual respect. Perhaps, with a little more patience and with a little more time, we might finally achieve mutual acceptance and the ultimate fruition of our cultural marriage.

Nearly half a million Koreans live in the state of California, and that many also live in all major cities throughout the country. How many of them will become fully integrated? And when? Let's add to the Koreans all the other newcomers from Asia, Latin America, Europe, and Africa.

To succeed, cultural marriage has to travel on a two-way street. Why must the world's peoples come and adopt the American way of life? Can't American people, too, learn and understand the cultures and languages of other lands? The study of foreign cultures could and should be part of the basic educational program from kindergarten through college. This is not only feasible, but may be essential to human survival.

Today, we have the capability to destroy the world as we know it. Some believe such a holocaust is inevitable. And in another million years, out of the ashes, a new living species with greater intelligence than the extinct Homo sapiens may emerge to build a new and more rational world. That is the most tragic and cynical view of man's future. I would rather cling to my faith that the human race is endowed with the potential to construct a world of peace and tolerance that our own sons and daughters will inherit.

# Chronology

1906    Peter is born on Kauai.

1907    Peter leaves with his family for Korea. He is only nine months old.

1918    Father appointed superintendent of Methodist Sunday schools in Korea.

1919    *Mid-February:* Father leaves Korea for Shanghai.
        *March:* Peter turns twelve, his last year at elementary school.

1920    The Hyun family leaves for Shanghai.
        *May:* Father appointed head of Korean Commission in Washington, D.C.

1923    *February:* Father returns to Hawaii as minister of Korean Methodist Church in Honolulu. Sister Alice accompanies him.

1924    *May:* At seventeen, Peter returns to Hawaii with Elizabeth, David, and Mary. He spends the summer washing pineapples for Dole and buys a violin with his earnings.

1925    Paul, Joshua, and Umma arrive in Hawaii.

1925–
1926    Peter attends Iolani High School and again spends the summer at Dole. This time he buys a Model-T Ford with his savings.

1926    *Fall:* Peter enrolls at McKinley High School for his sophomore year, then moves to Kauai with his family.

1927–
1929    Peter spends his junior and senior years at Kauai High School and receives his diploma.

1929    Off to college at DePauw University in Greencastle, Indiana. Peter spends Christmas in New York with Elizabeth, summer working at a hot dog concession in Rye Beach, New York.

1930    Sophomore year at DePauw. Peter attends a summer program at the Gloucester School of Little Theatre in Massachusetts to pursue his growing interest in theatre.

1930–  *Fall:* Peter enters New York City's theatre world as part of
1931   an apprentice group at Eva LeGallienne's Civic Repertoy
       Theatre.

1931   When the Civic Repertory Theatre closes down for a year,
       Peter finds his way back to Gloucester for the summer.
       Peter acquires financial backing for a new theatre group and
       the Studio Players debuts in Cambridge. The initial offer-
       ing is Ibsen's *When We Dead Awaken* in October. Shaw's
       *Great Catherine* follows in December.

1932   The Studio Players' success continues with Chekhov's *Uncle
       Vanya* in February and the Quintero brothers' *Fortunato* in
       April. Despite overwhelming success, Peter disbands his
       theatre group and returns to Kauai. There he wins the role
       of a butler in the movie *Cane Fire,* filmed on Kauai.

1932–  Peter heads east again to stage manage a play at the Austin
1933   Memorial Museum Theatre in Hartford, Connecticut. In
       New York he helps dramatize labor issues with the Work-
       ers' Lab Theatre.

1934   *Newsboy,* the most successful production of the Workers'
       Lab Theatre, was performed to acclaim in New York.

1935   *May:* Workers' Lab Theatre, now called Theatre of Action,
       produces its first full-length play, *The Young Go First.*
       With funds of the Theatre of Action group depleted, Peter
       moves to the New York Federal Theatre. As part of the
       children's theatre, Peter directs an unsuccessful production
       of Moliere's *The Miser* and a successful one of *The Emperor's
       New Clothes.* Peter attempts a marionette production of *Fer-
       dinand the Bull.* It is so successful it is tapped for the New
       York World's Fair.

1937   Peter directs *Revolt of the Beavers,* but his actors demand a
       new director for their Broadway debut. Peter leaves the
       world of the theatre.

1937–  Peter returns to Honolulu, where his family has moved, and
1939   joins them in ventures into fabric production and cucum-
       ber farming.

1940–  Peter becomes a "rodboy" at Pearl Harbor Naval Base.
1941

1941–  In October 1941 Peter is promoted from rodboy to sur-
1943   veyor and spends a year with the U.S. Corps of Engineers.

1944    Peter joins the U.S. Army at age thirty-eight and goes
        through basic training in Oklahoma. He is singled out but
        refuses officer training school in Minneapolis, where he
        instead studies Japanese in the military language school. His
        first assignment is to supervise a group of Korean POWs at
        Camp McCoy in Wisconsin.

1945    *September–October:* Peter is sent to Korea to interpret for the
        American military government. There he renews old fam-
        ily ties.

1946    Peter and Alice open a business, First Grand Liquor Store,
        in Los Angeles. The Hyun family completes its exodus
        from Hawaii to California.

1947    Peter courts and marries Anna Lee.

1949    *February 9:* Peter and Anna's first daughter, Paula, is born.

1950–   Korean War
1953

1951    *January 29:* A second daughter, Lena, is born. Peter and
        Anna attend the American Peace Crusade in Chicago.

1952    *October 15:* Douglass, a son, is born. Peter opens an insur-
        ance agency, Peter Hyun and Associates, and the Hyuns
        begin to prosper.

1953    Peter is subpoenaed by the House Committee on Un-
        American Activities.

1964    Peter and Anna divorce.

1965    Peter marries Marie Luisa Stuart.

# *Appendix*

**The Studio Players**

Brattle Hall, Cambridge, Massachusetts
1931–1932
Director—Peter Hyun

**Members of the company:**

Howard daSilva
Jane Kim
David Kerman
Sala Staw
Elaine Basil

**Guest members:**

Burgess Meredith
Robert Ross

**Staff:**

Promotion and publicity       Helen Thompson
Business manager              Lydia Walker
Set designer                 George McFadden
Lighting                     Harry F. Carlson
Costume                      Carlene M. Samoiloff
Stage manager                Walter Gomes

**Sponsors:**

H. W. L. Dana
Mrs. Alvan T. Fuller
Mr. and Mrs. Hugh Bancroft
Mrs. Richard M. Saltonstall
Mrs. William Dana Orcutt
Mrs. Charles T. Collens
Mrs. Steven W. Sleeper
Mrs. Guy Currier
Mrs. Edward Ingraham
Mrs. William Cox

Mrs. George L. Paine
Mrs. Charles Peabody
Mrs. Otis Weld Richardson
Mrs. Horace Morison
Mrs. C. Nichols Greene
Mrs. Carl P. Dennett
Mrs. Irving Babbitt
Mrs. Bliss Perry
Mrs. Henry I. Harriman

# THE STUDIO PLAYERS

Members and Students of

Eva LeGallienne's Civic Repertory Theatre of New York City

present

## HENRIK IBSEN'S

## "WHEN WE DEAD AWAKEN"

Staged and directed by Mr. Peter Hyun

Brattle Hall, Cambridge

Friday and Saturday, December 11th and 12th, 1931

Curtain promptly at 8:30 p.m.

∽

Ibsen's last play was called by Ibsen himself his "Dramatic Epilogue." It represents an epitome of his dramatic work and his thought on art and life. Bernard Shaw says of this play: "Ibsen's magic is nowhere more potent." This production offers for the first time an opportunity to see this remarkable drama at the lowest possible price—an opportunity which no one interested in drama and life should neglect.

PROFESSOR H. W. L. DANA, Cambridge School of the Drama

∽

Limited accommodations—please apply for tickets immediately at 42 Brattle Street — University 3439 — or Amee's Book Store, Harvard Sq.

Reserved Seats $1.00          Choice Seats $1.50

Performance announcement and order form from Peter Hyun's production of Ibsen's *When We Dead Awaken,* 1931.

**PRODUCTION:**               *When We Dead Awaken*
                              by Henrik Ibsen

## Comments and highlights of press reviews

"This production offers for the first time an opportunity to see this remarkable drama . . . an opportunity which no one interested in drama and life should neglect."
                    —Professor H. W. L. Dana, Cambridge School of Drama

*Boston Post* (December 12, 1931):
"To the limited stage of Brattle Hall, Cambridge, The Studio Players, drawn from the company and school of Eva LeGallienne's Civic Repertory Theatre, last night brought a sense of space and limitless power. The play was Ibsen's seldom done drama of artistic frustration, *When We Dead Awaken*. Both in direction and in playing, this newly organized company accomplished much of merit.

"Eagerness, born of a great love for their work, is apparent in the individuals forming this group. For these youthful players have spirit and humility. They possess not only an ability to act, but to build illusion, satisfying and complete."

*Boston Herald* (December 13, 1931):
"Ibsen's plays have a way of commanding attention, no matter how obscure their meaning may be, and his last work, *When We Dead Awaken,* is no exception. The Studio Players presented this play at Brattle Hall, Cambridge, and aroused considerable interest by their resurrection of a striking curiosity."

*Boston Transcript* (December 8, 1931):
"Last evening in Cambridge, a modest audience which cared nothing for the weather was privileged to see one of his [Ibsen's] rarest flights of imagination: *When We Dead Awaken*. The performance, in many ways an excellent one, contrived to get at the heart of the play's more cryptic scenes.

"Under the direction of Mr. Peter Hyun they gave imaginative propulsion to the characters. At no point did their interpretations obscure the symbolic possibilities of Ibsen's characters. In the most difficult passage of the play . . . they managed a level of acting well above the acceptable average of 'Little Theatre' standards.

"In a piece in which greater actors have failed and which better directors have hesitated to produce, this is something of an accomplishment."

**PRODUCTION:**                    *Great Catherine*
                                   by George Bernard Shaw

### Highlights of press reviews

*Boston Herald* (January 22, 1932):
"Last night's performance was a candid, energetic presentment; flourishes were plentiful, and G.B.S.'s license for the actors to tamper with their characters as they will did not go begging.

"The Studio Players succeeded in carrying out the unmistakable atmosphere of the play. Sentimental terms of endearment interchanged with the grossest appellations, coquetry alternated with insults . . . are fantastic enough to obliterate the line between acting and overacting."

*Boston Post* (January 23, 1932):
"Going with the swiftness and smoothness of magic from the unreality and mysticism of Ibsen's *When We Dead Awaken* to the brilliance and lightness of G. Bernard Shaw's *Great Catherine,* the Studio Players firmly established their reputation as an organization of exceptional worth in Brattle Hall, Cambridge, last evening.

"There is probably no finer test for the acting ability of a group of players than this fantastic satire by Shaw. The Studio Players met the test; passed it with distinction."

*Boston Transcript* (January 26, 1932):
"It might have been a more discouraging evening at Brattle Hall. The weather would have dampened an anti-saloon league convention.

"But the fun of Mr. Shaw's *Great Catherine* is almost unquenchable, and once things had gotten underway on the tiny Brattle stage, everyone present gave unmistakable evidence of amusement.

"By the time the program had drawn to an end, the balance was decidedly in favor of the Studio Players."

**PRODUCTION:**                     *Uncle Vanya*
                                   by Anton Chekhov

## Highlights of press reviews:

*Boston Transcript* (February 24, 1932):
"The intellectual ambitions of the Studio Players extend beyond their present capabilities of mind and imagery in the theatre.

"Last evening, as in the case of the two earlier productions of this group, a single note was not only struck, but maintained without any noticeable variations throughout the course of the four acts.

"In the third scene alone, where the disgruntled Ivan tries vainly to shoot the professor, did a stirring climax rise."

*Boston Herald* (February 25, 1932):
"The performances of Chekhov's *Uncle Vanya,* given by the Studio Players at Brattle Hall last evening and the evening before, are of sufficiently good quality to merit attention and appreciation.

"They also prove that this play, in order to produce the effect desired by the playwright, need not be given by a glittering cast. The players acquitted themselves earnestly and capably, projecting to praiseworthy degree the passive melancholy and curious fatalism of this quiet play.

"So much, indeed, did they identify themselves with the characters that the spectator felt almost like an intruder upon the intimate private life of this ill-assorted family group."

**PRODUCTION:**                       *Fortunato*
                              by Serafin and Joaquin Alvarez
                              Quintero

**Highlights of press reviews:**

*Boston Post* (April 3, 1932):
"The Studio Players gave the closing production of their season at Brattle
Hall, Cambridge, last evening, presenting most appropriately, Chekhov's
one-act play, *The Swan Song,* and *Fortunato* by the Spanish dramatists, Serafin and Joaquin Alvarez Quintero. Both plays moved smoothly and with
serene and unswerving artistry with which this gallant troup of young players have invested each of their several offerings.

"Not in many years has such fine, sensitive acting been brought to a contemporary stage by any similar group. They have given four widely different plays, Ibsen's *When We Dead Awaken,* Shaw's *Great Catherine,* Chekhov's
*Uncle Vanya* and *Fortunato* by the Quinteros. All have been splendidly acted,
and as splendidly directed by Peter Hyun."

*Boston Herald* (March 27, 1932):
"As their fourth and final production, the Studio Players offered last night
at Brattle Hall, Cambridge, the first local presentation of the Quintero
comedy, *Fortunato* . . . and they won unforced enthusiasm from the sizable
audience assembled to watch the first performance.

"Fortunato has fallen on evil days, without work and with a family to
support. Try as he will, he cannot beg, he cannot steal, he cannot bluff.
Driven desperate, he tries to steal from a blind beggar, only to put the
money back in the cup when he learns that the beggar, too, has children
dependent on him. Finally, after walking miles to answer an advertisement,
he finds that his job will be to stand against a target while Amaranta, the
champion woman shot, outlines him in bullets.

"Fortunato himself requires an actor of sensibility, resource, and unusual
perception who can convey the man's inescapable honesty, devotion to his
children, and pitiful determination that makes it possible for him to undertake the job of human target.

"Burgess Meredith acquitted himself admirably filling out his part [For-
tunato] with innumerable skillful little details of gesture and intonation that
made the spectator laugh at and pity the man at the same time."